MACHIG LABDRÖN
and the Foundations of Chöd

MACHIG LABDRÖN
and the Foundations of Chöd

Jérôme Edou

Snow Lion Publications
Ithaca, New York

Snow Lion Publications
Post Office Box 6483
Ithaca, New York 14851 USA
607-273-8519

First Edition USA 1996

Printed in the United States of America

ISBN 1-55939-039-5

Library of Congress Cataloging-in-Publication Data

Edou, Jérôme, 1952-
Machig Labdrön and the foundations of Chod / Jérôme Edou
p. cm.
Includes bibliographical references and index.
ISBN 1-55939-039-5
1. Gcod (Buddhist rite) 2. Labdrön Machig, 1055-1153.
I. Title.
BQ7699.G36E36 1995
294.3'923—dc20 94-40283
CIP

Table of Contents

PART TWO: THE MARVELOUS LIFE OF MACHIG LABDRÖN,
A Translation of Chapters I and II of *An Exposition of Transforming the Aggregates into an Offering of Food, Illuminating the Meaning of Chöd*

To the mother of all the Victors of the three times,
The inconceivable and sublime Prajñāpāramitā,
I bow down in full prostration.
She, the very essence of space devoid of all origin and cessation,
The selfborn sphere of primordial wisdom.

Prajñāpāramitā or Yum Chenmo, the primordial mother of wisdom, from a rare Newari manuscript. Photo courtesy of R. A. Kluenter.

Special thanks to:

Human and non-human ḍākinīs for their inspiration,
Khenpo Tsultrim Gyamtso for the motivation,
Janet Gyatso for her compilation,
Tashi Tsering, Cyrus Stearns, Matthew Kapstein and Matthieu Ricard for their suggestions,
Maruta Kalnins, Michelle Martin and Karry Moran for their corrections,
Dolpopa Tenzin Norbu for the illustrations,
Snow Lion for the publication, and the editor, Susan Kyser, for bringing it to completion,
Nicole, Jonathan and Kim for all the hours stolen from their attention.

Preface

> Look into the mirror of your mind,
> Mahāmudrā,
> The mysterious home of the ḍākinī.
>
> —*Mahāsiddha Tilopa*

It began at a farmhouse in the lower Alps where I was staying with a Tibetan lama recently arrived from India. That evening I heard resounding from his room the slow rhythm of a haunting melody which he intoned in his rich bass voice, accompanying himself with drum and bell, occasionally blowing the thighbone horn. Throughout the night I was held spellbound by this moving song, so different from any other ritual chant I had ever heard before. I suddenly found myself immersed in the strange and bewildering universe of Chöd, an ageless world of such antiquity as to have survived only in some forgotten isolated pockets of the Tibetan highlands.

Ever since that evening more than fifteen years ago, I haven't been able to let go of Machig Labdrön, the eleventh-century Tibetan lady who was the primary source of inspiration for the Chöd tradition. I looked for her in the Himalayan foothills and in the monasteries of Ladakh and Dolpo. I traced her footprint at Tiger's Den (Taktsang) in Bhutan and sensed her presence at her former retreat place of Copper Mountain (Zangri), among the nuns of Shuksep, as well as at Dampa Sangyé's hermitage at the foot of Mt. Everest. I read echoes of her passing and of her lasting influence in texts, on walls and along pilgrimage routes. On the banks of Lake Namtso, for instance, during the coldest month of the Tibetan winter, I found a group of nomads practicing the Chöd of Machig in a cave of Tashido, the Rock of Good Fortune.

Several lamas in the authentic transmission lineage of Chöd have advised me throughout this lengthy project, enabling me today to present this translation of the most famous biography of Machig Labdrön (1055-1153) together with an outline of her tradition, the Chöd of Mahāmudrā. This translation and most of the commentaries come from two main texts, the first of which is known as *An Exposition of Transforming the Aggregates into an Offering of Food, Illuminating the Meaning of Chöd* (henceforth *Transforming the Aggregates*[1]), the first two chapters of which comprise *The Marvelous Life*, generally considered to be an autobiography of Machig. This short version of Machig's life seems to come from a more extensive version which I have used as a reference, entitled *The Concise Life Story of Machig Labdrön, Derived from An Exposition of Transforming the Aggregates into an Offering of Food* (henceforth *The Concise Life Story*[2]).

Finally, while travelling in Dolpo just a few months before printing this book, I found at Lang Gonpa near Phyger a third version of Machig's hagiography called simply *A Biography of Machig*, an anonymous and unpublished manuscript,[3] quite different from the other two versions, which I have used as a reference.

The need to take up this research before the disappearance of the last witnesses of the living tradition of Tibet has lent a sense of urgency to the enterprise. The corpus of texts by now assembled has become quite overwhelming and the subject in itself is vast, even taking into account the loss of numerous sources of information in the twentieth-century cyclone of cultural devastation unleashed over Tibet. Within the limits of this study certain choices seemed imperative. Some aspects were expanded, others eliminated altogether. At the core remain a number of extracts from the available Tibetan literature, presented in the light of authentic commentaries from the oral tradition.

Having had the opportunity to live and study in close proximity to Tibetan lamas, yogins and erudite scholars, I have been able to address them with my numerous questions. Some replied, others merely smiled. From the Venerable Tenga Rinpoché I received the transmission of the rite. From the Venerable Gendün Rinpoché and Kalu Rinpoché I obtained the initiation of Machig (the latter, during a private interview, showed me a relic of Machig's son which he constantly carried on him in his personal *gau*). I received the explanations and commentaries on the practice, as well as the meditation transmission, from the Venerable Khenpo Tsultrim Gyamtso, accomplished yogin and incomparable scholar, who encouraged me to undertake the present work, and its completion is definitely thanks to his inspiration. In spite of remaining errors and imperfections for which I am solely responsible, I sincerely hope that

> Just like the dawn sun rising in the night sky,
> This authentic teaching aimed at cutting through demons
> Might cause the light to burst forth in all directions of space.
> PHAT!

J.E.
Bauddha, Kathmandu
June 1995

Statue of Machig Labdrön, Shukseb Nunnery near Lhasa. Photo: J. Edou.

Introduction

> All the Dharmas originated in India
> And later spread in Tibet.
> Only Machig's teaching, born in Tibet,
> Was later introduced in India and practiced there.
>
> —*The Marvelous Life of Machig Labdrön*

1 The Second Propagation of Buddhism in Tibet

After the Samyé debate of 792-794 sealed the victory of Indian Buddhism in Tibet, the apostasy of Langdarma, last king of the Tibetan dynasty, left institutional Buddhism in shambles, with its monasteries destroyed or abandoned and its monks dispersed or forced to marry. Following the death of Langdarma towards the end of the ninth century, the kingdom broke up into a multitude of principalities that wore themselves out in unceasing confrontations, while the Bönpo priests regained the power that had seemingly slipped from their hands.[1]

About a century later, the conflicts had come to an end and Tibet naturally turned towards India as a source from which to draw cultural and religious elements for its own renewal. The warlords, who had failed to impose any definite victory through military means, now tried to base their temporal power on an association with the reemerging power of religious authorities, while also actively supporting the arts, medicine and the translation of texts.

This cultural and religious renaissance, often referred to as the second propagation of Buddhism in Tibet, constitutes one of the most fertile periods in its history. Strangely enough, this renaissance first made its appearance in the outlying kingdoms of Gugé and Purang in the west. The rulers of these far-away kingdoms, all fervent Buddhists, invited to their courts Indian masters from the great monastic universities of India. Atiśa, the most famous of them all, arrived in Tibet in 1042, and having traveled and taught extensively, passed away there in 1054, just a year prior to the birth of Machig.[2]

In a parallel development, numerous Tibetans also crossed the Himalayas in their search for rare teachings and texts at these same Indian universities and at the feet of the mahāsiddhas.[3] In this way there appeared a new generation of great Tibetan translators, including Rinchen Zangpo (958-1055), who had been sent to Kashmir by the kings of Gugé; Drogmi (992-1072), the great translator and master of the tradition of "the Path and its Fruit" (*lam 'bras*); and Marpa the Translator (1012-1096) who laid the base for the Kagyü school.

These exceptional beings did not hesitate to undertake the long journey to the low-lying plains of India, braving dangers, disease and difficulties in order to bring back tantric texts and previously unknown teachings which they translated from Sanskrit and transmitted sparingly to chosen disciples. This corpus of translations known as "the new translations" (*gsar ma*) eventually brought about the emergence of new schools alongside the school based on the "ancient translations" (*rnying ma*) of the royal era.

At the time of Machig's birth in 1055 Milarepa was fifteen years old. The sacred biographies covering that period, for instance those of Marpa, Milarepa and Machig, create the impression that Buddhism was already firmly reestablished in Tibet, though black and white Bönpo priests, sorcerers, exorcists and other shamans remained powerful in the daily life of Tibetans.[4]

In the absence of any central political or religious power, informal communities developed around these Tibetan masters, often with the support of wealthy families. Some of these communities gradually turned into monastic institutions, for example Ratreng, founded in 1056, and the College of Sakya, established in 1073. Others retained their informal character, eventually producing the Tibetan tradition of "mad saints," in direct descent from the Indian mahāsiddha tradition. These wandering yogis, who remained outside any institutional framework, represent the Tibetan Buddhist ideal of renunciation and realization up to the present day. Such was the lifestyle of Milarepa and his disciples, and also of the small community that assembled around Machig Labdrön at Zangri, the Copper Mountain.

2 Machig Labdrön

Most western scholars seem to have confused Machig Labdrön, first revealer of the Chöd tradition (whose biography is presented in this volume), with her near contemporary Machig Zhama (1062-1153), who was a disciple of Ma Lotsāwa. This error goes back to George Roerich, who, in his translation of *The Blue Annals*,[5] identifies Machig Zhama as Machig Labdrön, though the Tibetan version clearly draws a distinction between the two women: their lives, teachings received, and the spiritual paths they followed are entirely different. Apart from their similar names, they hold little in common other than that both met the Indian paṇḍita Dampa Sangyé. In the translation of Machig's life presented here, it is he who once and for all clears up this error when he differentiates Machig Zhama, associated with the Path and its Fruit teachings, from Machig Labdrön, a native of E'i Lab, who disciplined beings on the basis of the system known as the Chöd of Mahāmudrā.

Beginning with her previous life as an Indian paṇḍita and continuing through her meeting with Dampa Sangyé—himself part of the Indian mahāsiddha tradition—Machig Labdrön appears at the very heart of the second propagation of the teachings from India to Tibet. But she also was a Tibetan woman, a contemporary of the founders of Buddhist lineages in Tibet, whom she eventually joined to become, like them, the founder of a new tradition, the Chöd, and the source of many transmission lineages.

Despite her important role, her biography is far from being a historical work in the modern sense. Like most Tibetan sacred biographies, Machig's life introduces us to a magico-spiritual universe where the marvelous occupies center stage and the historical facts often recede into the background. From the biographical evidence available, Machig appears as a controversial figure. Several sources (though not the main biography translated here) relate that she broke her nun's vows in order to marry an Indian yogin,[6] and as a result was rejected by the people of Ü and Tsang and forced to flee from Central Tibet. Next, in order for her teaching system to be recognized as authentic, she had to justify it in front of three Indian ācāryas who represented the authority of the paṇḍitas of Bodhgaya. During the period when the Buddhism of India was being transmitted to Tibet, these paṇḍitas of the great monastic universities of India (Nālandā, Vikramaśīla and Bodhgaya) were the undisputed guardians of Buddhist orthodoxy. It is easy to see how this woman, a native of a barbarian country, who

Jetsun Rigdzin Chönyi Zangmo (1852-1953), former abbess of Shukseb Nunnery and recognized incarnation of Machig Labdrön, ca. 1950. Photo courtesy of the author.

subjugated demons, performed miraculous cures and created her own doctrine, was bound to disturb them. They must have felt it their duty to duly test her claims.

While numerous female yoginīs, such as Yeshé Tsogyal, Jomo Menmo, Jetsun Mingyur Paldrön and Shukseb Jetsun Rigdzin Chönyi Zangmo[7] have left their mark on Tibetan religious history, it would seem that Tibetan society, not to mention religious authority, was not quite ready for the idea of a woman becoming a Vajrayāna teacher, let alone one who lived outside the range of any religious hierarchy and who single-handedly founded a new system. Had Machig failed to justify the authenticity of her teaching in front of the Indian paṇḍitas, there is every likelihood that she would have been considered a witch or, as the biography tells us in the words of the Indians, "an emanation of Māra or of some other evil spirit."[8]

This attitude towards women is no doubt the reason why very few women were officially recognized as incarnate lamas in Tibet, an attitude that prevails to the present day. Even the great Jetsun Rigdzin Chönyi Zangmo (1852-1953), abbess of Shukseb Nunnery and a recognized incarnation of Machig Labdrön, like many Buddhist nuns (and Tibetan women in general) made the wish to be reborn in a male body. Her present incarnation is a man (born in 1953), who renounced religious life to study in Beijing. While understandable in the strong patriarchal context of Tibet, it is suprising to note how widespread this attitude has become. After all, the venerable Ārya Tārā—in more than one way the feminine Buddhist ideal—vowed to reach enlightenment in the guise of a woman:

> There are many who wish to gain enlightenment in a man's form, and there are but few who wish to work for the welfare of sentient beings in a female form. Therefore may I, in a female body, work for the welfare of beings right until Saṃsāra has been emptied.[9]

Few have joined in this aspiration, and Machig is one of the rare examples of a man choosing rebirth as a woman in order to continue a spiritual career, despite Ārya Tārā's insistence:

> In this life there is no such distinction as "male" and "female," neither of "self identity," a "person" nor any perception (of such), and therefore, attachment to ideas of "male" and "female" is quite worthless. Weak-minded worldlings are always deluded by this.[10]

Machig's outstanding performance at the Red Fortress of the Copper Mountain (Zangs ri mkhar dmar, today known as Zangs ri khang dmar) silenced once and for all the opponents who had been disparaging her. Despite whatever controversy had surrounded her up to that point, she engaged from then onward, until her death at the age of ninety-nine, in vast activities to propagate Chöd.

So it is as a woman that Machig enters the very closed circle of founders of authentic and recognized lineages—a rare occurrence in the history of religions. She is woman and mother, but she is also ḍākinī and deity, legitimized as such by being an emanation of the "Great Mother of Wisdom," Yum Chenmo, as well as of Ārya Tārā, who transmitted to her teachings and initiations.[11] In this way she becomes an equal of the greatest Tibetan masters of her time. She furthermore personifies in the popular religious imagination the feminine ideal of ultimate realization and primordial wisdom.

3 The Chöd Tradition

Although Chöd has often been branded as shamanistic in origin, it is an established fact today that the Chöd tradition goes back to Indian Buddhist sources. *The Grand Poem* by Āryadeva the Brahmin,[12] for example, shows that by the tenth century Chöd existed as a complete system that combined the philosophical point of view of the Prajñāpāramitā with specific meditation methods and practical instructions regarding their application in one's activities.[13]

This Chöd tradition, according to the view of the Sūtras, was brought to Tibet by the Indian Dampa, also known as Pa Dampa Sangyé, who transmitted it to Kyotön Sönam Lama. He in turn passed it on to Machig Labdrön, together with the specific system of Dampa known as "The Pacification of Suffering" (*zhi byed*). Machig integrated these teachings and precepts with her meditation experience born from the Prajñāpāramitā and with the Vajrayāna instructions directly revealed to her by Ārya Tārā. Skillfully combining these three streams, she unified them into a single technique, named by her "The Chöd of Mahāmudrā,"[14] also known as the teaching "With the Object of Cutting Down Demons"[15] and further as "the Tibetan Chöd" (*bod gcod*). In response to the specific needs of her disciples, Machig Labdrön granted them different meditation methods that eventually generated separate lineages. Thus, one distinguishes the Sūtra lineages, the Tantra lineages, the lineages of the Combined Sūtra and Tantra, and the lineages of Recovered Treasure (*gter ma*) texts.[16]

No one can deny Chöd's status as an independent tradition; that much is clear, both in terms of historical development and in its doctrinal content. However, the existence of numerous transmission lineages suggests that Chöd was never a unique, monolithic tradition. One should really speak of Chöd traditions and lineages since Chöd has never constituted a school. Matthew Kapstein draws a distinction between schools (sects) and lineages: "By sect, I mean a religious order that is distinguished from others by virtue of its institutional independence; that is, its unique character is embodied outwardly in the form of an independent hierarchy and administration...."[17] Instead, the spiritual heritage of Machig and of Dampa was preserved through a teaching transmission of master-disciple channelled through different lineages, each of which in the course of time became increasingly independent, though not in matters of doctrinal content.

Two points should be considered regarding the historical development of Chöd: (1) the coexistence of different interpretations, according to Sūtra, Tantra or Recovered Treasure, all addressed to different kinds of disciples without reference to any unique corpus that could be called "*the* Chöd," which were transmitted in uninterrupted lineages up to the present day; and (2) the example of the early revealers, Dampa Sangyé and Machig, who preferred the (often outrageous) lay lifestyle of wandering yogis to that of the monastic community. Having received from a qualified master the meditational instructions, the Chödpa retreated from the world to practice in solitude, moving from one cemetery to the next, taking up residence in haunted houses or wilderness, often inspired by random encounters or circumstances, but always outside any institutional framework. This is how Patrul Rinpoché explains "The Accumulations of the Kusali" in one Chöd version derived from the Recovered Treasure tradition:

> The word "kusali" means beggar. To accumulate merit and wisdom, yogis who have renounced ordinary life—hermits who live in the mountains, for instance—use visualizations to make offerings of their own bodies, having no other possessions to offer.[18]

This nonconventional attitude of living on the fringe of society kept the Chödpas aloof from the wealthy monastic institutions and printing houses. As a result, the original Chöd texts and commentaries, often copied by hand, never enjoyed any wide circulation, and many have been lost forever.

This consideration allows us to evaluate the role of the monasteries in the codification and preservation of the teachings. The tradition of Dampa Sangyé known as "The Pacification of Suffering" has probably become extinct as a separate system because it remained outside the institutions. A similar fate was no doubt in store for the teachings of Milarepa, had not Gampopa—himself a monk—established the institutional foundations of the Kagyüpa school in order to preserve the distinct transmission of the famous yogin. Even if some Chöd lineages have managed to survive well apart from any institution—I personally encountered certain family transmissions in Tibet going back several generations—the majority of Machig's teachings have depended on a gradual integration into the other schools for their preservation.

4 Chöd as Viewed by the West

Strangely enough, amid the profusion of scholarly works on Tibetan Buddhism, not a single in-depth study devoted to the Chöd tradition has been published, with the exception of an excellent article by Janet Gyatso.[19] The majority of Western researchers have contented themselves with approximate accounts, often reducing the entire system to the offering of one's body to the demons, the most spectacular aspect of the rite. Consider, for instance, the following description by Bleichsteiner in 1937:

> To the sound of the drum made of human skulls and of the thighbone trumpet, the dance is begun and the spirits are invited to come and feast. The power of meditation evokes a goddess brandishing a naked sword; she springs at the head of the sacrificer, decapitates him, and hacks him to pieces; then the demons and wild beasts rush on the still-quivering fragments, eat the flesh and drink the blood....But despite this Buddhist coloring...[the rite is but] a sinister mystery going back to the most primitive times.[20]

Presented in such a way, it is easy to understand why Chöd could not be taken seriously by the first Western witnesses, still totally immersed in nineteenth-century rationalism. To them, this rite suggested cannibalistic practices which, together with the symbolic universe of tantric Buddhism and its use of sexual symbolism, could only be rejected in the name of the normative morals of the times. This attitude presented the added advantage of reconfirming the West in its own feelings of superiority and of reinforcing its self-justification of universal civilizer for a world immersed in obscurantism and superstition.

Alexandra David-Neel, who encountered Chöd adepts in the course of her peregrinations in Tibet, lingers over the morbid aspect of what she labels a "gruesome mystery," though parts of her description are closer to the real thing:

> Though [rites such as Chöd] may sometimes appear ridiculous or even repugnant, according to our ideas, their purpose is useful or lofty, such as liberating from fear, awakening feelings of boundless practical compassion leading to complete detachment and, finally, to spiritual illumination.[21]

Taking into account her pioneering work and acknowledging her genuine fascination for Tibetan Buddhism "in the field," it still remains difficult to differentiate in Mme. David-Neel's accounts the Parisienne in hot pursuit of "mystics and magicians" and the impartial witness relying on authentic source materials.

Evans-Wentz was the first Western researcher to publish, in his well-known *Tibetan Yoga and Secret Doctrines*, the complete translation of a Chöd ritual, "The Laughter of the Ḍākinīs" from the Revealed Treasure tradition,[22] a text apparently also studied by Alexandra David-Neel during her stay in Tibet. However, due to the confusing commentary that tends to equate Chöd with an exorcism rite, this work, considered authoritative for so many years, seems to have encouraged the most fanciful interpretations, including the idea of Chöd's origin in Bönpo and shamanistic rites. This interpretation was also taken over by Mircea Eliade, who mentions Chöd in his celebrated study on shamanism but unfortunately derives his data from Bleichsteiner.[23] According to Eliade, this rite, from a structural point of view, is to be defined as a "mystic revaluation of the basic stages in a shamanistic initiation," despite the fact that, according to him, the specific element of shamanism consists of "the ecstasy created by the shaman's elevation to heaven and his descent into the under-world." It should be noted that in the Chöd tradition there is no trace of either trance or ecstasy, nor of what in shamanistic terminology is referred to as the "initiatory journey." On the other hand, if the question is indeed one of "revaluation," this can only consist in a contribution *qua* meaning which, in the context of Chöd, would have to refer to the Prajñāpāramitā doctrine. As we will see, the Prajñāpāramitā is the conceptual source from which the Chöd system developed, and not the other way around. As for the specific methods of Chöd such as the offering of one's body, these seem directly derived from the Bodhisattva tradition, as described for example in the *Jātaka* stories.[24]

This shamanizing interpretation has been taken up of late by C. Van Tuyl in his article "Mi-la-ras-pa and the gCod Ritual," which tries to discover how the visualization of oneself as a skeleton "probably reflects a Tibetan memory of the original shamanistic ritual." Unfortunately, the author has no access to the Tibetan texts and relies on dubious source materials to back up a point of view that in itself is not very clear:

> Then [Milarepa] goes on in prose to enumerate each item of the body which he gives the demons to eat. This enumeration of the parts of the body is a characteristic of the shamanistic initiation ritual of the Eskimo peoples and its appearance in the Milarepa account suggests that the *mgur-'bum* [*The Hundred Thousand Songs of Milarepa*] preserves a very old version of the ch'ö.[25]

The reasoning is sufficiently confusing for one to wonder whether Van Tuyl is trying to demonstrate that Chöd's origins are to be traced back to the shamanistic rites, or would like us to believe that the "very old version of Chöd" conceals the shamanistic rites of dismemberment. Furthermore, as discussed below in the chapter on offering the body, one should differentiate the generic term "chöd" that refers to cutting through the ego and its emotional entanglements (and in this sense would seem as ancient as Buddhism itself), and the Chöd doctrine of "cutting through demonic objects" (*bdud kyi gcod yul*), for which Machig was the source and inspiration. *The Concise Life Story* insists:

> Although numerous Buddhas and mahāsiddhas did appear in this country [Tibet], [prior to Machig] no tradition existed about how to transform the aggregates into a food offering and thereby to satisfy [the gods and demons] with flesh and blood.[26]

Whatever the interpretation proposed, historical research cannot accept this kind of reductionist interpretation, nor feel satisfied with structural comparisons that, willfully or otherwise, ignore the actual meaning. Even if certain elements of Chöd present lexicographical similarities with certain shamanistic rites, the latter are considered "erroneous forms of Chöd" (*gcod log*), simple superstitions (in the etymological sense of the word) which Patrul Rinpoché describes as follows:

> What today's so-called Chö practitioners mean by Chö is a grisly process of destroying malignant spirits by slashing, chopping, chasing and killing them. Their idea of Chö involves being constantly full of anger. Their bravodo is nothing more than hatred and pride. They imagine that they have to behave like the henchmen of the Lord of Death. For example, when they practise Chö for a sick person, they work themselves into a furious display of rage, staring with hate-filled eyes as large as saucers, clenching their fists, biting their lower lips, lashing out with blows and grabbing the

> invalid so hard that they tear the clothes off his back. They call this subduing spirits, but to practise Dharma like that is totally mistaken.[27]

The history of religions teaches that each new religion tends to incorporate within its system the beliefs already established, "because it takes root in everything the past has left of imagery, symbols and particular modes of sensibility."[28] During the second propagation of Buddhism in Tibet, throughout the tenth and eleventh centuries, the indigenous religion was, in the words of Giuseppe Tucci, "a true 'folk religion'. The beliefs, myths and customs of this folk religion are widely known and followed among the ordinary people."[29] In this sense, it seems more than likely that Chöd, while already constituting a coherent religious system in India (defined there as the practical methods of the Perfection of Wisdom), incorporated elements from the popular tradition and Tibetan imagination—such as a pantheon of autochthonous gods and demons—in order to integrate itself into the cultural and religious environment of the tenth century. Beyond this, it contributed a new meaning to that environment, based on the teaching of emptiness.

PART ONE: THE CHOD TRADITION

This authentic tradition,
The Chöd of Mahāmudrā,
Is similar to the well-known Prajñāpāramitā
And its practice is the secret Vajrayāna.

—*Machig Labdrön*

Dampa Sangyé. Clay statue preserved at his hermitage of Langkhor near Dingri. Photo: J. Edou.

I The Grand Poem on the Perfection of Wisdom

by Āryadeva the Brahmin

In Sanskrit: *Ārya-prajñāpāramitā-upadeśa*
In Tibetan: *'Phags pa shes rab kyi pha rol tu phyin pa'i man ngag*
The Instructions on the Perfection of Wisdom[1]

To all the Buddhas and bodhisattvas I offer salutation with full prostration.

By the sun and moon of your realization, you vanquish the misconceptions born from ignorance,
While the moisture of your compassion brings living beings to spiritual maturity.
To Mañjuśrī, Lion of Speech, who perfectly accomplishes both aims,[2]
I bow down in pure devotion with body, speech and mind.

Here I will explain to the best of my abilities and for others' benefit
[The ultimate nature of the mind], the actual meaning of the nondual Perfection of Wisdom,
The heart essence of what is to be practiced, devoid of any support
And free from conceptually conceived extremes such as eternalist and nihilist views.[3]

Through [spontaneous] awareness free of artifice and corruption
Recognize your mind as the root of both saṃsāra and nirvāṇa.

It is not produced by causes or conditions,
Unborn, naturally serene, its nature is emptiness.

To realize [this nature] is like cutting down a tree trunk at the root:
No more branches of thoughts will ever grow forth from there.
Whatever appears in your mind, real or imaginary,
Give as vast offerings to the Lama [and the Triple] Gem.

Offer salutation with full prostration, present homage and offerings,
Then, with devotion, go for refuge and generate the altruistic mind set on enlightenment.[4]
Once you have obtained the oral instructions, guard them like your eyes.
Even at the cost of your life never abandon the instructions on the bodhisattva's [way of life],
And show perseverance in sticking to the training.

Abandon the ten negative acts such as killing and the rest,
And encourage others to do likewise.
Follow meticulously these instructions to renounce killing and other such acts.
Live your life that way.

However, by merely abandoning the ten negative acts
You will not find the supreme path.
You should put into practice the six perfections
And encourage others to do likewise.
Follow meticulously these six perfections.
Live your life that way.[5]

As you get [increasingly] involved in the practice of positive activity
Such as the six perfections and more,
Exaltation should be rejected as soon as it arises.

As long as you fail to realize the profound meaning of the Perfection of Wisdom
As utterly nondual and devoid of every extreme
Such as virtue and fault, acceptance and rejection, hope and fear,
Even though each inclination [of the mind] is transformed into virtue,
In this very life you will not attain liberation.

So, with regard to all phenomena,
Composite and noncomposite [material and imaginary],
Whether the karmic impact is positive or negative,
Don't turn anything into a fixed reference or support, not even so much as an atom.

Without, however, relying on skillful means as well,[6]
Perfection of Wisdom will not manifest itself,
Just as without preparing the field
No harvest will ever appear.

And without first having gained certainty about the [definitive] meaning of Prajñāpāramitā,
Even if you practice [the other perfections of] generosity, discipline and patience, perseverance and meditative concentration,
[It will be like] a blind man who has lost his stick:
How could he possibly figure out the path?

The meaning of the Prajñāpāramitā
Is not to be looked for elsewhere: it exists within yourself.
Neither real nor endowed with characteristics,
The nature [of the mind] is the great clear light.[7]

Separate from any kind of mental fabrication
And naturally purified of conceptual recollection
Is the Buddha, whom one keeps in mind while practicing meditation.

Neither outer nor inner, neither god nor demon,
Not existence in saṃsāra's cycles nor nirvāṇa's beyond,
Neither manifest nor empty:
[Mind is] free from any such dual appearances.
This is the Buddha's true intention, his flawless uncontrived view.
If looking for a simile, one could say it is like space.

The supreme method here [to realize the nature of mind]
Is to unite space and awareness.[8]
When thus mixing space and awareness,
You spontaneously purify fixed notions
Such as reality and characteristics, negating and establishing,
And you abide in the truth of suchness, dharmatā,
Free from dualistic subject-object cognition.

With body and mind thus [in their natural state],
Without further intervention, a fresh awareness arises,
Extending just as far as the reach of empty space,
In this vast expanse remain absorbed without constraints or limits.

At that time you will experience a state of consciousness
Free from any support, from any sort of foundation,
An awareness abiding nowhere,
Not absorbed in either the five aggregates or any outer object.

In desolate rocky mountains or among snowy peaks,
In charnel fields and cremation grounds, in wilderness,
In villages and in towns, in caves and lonely grottos,
Wherever you may be, meditate on nonduality.

Put into practice during all four activities of life [—walking, sleeping, sitting down and eating—]
The meaning of the unborn [nature of mind] as the guru has taught.

In the course of your practice,
Through the blessing of the pāramitās
And the realization of phenomena as empty,
Obstacles will not occur.
Within emptiness,
How could [obstacles] arise from emptiness?

Once the essence of reality is realized as empty
And beyond any signs and characteristics,
Resting in this emptiness you will purify to the utmost
All the objects of the five gates [of the senses]:
Forms and sounds, odors, tastes and that which can be touched.
Though coarse emotional afflictions
Will still arise within and subtle ego-grasping too,
In nonduality they'll become self-liberated, and of no more importance.

Having gained such realization, abide in suchness and become liberated;
This is like reaching the Golden Islands[9]
[Where there are no impurities, no earth or stones].

When someone is killed, his life cut off at the root,
There is no further need [for the murderer] to also block the gates
Of the [victim's] sense organs, eyes and the rest.
Likewise, when mind itself is cut off at the root,
You will realize all phenomena as empty.

Thus to cut off mind itself at the root,
To cut through the five poisons of mental afflictions,
To cut through extreme views and mental formations during meditation,
As well as anxiety, hope and fear in actions
And to cut through arrogance [which is grasping at a self[10]]—
Since all this is a matter of cutting through ["chöd pa"],
This is the real meaning of Chöd.

Now as for the tangible demons[11] of strong longing for manifest reality,
Of passionate attraction, of hatred or aversion,
How does one cut through these?
Depending on whether your experience is excellent, medium, or ordinary,
Remain in spontaneous absorption free of thought, similar to a dense forest;
Meditate with your concentration aimed at these [demons], as if you were endowed with supernatural powers;
Or, like [using] a sharp axe, firmly establish [their non-existence] by analysis and reasoning.[12]

What are known as the intangible demons[13]
Consist of magical manifestations of gods and demons, and of arrogance.
If overcome with fear, remain absorbed in this fear,
Just like directing the burning needle of moxibustion with sharp precision onto the flesh.[14]

With the Three Jewels for your sole shelter and refuge,
Remain as one who lives below the constellations of the starry sky.
Any dealings, close or distant, with gods or demons should be abandoned.
Once and for all sever [all ties with] close friends and relatives.

The definitive sign [of realization] in Chöd is to be free from fear.
The level of final accomplishment in the practice
Is the spontaneous pacification of magical interferences [of gods and demons].[15]

But if your practice is not right you will run away in panic
[Chased by such magical interferences].
Don't flee but remain unwavering, solid like a doorframe,
Even if terror or panic arise.
Immutable, like a wooden stake, eradicate all negativity,
Force down and subdue [any demonic interference].

Such are the authentic oral instructions [on Chöd].

When you are thus meditating on nondual Prajñāpāramitā,
The local gods and demons can't stand it,
And in despair cause magical interferences of all kinds,
Real, imaginary or in dreams.
In dealing with these,
Those of most excellent [meditational capacity] should remain absorbed in the meaning of the nondual [nature of mind];
Those of medium capacity should concentrate on those very wonders;
Those of average capacity should transform their aggregates into an offering of food.
Next, generate an awareness that experiences mind free of any reference points [or mental fabrications].

Having moved to desolate spots,
When magical displays of gods or demons arise,
Separate awareness from the material body [through transference of consciousness].[16]
The physical body is like a stone—nothing can harm it—
And mind has no real existence, being similar to space.
So who or what could possibly be harmed?
Pondering this, remain in suchness, with no anxiety, no fear.
Even when it feels as if gods and demons are carrying away your body,
That inanimate corpse,
Don't move an inch from the seat you have taken,
Nor feel scared or think of danger.

Whatever wandering thoughts arise are demons that arise from
your own mind.
And mind has not even an atom of existence: no place where it
comes from,
No place where it abides, no place for it to go to, either.
Once liberated, it is not where Buddhahood comes from;
Still confused, it could not possibly be drifting through saṃsāra

[For this natural state is beyond both liberation and confusion].
All virtuous and negative deeds are totally pure,
Primordially pure, primordially liberated, primordially Buddhahood.
Still, not to shun faults and negative acts, that's a mistake!

Attachment to a philosophical tenet is obscuration.
Nondual, self-liberated is the ultimate nature [of the mind].
Take refuge in the essence of reality
And generate the mind set on enlightenment.

When encountering inner obstructions,
Meditate on nonduality in the wilds.
If you wish to benefit someone [through the practice of Chöd],
Generate compassion as a preliminary,
Then realize how yourself, the sick person, the demon and the illness
Are all empty [devoid of inherent existence].
Then cleanse by means of mudrā and meditate upon emptiness.
The patient should then lie down facing you.
If thereby the disease is not pacified
Take the patient to a desolate spot, take refuge and generate the mind
set on enlightenment.
Three times step over the sick person and follow this by meditation
[on emptiness]
Free from extremes [and reference points].
Next [in the patient's name] present a maṇḍala offering
Together with the small sticks and pebbles over which you have
invoked the blessing.

The gods of the upper regions should be viewed as sacred
And the nāgas of the lower regions should be subdued.
Any task you request from them, the nāgas will accomplish.

Thus befriend through rites the gods from wherever you reside
And force all nāgas into submission, making them act as your servants.
Towards guru, yidam-deities, ḍākinīs and protectors, you should feel like their only child.

Once the tangible demons are cut off,
The visual world will no longer appear as an enemy.
Once the intangible demons are cut off,
Male and female harm-bestowing yakṣas will be bound by oath.

These and other excellent qualities by means of which to benefit [others]
Will eventually become immeasurable.

Advice given by the Brahmin Āryadeva, *The Grand Poem Explaining the Perfection of Wisdom,* [is hereby completed].

[*Colophon*]
Following direct oral translation made by the Precious Master Dampa Rinpoché, the paṇḍita from India, in Dingri at the Fern Forest Retreat, Zhama Lotsāwa revised [the Tibetan text] and established the definitive version.

[*Prayer for Auspiciousness*]
OM SVASTI!
In the vast cloud of the profound and secret [teachings] by "the descendant of Ikṣvāku" [Śākyamuni],
If the drum of summer [thunder] of the feats in the equally profound Chöd practice
Resounds even just a little thanks to this composition,
The joy in the play of the peacocks [beings to be tamed] is bound to increase.

On the meaning of the wisdom, the Conqueror's middle turning of the wheel,
Space of the Vajra Queen, space of the Triple Gate to liberation,
This very explanation by the supreme authority Āryadeva himself
Has been reprinted, motivated by the three kinds of devotion.
By the moon's crystal orb of merit thereby accumulated,
May the dense darkness of karma and delusory obscurations be lit;
And by the festive banquet of the utterly white light, highest of all,
May the kunda flower of mind blossom throughout the triple world.

Prajñāpāramitā or Yum Chenmo. Drawing by Dolpopa Tenzin Norbu.

II The Prajñāpāramitā

The meaning of the Prajñāpāramitā
Is not to be looked for elsewhere: it exists within yourself.
Neither real nor endowed with characteristics,
The nature [of the mind] is the great clear light.

—*Āryadeva the Brahmin*

1 The *Heart Sūtra*

By the late tenth century the Theravāda tradition was still the predominant force within Indian Buddhism, but beginning in the seventh century two trends had developed at Nālandā, Vikramaśīla and Odantapurī, the great monastic universities of northern India: (1) the Prajñāpāramitā, or Perfection of Wisdom, the philosophical foundation of the Mahāyāna, which emphasized the emptiness of all phenomena as systematized by Nāgārjuna (ca. second century); and (2) the Vajrayāna, based on the tantras, which borrowed from the Mahāyāna the conceptual point of view of emptiness, but applied specific techniques for spiritual realization. While accepted and recognized by the monastic institutions and taught at some of them from the thirteenth century onwards, it had already reached its full blossoming in the tradition of the mahāsiddhas.

The Prajñāpāramitā became particularly widespread starting from the thirteenth century, mainly due to the extensive commentaries by Śāntideva and Śāntarakṣita, first in India, later in Tibet itself, where the teachings of Śāntarakṣita and of his disciple Kamalaśīla formed the conceptual foundation of Tibetan Buddhism.

The Prajñāpāramitā was first taught by the Buddha at Vulture Peak near Rājgir in the course of what came to be known as the Second

Turning of the Wheel. After giving the teachings related to suffering, its causes, cessation and the path of liberation, the Buddha taught the ultimate meaning of the Dharma, the emptiness of inherent existence of all phenomena. This teaching finds its most concise expression in the famous *Heart Sūtra*.[1]

This sūtra takes the form of a dialogue between Avalokiteśvara and Śāriputra at the feet of the Buddha. Avalokiteśvara applies reasoning by negation to show Śāriputra ultimate truth. The form of this reasoning presents certain features analogous to the scholastic tradition of negative theology of Eastern Christianity. It is by definition impossible to express the ineffable, what is beyond expression, and the same holds true for absolute truth, which is beyond words and concepts. At the very most one may express what it is not, by exclusion: "Thus, Śāriputra, in emptiness there is no form, no feeling,...no suffering,...no cessation [of suffering],...no attainment, and also no non-attainment."[2]

The term *emptiness*[3] does not carry here any connotation of void or of absolute nothingness. It should be understood as the naturally open and serene state of the mind. Thus, to affirm the emptiness of phenomena does not in any way mean that they do not exist in the way that the horn of a hare or skyflowers do not exist. Instead, emptiness refers to the insight that, at the ultimate level, both interior phenomena—sensations, perceptions and the "I"—and exterior phenomena—all the appearances of the phenomenal world—have no real existence, although they do appear in different forms. The *Heart Sūtra* summarizes this as follows:

> Form is emptiness, emptiness is form,
> Emptiness is not other than form,
> Form is not other than emptiness.

"Form is emptiness" is the insight (Skt. *prajñā*) that challenges materialism and the realistic conception of the universe by establishing that phenomena—from the tiniest particle to the Buddhas' omniscience—ultimately do not possess any existence on their own. "Emptiness is form" is the affirmation of relative truth and the rejection of nihilistic conceptions. Emptiness manifests as form in all things, material as well as imaginary, and cannot be found outside these phenomena. In this way, bodhisattvas cannot cut themselves off from the world, nor find individual delight in emptiness, but they must make use of skillful means (Tib. *thabs*) such as loving-kindness and compassion in order to realize the ultimate truth. With this aim, they must develop the qualities of generosity, discipline, patience, perseverance and meditation, the five relative perfections that are the means to realize the sixth perfection, wisdom or insight (*prajñā*). "Emptiness is not other than form, form is not other than emptiness" expresses the interrelatedness of these six perfections, how it is impossible to separate emptiness and appearances, the necessary union of relative truth and absolute truth according to the principles of exclusion and mutual contradiction. Emptiness does not deny or refute form, and likewise form does not deny or refute emptiness.

In order to illustrate the emptiness of inherent existence of phenomena, the commentators often use the example of the dream. Indeed, dream images are devoid of any material reality on their own, since they are not composed of atoms or particles. Likewise, neither the eye sense nor the eye consciousness that are at the basis of vision of these images has any real existence. The fire one perceives in a dream does not really exist; it simply appears as a play of mind and, having never existed, cannot perish either. Hence the level of existence of dream images is nothing but a convention, a term applied to define mental experience. One cannot affirm that dreams don't exist, for in the consciousness of the dreamer they produce emotions, suffering or joy, tears or laughter. Neither can one affirm that they really do exist, for they are devoid of any intrinsic reality of their own, outside the consciousness that created them in the first place. In the same way, according to Mahāyāna, phenomena seem to exist, but in reality their essence is emptiness. They are like a mirage or an illusion created by a magician.

The school of thought that articulates this view is called the Middle Way (Madhyamaka), because it establishes that phenomena are neither existing ("form is empty"), nor non-existing ("emptiness is form"), nor any other combination of these two extremes. It therefore situates itself in the middle, between the eternalist and nihilist points of view, insisting on the impossibility of separating the two truths (relative and ultimate), of separating saṃsāra and nirvāṇa. Therefore the nature of all phenomena cannot be reduced to concepts, however profound. It is beyond all conceptualization (Tib. *spros bral*).[4] This Madhyamaka doctrine was systematized by Nāgārjuna in his *Fundamental Treatise on the Middle Way, Called Wisdom,* later commented upon by Candrakīrti (sixth century) in his *Entering the Middle Way: A Commentary to (Nāgārjuna's) "Fundamental Treatise on the Middle Way"*. To the present day these remain the foundational Madhyamaka treatises used by the four Buddhist schools of Tibet.

2 The Mother of the Buddhas

Among the wide variety of analytical and meditational techniques of both Mahāyāna and Vajrayāna, only the realization of emptiness allows one to cut through the erroneous belief in a self and reach Buddhahood. In the Chöd terminology, this notion of the reality of a self is the most powerful demon of all which must be cut down by the realization of emptiness—the meaning of the Prajñāpāramitā. Hence the Prajñāpāramitā is called "the Mother" (Tib. *yum*), because she is the matrix that gives birth to the realization of all the Buddhas. In the words of H. H. the Dalai Lama:

> The difference in vehicles must be determined through either wisdom or method. Because the wisdom cognising emptiness is the mother common to all four sons—Hearer, Solitary Realizer, Bodhisattva, and Buddha Superiors—Hinayāna and Mahāyāna are differentiated by way of method, not by way of wisdom. For the same reason, the Perfection and Mantra Vehicles are differentiated by method, not wisdom.[5]

In the biography of Machig, Prajñāpāramitā is called Yum Chenmo, the Great Mother, spontaneous Dharmakāya free of origination, existence and cessation. She appears as a four-armed deity, seated in meditation posture, adorned with many attributes, but her real nature is explained to Machig by Ārya Tārā:

> The Primordial Mother, Yum Chenmo, is the ultimate nature of all phenomena, emptiness, suchness [Skt. *dharmatā*], free from the two veils.[6] She is the pure essence of the sphere of emptiness, the insight of the non-self. She is the matrix who gives birth to all the Buddhas of the three times. However, to give beings the opportunity to accumulate spiritual merits, she manifests herself as an object of veneration.[7]

Just as emptiness is referred to as the Mother of the Buddhas, so the three fundamental texts of the Prajñāpāramitā are traditionally known as the three "mother" texts (Tib. *yum gsum*): *The Prajñāpāramitā Sūtra in One Hundred Thousand Lines, The Prajñāpāramitā Sūtra in Twenty-Five Thousand Lines*, and *The Prajñāpāramitā Sūtra in Eight Thousand Lines*. By further analogy, seventeen texts are called the "sons" of Prajñāpāramitā; they include the *Heart Sūtra* and the *Diamond-Cutter Sūtra.*

These three versions of the Prajñāpāramitā are constantly cited in the biography of Machig as the principal source of her inspiration. Machig herself is considered a wisdom ḍākinī and an emanation of Yum Chenmo, as Tārā states in her biography: "Yum Chenmo finally took birth in Tibet and is no one but you, Machig Labdrön!" From her earliest youth, Machig showed a particular attraction for the Perfection of Wisdom, of which she recited several volumes every day. Having mastered this doctrine—so the text informs us—"at the chapter of the Prajñāpāramitā that deals with the topic of demons, an exceptional realization was born in her."[8]

In fact, the very idea of "cutting through" (Tib. *gcod*) attachment appears at a very early stage in Buddhist literature, in a context closely related to the Prajñāpāramitā doctrine. For example, in the well-known *Diamond-Cutter Sūtra*, the Perfection of Wisdom is said to resemble an indestructible diamond (Skt. *vajra*) that cuts through all attachment to the reality of phenomena and establishes their non-existence. Likewise, as Janet Gyatso has pointed out, this metaphor is already in use in the Pāli canon, where Buddhaghosa defines the technique of "abandoning by cutting off" (*samuccheda*) as the "supramundane path that leads to the destruction (of defilement)."[9] One should of course refrain from identifying the generic term "cutting off," as it occurs in Buddhist literature in general, with the specific system of Machig. Nonetheless, it seems certain at present that Machig's tradition, generally considered a Tibetan doctrine, has its origins in the Indian tradition of the Prajñāpāramitā as taught by the Buddha.

3 The Indian Tradition

According to Karma Chagmé, the Indian Chöd tradition divided into four main streams exemplified by four texts: (1) *The Grand Poem on the Perfection of Wisdom* of Āryadeva the Brahmin; (2) *The Single Taste* of Nāropa;[10] (3) *The Pacification of Suffering* of Dampa Sangyé; and (4) *The Elimination of Confusion* of Orgyen [Padmasambhava].[11]

The Indian origin of the latter three texts are above all suspicion, for these authors are well attested in the Indian Buddhist tradition between the sixth and twelfth centuries, even if, among commentators, there are noteworthy differences in the titles of these works. Machig may have had access to these teachings, though none of our sources explicitly mentions her receiving the transmission of Nāropa's *Single Taste* or of Orgyen's *Elimination of Confusion*. By contrast we know that Dampa passed on to her the teachings on the *Pacification of Suffering*, and it is more than likely that he also transmitted to her Āryadeva's *Grand Poem on the Perfection of Wisdom*, which he himself had brought to Tibet. Carrying with him the Sanskrit text, he gave an oral translation thereof at Dingri to Zhama the Translator, who later revised it and established the definitive version in Tibetan—that much is said in the colophon to *The Grand Poem*.

Each of these four texts belongs to the Sūtra tradition and consists of a commentary to the Prajñāpāramitā. Only *The Elimination of Confusion* seems never to have been openly revealed in India, but was hidden by Padmasambhava, later discovered as a terma or Treasure (Tib. *gter ma*), and then propagated in Tibet.[12]

The Grand Poem on the Perfection of Wisdom by the Brahmin Āryadeva is the most concise of the four and contains an explicit reference to an Indian Chöd tradition. The Tibetan sources make a clear distinction between its author, Āryadeva the Brahmin, and Lopön Āryadeva,[13] the well-known disciple of the philosopher Nāgārjuna. The former seems to belong to the ninth century and he is often quoted in the transmission lineage (Tib. *bka' brgyud*) of the Prajñāpāramitā.

The text by Āryadeva follows the standard explanation of the Madhyamaka point of view. It teaches the inseparability of transcendent wisdom and the means of realization, and establishes the nonduality that rejects the eternalist and nihilist assertions. It emphasizes, however, understanding the emptiness of mind as a means for understanding that all phenomena are empty, an approach that has been carried on within the Mahāmudrā tradition. Thus Āryadeva borrows from Tilopa's *Mahāmudrā Upadeśa*[14] the analogy of the tree and its roots in order to illustrate the means for realizing the nature of mind:

> To realize [this nature] is like cutting down a tree trunk at the root:
> No more branches of thoughts will ever grow forth from there....
> Likewise when mind is cut off at the root [if you realize its true nature]
> You realize all phenomena as empty.

Mind is the source of all manifestation of the phenomenal world: happiness and suffering, saṃsāra and nirvāṇa, gods and demons. When one thus cuts off mind at the root, that is, when one realizes its nature as purified of contingent impurities and when one remains absorbed in emptiness, free from subject-object duality, all emotional afflictions such as ignorance, attachment and aversion disappear by themselves.

In order to realize this unborn nature of the mind, Āryadeva's advice is "to unite consciousness and space," the means that constitute the very foundation of the Chöd tradition of Machig. In the last instance, what must be cut off is the erroneous conception of self as inherently existing, the very source of ignorance:

> Thus to cut off mind itself at the root,
> To cut through the five poisons of mental afflictions,

To cut through extreme views and mental formations during
meditation,
As well as anxiety, hope and fear in actions
And to cut through arrogance—
Since all this is a matter of cutting through ["chöd pa"],
This is the real meaning of Chöd.

This definition, so often repeated by Tibetan commentators, summarizes the Indian Chöd tradition based on the Prajñāpāramitā and known as the Sūtra tradition. Up to now no trace of any Indian Chöd rite has been discovered, hence it is difficult to know how it was practiced. The only information to have reached us comes through Dampa Sangyé, who passed this tradition on to Tibet.

4 Dampa Sangyé and the Tibetan Tradition

Dampa Sangyé (Dam pa sangs rgyas), "the Indian," is traditionally considered the guru of Machig. As with most biographies of Indian siddhas, the accounts of his life abound in fabulous tales, and versions vary greatly from one to the other.

Born in a Brahmin family of Tsarasingha in the Beta region of South India,[15] at the age of thirteen he was sent to Vikramaśīla University where he received monastic ordination. Upon completion of his monastic studies, he set out on the life of a wandering yogin and studied at the feet of the greatest masters of India. From fifty-four siddhas, both male and female, he received teachings on the Sūtras and initiations and instructions in the Tantras. Since the biographical sources do not always draw a clear distinction between masters actually encountered and teachings received through visionary experience, there is plenty of obvious anachronism in the enumeration of his masters who include, for the Sūtra tradition, Nāgārjuna, Āryadeva,[16] Asaṅga, Śāntideva and Dharmakīrti; among his principal tantric teachers Kukuripa, Saraha, Maitrīpa, Tilopa and the ḍākinī Sukhasiddhī are mentioned. According to the *Blue Annals*, he meditated for a period of fifty-nine years at different sacred spots in India and Nepal, including Bodhgaya and Swayambhū,[17] and attained both the ordinary and extraordinary accomplishments (Skt. *siddhi*). He became known for his supernatural perception, developed the power of swift-footedness (Tib. *rkang mgyogs*) and realized the path of vision and later supreme Mahāmudrā.[18]

Dampa remains primarily associated with the doctrine of the Pacification of Suffering (Tib. *zhi byed*), of which he was the first revealer and which he passed on to his Tibetan disciples, the latter being, in his own words, "as numerous as the stars in the sky of Dingri." At Langkhor, close to Dingri, in the large valley dominated by Mount Everest, he established his Tibetan residence, but he remained a formidable traveller whose wanderings even led him to China. According to Tibetan sources he travelled five times to Tibet. In the course of his fifth Tibet trip he continued on to China where he spent twelve years and was known as Bodhidharma. He finally returned to Dingri where he passed away in 1117.[19]

Quite a different version of his life is given by Karma Chagmé: Kamalaśīla, after his triumph at Samyé, did not die in Tibet as is generally believed, but travelled to South India. There, out of compassion for the local villagers none of whom dared to remove the polluting corpse of a leper, he temporarily transferred his consciousness into the leper's corpse. Meanwhile his own body was stolen by a horrible-looking sadhu. Left without any alternative, Kamalaśīla had to take over the sadhu's body and returned thus to Tibet, where he became known as Pa Dampa Sangyé.[20] This version would explain why

Bodhidharma and Dampa Sangyé are both, in iconographical tradition, represented with very unattractive features.

The version of this episode given in *The Concise Life Story* has an even more surprising development involving Machig's direct intervention. As an extraordinary example of the hagiographically marvelous, it deserves to be quoted extensively:

> One morning, at dawn, while she [Machig] resided in the lama's shrine room, a lion-headed ḍākinī appeared and said, "Labdrönma, Wisdom Ḍākinī, Dampa Sangyé is about to depart for the Pure Land of the ḍākinī realm [*mkha' spyod*]. How do you feel about that? If you mount this lioness, we could travel there together."
>
> In the sky was a white lioness that had guided the ḍākinī. Machig went outside and right away they set off into illusory space [*sgyu 'phrul*] under the guidance of the ḍākinī. Without any delay they reached Nepal.
>
> The Indian Dampa Sangyé and Dampa Nagchung ["Little Black Dampa"], on their way back to Tibet, had just arrived in a valley of Nepal where the people were afflicted by a terrible epidemic. The two Indians inquired about the cause of this epidemic and were told, "Uphill, on a slope of the valley, an elephant has died and is still there, at the spring. Its saliva has polluted our water and we all drank from it and became ill."
>
> Dampa then asked Dampa Nagchung, "Shall the two of us take it upon ourselves to get the elephant out and carry it to the other side of the river?"
>
> Dampa Nagchung agreed and Dampa Rinpoché told him, "Since you are an expert in the oral instructions [on entering a corpse with one's own consciousness], why don't you carry the elephant across to the other riverbank while I watch your body?"
>
> But Dampa Nagchung replied, "I'm unable to do so. You are the one [capable of accomplishing] the well-being of all beings without exception!"
>
> "Okay then, but make sure that no birds or dogs come to feast on my body—guard it well!"
>
> And with these words the body of Dampa Rinpoché became resplendent and bright; his black hair, reaching down his back, gleamed and he displayed the thirty-two marks [of a superhuman being]. His body, so splendid it was hard to divert one's eyes from it, was seated in the vajra posture, then rose into space, and settled one cubit above the ground. His mind entered the elephant's remains, thereby reviving it, and then it marched to the opposite riverbank.
>
> In the meantime, Dampa Nagchung looked at his own body and found it very ugly. So he lay down on his back and, leaving his body right there, he entered the now corpse-like body of Dampa

Sangyé and carried away with him the corporal form of Dampa Sangyé to India....

Back there [in Nepal], Dampa Sangyé had now deposited the elephant corpse across the river and returned to the previous spot, yet was unable to find his own body. He thought it over and spoke, "For me to succeed in benefiting all living beings, they'll need a support for their faith and devotion; but if I now enter these physical remains [of Nagchung], no one will feel any faith or devotion for me. Unable to benefit others, I'd better depart right away for the ḍākinī realm."

At that very moment, Machig thought, "If Dampa Rinpoché departs for the ḍākinī realm, he will thereby take away the good fortune of beings. This should be avoided at all costs. Maybe if I address a hymn of praise to the body of Nagchung, Dampa Sangyé might enter it." And so she composed this hymn:

> *HUNG!* Great Black Father with the splendor of glory endowed,
> Your chest is powerful like the lion's
> Whose claws tear apart the four kinds of demons.
> Your sides gleam like a peacock's feathers
> As the sign that you break up the five poisons.
> Your waist is thin like the heart of the Vajra
> Because you cut through the source of confusion, at its root.
> Your two legs are planted parallel to one another, like young bamboo shoots,
> For you travel the direct path to enlightenment.
> Your body color is a shining black
> Since you are unwavering in the suchness of phenomena.

Upon Machig's completion of these praises, Dampa Rinpoché thought, "At present, even with my appearance not exactly the best to inspire devotion and faith for suffering beings, the wisdom ḍākinī Labdrönma, truly Samantabhadri, mother of all Buddhas of the three times, has composed a marvelous hymn [to this Nagchung's body]. I just couldn't act against her words."

And so he took over Dampa Nagchung's body and pursued his trip to Tibet.[21]

Most Tibetan compendia classify Chöd as a branch of the Pacification of Suffering (*zhi byed*), in other words, of Prajñāpāramitā. Two reasons seem to be involved in this assimilation. To start with, the Sūtra tradition of Chöd is very close to Dampa's Pacification of Suffering system, which itself occupies an important place in the transmission of the tradition he received from Āryadeva and in turn passed on to his disciples, no doubt including Machig herself.

On the other hand, popular belief tends to consider Dampa the guru of Machig, probably on the basis of source materials like those contained in *The Blue Annals* which hold the view that during his third visit to Tibet, Dampa transmitted "the Chöd precepts that belong to the intermediate lineage [of Dampa]" to Machig Labdrön. The various sources present two mutually exclusive interpretations: (1) According to one version, Dampa and Machig met only occasionally. *The Blue Annals* reports that "Dampa Sangyé used to say that he had given to the noble Ma, who recites texts at Rogpa in Yarlung, three secret instructions, by means of which she attained liberation."[22] The *Transmission History* confirms this version: Machig requested from Dampa an empowerment, and the latter granted her the Opening of the Gates of Space, together with four sets of instructions (*gdams pa*). Machig felt no need to request any further instructions, because by means of these she achieved liberation.[23] (2) Other sources seem to reinforce the connection between Machig and Dampa. In *The Marvelous Life* as well as in *The Concise Life Story*, from where the anecdote above was taken, the encounters between them are multiple, and the texts suggest that at the time of their first meeting they at least knew about each other: Dampa is in search of an Indian paṇḍita supposedly reincarnated in Tibet, while Machig welcomes him with the words: "What a great marvel that you, Dampa Rinpoché, have come to Tibet!" Occasionally, two versions of the same anecdote illustrate these two different hagiographical tendencies in the biographical materials. Thus, after long wanderings in Central Tibet, Machig returns to Latö, then travels to Dingri in order to meet Dampa. According to the *Transmission History*, she stays a mere three or four days, then sets out for Zangri, the Copper Mountain. In *The Marvelous Life*, she remains with Dampa for one and a half months.

Perhaps the most disturbing element in the text here translated, as in *The Concise Life Story*,[24] is the nearly identical repetition of the names of the initiations which Machig receives from Sönam Lama first, then again from Dampa a few pages further—empowerments that go unmentioned in all other sources. Even though Dampa passes on to Machig more initiations and instructions than Sönam Lama does, still, it is difficult not to feel that this part of the text might well have been interpolated in order to reinforce the links between Machig and Dampa. The *Transmission History* ignores these initiations and only mentions the first meeting between Dampa and Machig, on which occasion he transmits to her instructions that evoke, between the lines, Āryadeva's Indian Chöd tradition:

> Turn away from all negative aims and eradicate all resistance.
> Cultivate what seems impossible to you.
> Cut through entanglements and recognize your desires.
> Wander in desolate places that inspire fear.
> Understand that all beings are similar to empty space.
> While in the wilderness, look for the Buddha within yourself
> And your teaching will be like a sun illuminating space![25]

These two trends seem to confirm the hypothesis that the historical chronicles such as *The Blue Annals* were composed "by erudites for an erudite public"[26] concerned with the preservation of historical truth, especially as related to the transmission lineages of teachings, commentaries and initiations. Hagiographies, by contrast, tend to favor the marvelous and mysterious, and thus are closer to myth. They are "thought to express the absolute truth because [they] narrate a sacred history."[27] For collective memory, it is no doubt as important to know with some degree of precision what initiations Machig received from Sönam Lama as it is to remember that she was the spiritual daughter of Dampa Sangyé—even with Sönam Lama serving as the intermediary between the two of them.

Thus, even if the hagiographic tradition has, as it seems, gradually diminished the importance of (the relatively little-known) Sönam Lama in favor of viewing Machig as a direct disciple of (the celebrated) Dampa, historical evidence suggests that all the lineages held by Sönam Lama come to him from Dampa, with Sönam Lama passing them on, in turn, to Machig. She herself insisted that Sönam Lama was her root guru, not Dampa.[28]

In fact, all sources agree in recognizing that Dampa transmitted to Sönam Lama the Indian Prajñāpāramitā teachings as well as the Chöd of the Combined Sūtra and Tantra tradition. It would seem that Dampa authored one text known as *The Six Precepts of Chöd*[29] which contained among others the Opening of the Gates of Space and numerous other practices by means of which to perceive how "all phenomena are not other than mind and mind is not other than Buddhahood." Again, *The Blue Annals* have it that Dampa, during his third visit to Tibet, "bestowed many hidden precepts of Chöd on Kyo Sönam Lama."[30] The *Transmission History* points out that Dampa gave "his nephew Sönam Lama" the precepts of the written tradition, with no mention of the oral tradition.

Moreover, in our version, Dampa granted to Machig the instructions on the Prajñāpāramitā according to the oral transmission of Sūtras and Tantras in the course of a spiritual empowerment[31] called "The Four Empowerments of Meditative Stabilization and the Opening of the Gates of Space." Apart from the Pacification of Suffering and the Six Precepts teachings, Dampa also passed on to her the means to "unite in a single practice four of the Six Yogas of Nāropa" and instructions on the Vajrayāna exercises,[32] as well as the visualization of the Eight Great Cremation Grounds and the Chöd To Be Practiced Without Leaving One's Meditation Seat.[33]

Other sources seem to indicate that Dampa gave out these precepts only to Kyo Sakya Yeshé, to his two disciples suffering from leprosy and to Lama Mara Serpo. The texts dealing with this transmission are confused indeed and often contradictory: "Mara Serpo transcribed them and personally put them into practice, without passing them on to anyone," yet "at the end of his life gave them to Nyönpa Boré." Likewise "Kyo Sakya Yeshé practiced them without transmitting them" but, fearing that they might be lost, "eventually gave them to Önpo Sönam Lama" and next gave four of them to Machig Labdrön. Our biography makes no mention of this transmission by Kyo Sakya Yeshé to Machig; however, this lineage from Dampa to his male disciples is usually referred to as the male lineage of Chöd (*pho gcod*).

According to our biography, Sönam Lama did not give a single Chöd precept to Machig, but on the other hand she received from him her first initiation. Through the playing out of their aspirations from previous lives, the young girl was to attain the siddhis through his precepts.

So, to summarize this mass of vague and often contradictory source materials: Dampa and Machig definitely met and he transmitted the Pacification teachings to her, even though it is not established that he directly passed on to her the Chöd precepts and the Indian Sūtra tradition which he himself had obtained from the Brahmin Āryadeva. This Indian tradition would have reached her via either Mara Serpo, Kyo Sakya Yeshé or Sönam Lama. All the same, Machig appears as the privileged vessel of the teachings that Dampa brought to Tibet. She integrated these teachings with her meditative experience and subsequently transmitted the corpus known as the female lineage of Chöd (*mo gcod*).

Karma Chagmé summarizes as follows the distinction between the Indian Chöd and the Tibetan Chöd:

> These four texts [cited above] constitute the Indian Chöd.
> What was born in the mind of Machig Labdrön, emanation of Yum Chenmo, and her subsequent activity is called the Tibetan Chöd.
> It was transmitted to India by the three ācāryas.[34]

In turn, Jamgön Kongtrul Lodrö Thayé summarizes this as follows:

> This Tibetan Dharma that spread in India consists of the means to practice the meaning of the Prajñāpāramitā and came to be divided in different lineages so that all might gain confidence in this authentic method that cuts through demons.[35]

III The Chöd of Machig

To annihilate the four demons
Is the teaching of the Great Vehicle.
To neither reject nor pursue saṃsāra or nirvāṇa
Is the meaning of the Prajñāpāramitā.
Making use of unfavorable conditions
Was taught by the venerable Machig.
To consider adversity as a friend
Is the instruction of Chöd.

—Machig Labdrön

1 The Practice of the Bodhisattvas

According to Jamgön Kongtrul, the term "Chöd" (Tib. *gcod*), "cutting through," also covers the meaning of its homonym "Chöd" (Tib. *spyod*), the "practice" or "conduct" of the bodhisattvas. He combines both meanings in his own definition of Chöd:

> The profound practice (*spyod*) of the Prajñāpāramitā,
> The Chöd (*gcod*) that aims at cutting through demons.[1]

Kongtrul explains that these two terms differ according to the point of view from which one defines Chöd. From the point of view of method and of stages in meditation, it is called the practice or the profound action (Skt. *caryā*, Tib. *spyod*), with the same meaning this term carries in the Cakrasaṃvara Tantra or the Hevajra Tantra when they describe the secret practice, the practice with consort, or the group practice.[2] In this context, Chöd is considered a set of meditation methods and a gradual path to put the Prajñāpāramitā into practice.

If, on the other hand, one views it as a remedy that uses the afflictive emotions to be cut through as a spiritual path, it is then called "cutting through (in the presence of) the object" (*gcod yul*). This is the reason why Jamgön Kongtrul, like the author of *The Blue Annals* before him, accepts the double meaning of Chöd as expressed through its homonyms *spyod* —the action—and *gcod*—to cut through.[3]

Jamgön Kongtrul comments upon the first definition of Chöd as the practice of a bodhisattva by a quotation from *The Verse Summary* (*sDud pa tshigs su bcad pa*):

> The four demons will have difficulties controlling and deceiving the bodhisattva who has mastered these four fundamentals [of Chöd]: (1) to abide in emptiness, (2) not to exclude any being, (3) to follow exactly the instructions received, and (4) to be endowed with the spiritual influence of the sugatas.[4]

Since all delusions, which grasp at the reality of inner and outer phenomena, are nothing but illusions, in order to pacify them, the practitioner should remain in the view of the emptiness of phenomena as expressed in the Prajñāpāramitā and also in Chöd. The bodhisattva actualizes this realization of emptiness by the power of compassion, which does not exclude any being, even enemies, gods or demons. The practitioner follows the instructions regarding the enlightenment mind (Skt. *bodhicitta*) aiming at the benefit and welfare of others, as opposed to striving for his or her own happiness and peace. Finally, by taking refuge and invoking with faith and devotion the Buddhas, bodhisattvas and lineage lamas, the aspirant will come under the spiritual influence of those "gone to bliss" (Skt. *sugata*). These four fundamentals are described as the essence of the Chöd practice.

When starting the rite of offering one's body (Tib. *lus sbyin*), the meditator mentally invites eight groups of particularly honored guests who represent the beings of the three worlds. The first three groups include the three outer malignant forces: (1) the visible or imaginary enemies that bring forth anger and aversion (*sdang ba'i dgra*); (2) the negative forces that cause hindrances (*gnod par byed pa'i bgegs*), affecting body and mind by illness and disturbances; and (3) the conditions that cut apart (*bar du gcod pa'i rkyen*) merit or interfere with one's practice. The next three types of guests are the three inner malignant forces: (4) the demons of karma (*las gdon*), such as the clinging to the notion of a self, or the ignorance which led to rebirth in this present life; (5) the physical demons (*lus gdon*), for instance those involved in identifying the psycho-physical aggregates as being an "I"; and (6) the demons of frightful places in the wilderness (*gnyan sa'i gdon*). The last two guests are (7) one's father and (8) mother in this present life, representing all beings, each of whom has been one's parent in the course of previous existences.[5]

This is how Machig evokes the compassion that "does not abandon any single being," even demons:

> With the hook of compassion I catch those evil spirits. Offering them my warm flesh and warm blood as food, through the kindness and compassion of bodhichitta I transform the way they see everything and make them my disciples.[6]

By contrast, in accordance with the second definition as *gcod yul*, "the Chöd with the aim to cut through the demons," the general attitude of the Chöd practice is that the meditator does not renounce the world by protecting him- or herself from afflictive emotions as in the Theravāda approach, but deliberately evokes these emotions by entering situations or encountering objects (*yul*) that will make them arise, in order to cut through (*gcod*) them and use them on the path of meditation. This is expressed in the verse of Machig: "To consider adversity as a friend is the instruction of Chöd," for adversity will generate fear, anger or attachment to one's body, afflictive emotions which the yogi will instantly recognize as the unlimited play of the clarity of mind, Mahāmudrā, and thereby transform.

This second definition of Chöd may be summarized as follows:

> One might ask: that which is known as Chöd, what does it cut through?
> As it cuts through attachment to body, it is Chöd.
> As it cuts through the root of mind, it is Chöd.
> As it cuts through the very base of all partiality, it is Chöd.
> As it cuts through acceptance and rejection along the path, it is Chöd.
> As it cuts through hopes and fears with regard to the results, it is Chöd.
> As it cuts through all thoughts, wherever they come from or wherever they're going, right there, it is Chöd.
> Therefore, it is called Chöd![7]

Formulated this way, the Chöd practice might present some similarities with the techniques applied in the Tantras, but the use of desire and emotion—the objects—on the spiritual path is not a technique exclusive to the Vajrayāna, as the Fourteenth Dalai Lama reminds us:

> Some say that the difference between Sūtra and Mantra is that Mantra [yāna] was taught for those who can use desire as an aid

> in the path whereas the Perfection Vehicle [of the Mahāyāna Sūtras] was taught in order to tame beings within the context of separation from desire. This opinion is wrong because both the Perfection Vehicle and the Mantra Vehicle have modes of advancing on the path without having abandoned desire and both have modes of progress by cultivating paths to abandon desire. In Sūtra it is said that just as the filth of a city is helpful to the field of the sugarcane grower who knows how to utilise a substance which itself is not helpful, so the afflictions can be useful in the path...although, from the viewpoint of the entities of the afflictions, they are indeed to be abandoned.[8]

If the philosophical point of view of all Chöd traditions is undeniably the exposition of emptiness according to the Prajñāpāramitā, one should look into the variety of its meditation methods to answer the question, Is Chöd a Mahāyāna practice in which one must recognize all outer and inner objects as similar to an illusion or a mirage, or is it rather a set of Vajrayāna methods, a way of transforming appearances into wisdom and poison into a remedy?

In *The Concise Life Story,* Machig points toward an answer when she explains, in response to the questions of Pamtingpa, how her teachings appeared and how they developed. Starting from the teachings of her three main lamas, Sönam Lama, Lama Trapa and Dampa Sangyé, this tradition is called "the Chöd of Mahāmudrā with the Object of Cutting Through Demons," for it unites in a single doctrine the Tripiṭaka, the Prajñāpāramitā and the four classes of Tantra and, "in particular the Mother Tantras of the Highest Yoga Tantra."[9] The *Transmission History* adds that Chöd practitioners, on the Mahāyāna foundation of the practice of the perfections of generosity, discipline and so forth, should use the fast and deep methods of the Vajrayāna to actualize their realization of Chöd. The text quotes Machig:

> This authentic teaching called the Chöd of Mahāmudrā
> Is similar to the famous path of the [Prajñā]pāramitā.
> Its practice is the secret path of the Vajrayāna.[10]

2 The Chöd of Mahāmudrā

All commentators agree that the expression "Chöd of Mahāmudrā"—at first glance paradoxical—refers exclusively to the specific Chöd tradition coming down from Machig. As she stated:

> My tradition is the Chöd of Mahāmudrā.
> After the appearance of the sun of Mahāyāna,
> Chöd chases the darkness of ignorance.[11]

The term *mahāmudrā* (Tib. *phyag rgya chen po*) literally means "the great seal," an analogy to the immutable authority of a royal seal. It symbolizes the ultimate nature of the mind free from any subject-object duality—the naturally serene and open state of mind which is not other than Buddhahood. The immutable character of Mahāmudrā is the continuity of mind as pure from the beginning, the nature of all thought in essence inseparable from the dharmakāya, the emptiness body of the Buddhas. Machig defines Mahāmudrā as follows:

> My Chöd instructions consist in the authentic teaching of
> Mahāmudrā,
> And the Mahāmudrā cannot be explained [by words].
> Yet though it cannot be explained, this is the way it is:
> *Phyag* is the nature of emptiness [of mind];
> *rGya* is the liberation from the vastness of saṃsāra ['s appearances];
> *Chen po* is the inseparable union [of appearances and emptiness].[12]

According to the Mahāmudrā, mind itself is the object of meditation in both Sūtra and Tantra. It is the basis of all suffering and illusion as well as the basis for liberation from suffering and illusion. In the words of Mahāsiddha Saraha:

> Mind is the sole origin of everything;
> Of cyclic wandering in saṃsāra,
> Of liberation in nirvāṇa.

Or in other words, as presented by the Third Karmapa in his *Mahāmudrā Aspiration Prayer*:

> When you look for an object,
> There is no object, there is only mind.
> When you look for mind,
> There is no mind, its essence is emptiness.
> When you look for both, duality becomes self-liberated.
> May I realize the clear light nature of the mind.[13]

Accordingly, Mahāmudrā represents the ultimate teaching on the nature of mind. Beyond all characteristics and all terminological and philosophical limitation, it is the very mind of the Buddhas that must be realized. However, the means of realization differ according to schools and philosophical views, and thus one distinguishes three different approaches to Mahāmudrā:

(1) The Mahāmudrā free from conceptualization, according to the Sūtra tradition, following the philosophical views of the Prajñāpāramitā. This approach is based on reasoning and analysis, and establishes that the ultimate nature of mind, Mahāmudrā, is be-

yond or devoid of all conceptualization (Tib. *spros bral*).

(2) The bliss-emptiness (Tib. *bde stong*) Mahāmudrā of the Tantras, based on the philosophical view of the Sūtras, but using the techniques of deity yoga, mantra recitation, maṇḍalas, and the four mudrās in order to realize the ultimate nature of the mind. This approach is considered the quintessence of Highest Yoga Tantra.[14]

(3) The essence Mahāmudrā (Tib. *snying po*) according to the oral transmission of the mahāsiddhas Maitrīpa, Saraha and Tilopa. This tradition does not follow either the Sūtra or Tantra methods but directly introduces the disciple to the recognition of the ultimate nature of the mind through the oral instructions of the spiritual master, who points out or makes the disciple recognize (*ngo sprod*) this ultimate nature of the mind.

In *The Grand Poem on the Perfection of Wisdom,* Āryadeva follows the first approach of Mahāmudrā according to the Sūtra tradition:

> The meaning of the Prajñāpāramitā
> Is not to be looked for elsewhere: it exists within yourself.
> Neither real nor endowed with characteristics,
> The nature [of mind] is the great clear light.

This point of view seems to be also followed by Machig:

> All phenomena—the outer container and its inner contents [the world and the beings that inhabit it]—down to the tiniest hair are without inherent existence since the beginning: they have the nature of emptiness. This is called Mahāmudrā.[15]

Machig did, however, also hold a Mahāmudrā transmission according to the Tantras, directly given to her by Tārā, who enjoined her to keep united "as an indivisible whole the exceptional means of the four mudrās in the way I have taught them to you, and the view of the heart of Prajñāpāramitā."[16] Machig defines these four (mahā) mudrās in *Transforming the Aggregates*:[17]

> Once the yogi has reached an intellectual understanding of the meaning [of emptiness] and has integrated it with the mind, he will be able to utilize this emptiness on the path (*lam du 'khyer*). Next, having mastered the yogic exercises (*'khrul 'khor*) on the pathways, winds and drops, with the assistance of a knowledge woman (*shes rab ma*) the yogi will utilize great bliss as a path of meditation. Through the experience of great bliss he will develop immense bodily powers. This is known as Karma Mahāmudrā.
>
> Next the yogi will practice while hiding all these qualities, without abandoning the samaya of the outer substances:[18] this is known as Samaya Mahāmudrā.

> Likewise, as the yogi maintains this extraordinary bliss in emptiness without attachment, "the vapors of heat" [will manifest]: that is the Mahāmudrā of Bliss Emptiness.
>
> Finally, to this yogi now free from the veil of the emotional afflictions [*kleśa*] or from the turbulence thereof, all appearances will manifest as devoid of any actual reality and as empty, similar to dream images or to a magical show. Such is the Mahāmudrā of Clear Light Emptiness.[19]

At the ultimate level of essence Mahāmudrā, there is nothing to be rejected or added to this clear light nature of mind. The definitive view is the non-view, beyond the duality of observing subject and observed object. The ultimate meditation is the non-meditation, beyond the duality of meditating subject and object meditated upon—for as long as mind is not freed from all support, it cannot manifest its natural, serene state.

These paradoxes are summarized by Tilopa:

> Don't think [about the past], don't conceive [any present],
> Don't fantasize [about the future], don't meditate [on the emptiness of phenomena and of mind],
> Don't analyze [an object or subject],
> But leave the mind in its natural state.[20]

And so too, in Chöd terminology, at the ultimate level there is nothing to cut, nor anything that cuts, as is reflected in Machig's words:

> The supreme conception of Chöd is non-conception.
> The supreme meditation is the samādhi of non-meditation.
> The supreme activity is non-activity. Thus it has been stated.

And the perspective of ultimate Mahāmudrā is also summarized in Tilopa's dictum:

> Cut through all attachment and aversion towards any phenomena of saṃsāra.
> Meditate in the solitude of a forest or hermitage.
> Remain in a state where there is nothing to meditate upon.
> When you have realized what cannot be realized,
> You will have realized Mahāmudrā.[21]

The above verses suggest that these three approaches of Mahāmudrā were known to Machig, who then combined them into a single system utilizing the specific Chöd methods either received from different traditions or born from her own experience. By cutting through mental afflictions, the illusion of saṃsāra and the erroneous attachment to a self, and finally by cutting through everything that hinders the realization of the nature of mind, its unchanging nature will manifest naturally and immediately: this is nothing other than Mahāmudrā. Khenpo Tsultrim Gyamtso has called this connection between Chöd and Mahāmudrā "the Mahāmudrā related to the Chöd tradition."[22]

In a similar vein Jamgön Kongtrul distinguishes two stages within the Chöd practice: the stage of meditative stabilization that consists in letting the mind remain in its own nature, Mahāmudrā; and the post-meditation stage during which the meditator must apply the particular Chöd methods such as the transference of consciousness, the union of mind and space or the offering of the body, as well as the various techniques to make the winds enter the central channel according to the Mother Tantra methods. Machig summarizes the Chöd of Mahāmudrā as follows:

> Once the yogi has realized the non-existence of both inner and outer phenomena, through the ability to make mind and wind enter the central channel, he or she will gain the extraordinary experience of unlimited bliss and clear light. From this experience, the perfect knowledge of past, present and future will come forth, as well as the understanding [of the nature] of all phenomena. Having penetrated the clear light, the yogi will be able to discipline vast numbers of beings through numerous qualities derived from this realization of the clear light, such as limitless forms of teaching, debate and exegesis. [The teaching] that possesses the power to accomplish this is known as the Chöd of Mahāmudrā.[23]

The Mahāmudrā viewpoint resembles those of the Great Middle Way (Skt. *madhyamaka,* Tib. *dbu ma chen po*) and the Great Perfection (Tib. *rdzogs pa chen po*) traditions that developed in Tibet. Machig explains them as follows:

> The middle or center (*dbu*) of mind itself unites all phenomena. If one knows the center of mind [i.e., when one realizes the heart or ultimate nature], that alone guarantees that one knows the center of all phenomena. Accordingly, my tradition is the Great Middle Way (*dbu ma chen po*).
>
> The fruit of my tradition is the great perfection (*rdzogs*) of all phenomena, for all apparent phenomena of saṃsāra and nirvāṇa can only be perfected in the mind. In this way, if one knows how to accomplish the ultimate meaning of mind itself, that guarantees one's knowledge of the meaning of the perfection of all phenomena, in other words the Great Perfection (*rdzogs chen*).[24]

Therefore the Chöd tradition of Machig is in agreement with the principal philosophical systems transmitted from India to Tibet: (1) the Great Seal (Mahāmudrā) systematized by Gampopa which up to the present day constitutes the Kagyü corpus of teachings; (2) the Great Middle Way founded by Nāgārjuna and transmitted within the Gelug school mainly on the basis of Tsongkhapa's commentaries; and (3) the Great Perfection of Padmasambhava, as passed on through the lineages of the masters of the Nyingma school. All these oral traditions eventually lead to the realization of the ultimate nature of mind, emptiness, as expressed in the Third Karmapa's *Mahāmudrā Aspiration Prayer*:

> May I obtain the certainty that by knowing one [of these traditions],
> I realize the meaning of all the others.[25]

3 Union of Consciousness and Space

Usually the first steps on the meditational path leading to Mahāmudrā include the development of calm abiding (Skt. *śamatha*, Tib. *zhi gnas*) to pacify mental agitation, and the practice of profound insight (Skt. *vipaśyanā*, Tib. *lhag mthong*). In the Chöd tradition, on the contrary, emphasis is put on the need to let the emotions arise so as to cut through them as soon as they appear within the mind itself. The Chödpa does not guard against mental afflictions such as attachment, hatred, fear, etc. by retreating from worldly life, but goes out to meet, head-on, the objects (Tib. *yul*) and circumstances that provoke terror or bodily attachment, in order to experience the empty nature of these mental afflictions:

> This authentic Dharma that cuts through the demonic objects[26]
> Is different from any other meditational instruction, since the others
> Only eliminate [attachment to self and afflictive emotions] at a later stage,
> Whereas this technique cuts through them right away . . . .
> Others only gradually eliminate discursive thought,
> Whereas Chöd instantly unites it [with emptiness].[27]

In Chöd terminology, the mental afflictions (Skt. *kleśa*, Tib. *nyon mongs*),[28] including all negative emotions, are symbolically identified with demonic forces that need to be conquered and annihilated. The most powerful of those demons—the one which definitely must be cut through—is the holding on to a real and permanent self, source of all inner and outer demons. This is called arrogance (Tib. *snyems byed*) in the Chöd terminology. From the perspective of the Middle Way, this comes down to recognizing the illusory nature of, and cutting through the identification with, the psycho-physical aggregates[29] that seem to constitute an "I." As in a dream, as long as the dreamer identifies with the dream images, he or she experiences all sorts of pleasant and unpleasant sensations, fears, desires and sufferings associated with the strong impression of an "I." But as soon as the dreamer becomes aware that he or she is dreaming, the suffering evaporates and the fears and so forth are seen to be nothing other than the play of mind. Indeed there is no duality between the subject dreaming and objects dreamed about. Understanding in this way that this "dream-I" is devoid of inherent existence, all identification with it ceases, together with the sensations and perceptions attached to it. This is what Sönam Lama explains to Machig:

> Then, liberated from attachment to reality, you will be totally free of the conception of subject and object, equally divorced from all mental states related to action and agent. This understanding of nonduality is a great fire which destroys the darkness of ignorant clinging to a self...
>
> Free from any conceptualization, Machig eliminated the demon of ego-clinging and self-centeredness. This insight of realizing the non-existence of a self was like the sun dissipating darkness: the erroneous belief in the existence of a self was forever silenced.[30]

Āryadeva describes the Chöd methods to free oneself of this duality:

> Here, the supreme method [to realize mind]
> Is to unite space and awareness.[31]
> In the course of the periods when you mix space and awareness,
> You are spontaneously purified from hanging on to such fixed notions
> As reality and characteristics, negating and establishing,
> And you abide in the truth of suchness, dharmatā [32]
> Free from dualistic subject-object cognition.

This fusion of consciousness in empty space is brought about by the Opening of the Gates of Space, one of the techniques Dampa transmitted to Machig. This technique, known as the "consciousness transference [Tib. *'pho ba*] for recognizing [the nature of mind],"[33] should not be confused with the numerous other traditions of consciousness transference. There exist different methods to perform it.

The first method of consciousness transference for recognizing the nature of mind is the transference with support in the heart of the deity: one ejects one's consciousness in the shape of a drop (Skt. *bindu*, Tib. *thig le*) into the heart of the deity visualized at the crown of one's head, usually Machig Labdrön or Yum Chenmo. Commentaries on the rite describe various visualizations to eject the consciousness, to be applied either simultaneously or progressively.[34] Next, the bindu comes back down through the Brahmā aperture, and the meditator instantly changes into Vajravārāhī (rDo rje phag mo) or into the Wrathful Black Lady (Khros ma nag mo), according to the system followed.

The second method mentioned by Āryadeva is called "without support but with representation." It consists in melting consciousness and empty space and resting in a non-conceptual state of absorption. This method is described by Jamgön Kongtrul:

> Thinking of awareness and dynamic space, one mixes them, and with *PHAT!* one's consciousness flies up into the sky. Wherever space penetrates, awareness penetrates; wherever awareness penetrates, the dharmakāya penetrates. [One] rests in sameness with the dharmakāya mind of the ultimate Machigma.[35]

When one realizes that neither mind nor body inherently exist, one understands that mind is not connected to the body and that the body is not connected to mind. Likewise, all phenomena, real or imaginary, are beyond all notions of attachment or non-attachment: their nature is emptiness. This technique is further referred to as the transference of the formless dharmakāya, the very essence of Mahāmudrā realization. Machig illustrates this process as follows:

> The body? Drop it as if it were a corpse.
> Leave it as if it had no owner.
> Mind? Let it [be] as if it were the sky.
> Leave it alone as if it had no object (*dmigs pa*).[36]

The third method, called "with neither support nor representation," is described by Jamgön Kongtrul:

> To remain forever poised in the unchanging and unaltered mind, which is empty clarity and awareness at its heart, is the king of all transferences. The great opening of the gates of space is the very essence of the meaning of the authentic doctrine of Chöd as taught by Machig Labdrön.[37]

During the stage of meditative absorption in nonduality, the meditator must face everything that appears, gods or demons, terror, wonders or sufferings, in complete equanimity, impassive "like an elephant that crosses a thorny bush or like a fish for which the waves mean nothing."[38] In fearful places or sky burial spots one must remain seated, as unmoving as "a wooden stake," even if one sees one's own corpse being carried off by demons.

Although Opening the Gates of Space is the best-known technique, *The Profound Meaning of the Essence of Mind*[39] describes ten different "openings" (*sgo 'byed*), and Jamgön Kongtrul adds that these ten openings are the main instructions on Chöd practice: (1) the initiation called "Opening the Gates of Dharma" contains the Chöd tradition's refuge and the development of the mind set on enlightenment in eight points.[40] This initiation is not a proper Vajrayāna empowerment, although it is said to be equivalent to the fourth initiation of Highest Yoga Tantra. In the sacred biography, it is described as belonging to the Sūtra lineage which Machig received from Dampa Sangyé and which she defines as follows:

> It is not an initiation into a deity transmitted to the body,
> It is an initiation of the ultimate meaning (*chos sbang*) transmitted to the mind.[41]

(2) The sādhana called the "Opening of the Gates of Blessing" involves the separation of body and mind. The next four openings are specific techniques belonging to this Opening of the Gates of Blessing: (3) the recognition of the nature of mind, known as "Opening the Gates of Space" [proper]; (4) the dream practice called "Opening the Gates of the Sun and the Moon"; (5) the consciousness transference called "Opening the Gates of Liberation"; and (6) the transference in the intermediate state called "Opening the Gates of the Clear Light." Then: (7) the elucidation of adversity, called "Opening the Gates of the Interdependent Origins," which is only transmitted orally by the lama; (8) the enhancements (*bogs 'don*), called "Opening the Gates of Qualities"; (9) the benefit of others, called "Opening the Activity"; and (10) the goal of the practice, called "Opening the Gates of the Supreme Āryas." The temporary goal is to appease the four demons of physical disease and mental suffering; the ultimate goal is the realization of the three Buddha bodies (Skt. *kāya*).[42]

As a conclusion, according to Jamgön Kongtrul:

> The Opening of the Gates of Space is the essence of Machig's intention and the heart of the Chöd tradition. To remain totally absorbed in the expanse of manifestation, the dharmadhātu, is the innermost meditation method of this extraordinary tradition.[43]

4 Transforming the Aggregates into an Offering of Food

> Those of most excellent [meditational capacity]
> Should remain absorbed in the meaning of the nondual [nature of mind];

> Those of medium capacity should concentrate on these very wonders [produced by gods and demons];
> Those of average capacity should transform their aggregates into an offering of food.[44]

This description of the Chöd methods, given by Āryadeva in *The Grand Poem*, is echoed by Machig, who explains the procedure thus:

> Having separated body and awareness, unite awareness and space.
> Uniting inseparably awareness and space,
> Remain as much as you can in emptiness
> And practice the transformation of the aggregates into an offering of food.[45]

Apart from the striking fact that Āryadeva considers the method of "transforming the aggregates into an offering of food" as the most ordinary level of Chöd practice, in his words, this expression, which is the very title of Machig's sacred biography and is usually attributed to her, distinctly shows the Indian origin of the Chöd tradition. According to *The Concise Life Story*, when Machig's son Thönyön Samdrup returned to his cave to continue his retreat, a ḍākinī addressed him in a dream:

> "Isn't there anything in Machig's tradition which you don't know?"
>
> He replied that he was acquainted with all of Machig's teachings, but she told him: "Yogin, you are most learned in Machig's tradition...but you still must receive from her the methods of the meaning of the Sūtras, in order to practice the three traditions [according to the Sūtras, the Tantras, and the Combined Tradition] of Machig, known as 'Offering the Body Through Transforming the Aggregates into an Offering of Food'."[46]

What is the meaning of "transforming the aggregates into an offering of food"? The term *food* is a translation of the Tibetan *zan* or *gzan*, actually a ball of tsampa (roasted barley) which one throws as food for the dogs. In this way the Chödpa should first mentally separate body and awareness through the technique of consciousness transference and dwell in the emptiness, similar to empty space, that is the nature of mind. Next, in order to cut through attachment to the reality of "I," the yogi must offer his or her bodily remains to the gods and demons as if throwing them away to feed the dogs.

The five aggregates are form, feelings, perceptions, compositional factors, and consciousness. They are the components of individuality. In the present context, however, offering the aggregates is to be understood as referring to the aggregate of form, the body composed of flesh and blood, the coarsest source of attachment to a real and permanent self.[47] One starts by renouncing one's own body, gradually abandoning the notion of any real self.

Once the consciousness has been transferred either to the heart of the deity or to empty space, the meditator instantly appears as Vajravārāhī (or as the Wrathful Black Lady). With her meat-chopper she cuts up the mortal remains that lie inanimate at her feet. Through a series of visualizations, the corpse is transformed into various offerings. The offerings of the body to the demons are quite well known, but different banquets (Tib. *'gyed*) are referred to and should be clearly distinguished. Patrul Rinpoché enumerates them briefly:

> In the Chö texts there are usually four great feasts: white, red, variegated [multicolored] and black. But in this one there is no red or black feast.[48]

In the white banquet, the mortal remains of the physical body are transformed into wisdom nectar and a hundred marvelous substances which assemblies of offering-goddesses present to the lineage lamas, the yidam deities of the four classes of Tantra, the ḍākas and ḍākinīs, and the guardians and protectors of the teaching, as well as to all beings of the triple world. Certain commentators distinguish three ways to practice the white banquet: according to the outer view of the Prajñāpāramitā, the inner view of the lower Tantras, or the secret view of the Highest Yoga Tantra. Yet notwithstanding the differences in the visualizations, the white banquet remains in substance the same in all three cases.[49]

In the multicolored banquet, the meditator offers his or her body in the form of sense gratification and whatever else is desirable to the guests of the upper regions (the lamas, Buddhas, yidams and protectors) as well as to the guests of the lower regions (all the beings of the triple world).

The red banquet is dedicated to gods and demons such as the lords of the locality, of bodily demons, cannibal demons, etc. Inviting them to gather for the feast, the meditator (identified with Vārāhī) gratifies them with heaps of flesh, blood and fat:[50]

> I make an offering of this body. May those in a hurry devour it raw, may those with leisure partake of it cooked....Eat it the way you prefer, cooked, roasted or raw. Take as much as your stomach can contain. May the strong ones carry away as much as they can carry....Take this offering till nothing remains of it![51]

The main purpose of all these offerings is to complete the accumulations of meritorious actions, to purify obscurations and to repay karmic debts towards all beings, who have been our mothers since beginningless time. Each banquet should be followed by a stage of profound nonconceptual absorption on the emptiness of the three spheres (the subject, the object and the action of meditating), in order to accumulate wisdom. In the *Quintessence*, Machig explains the food offering in three stages:

> (1) the preliminaries, a meditation on love and compassion;
> (2) the actual practice, the offering of one's own body, intended to cultivate the six perfections [*pāramitās*];
> (3) the conclusion, a dedication of the [preceding] meritorious activity for the realization of unsurpassable enlightenment.

She summarizes the instruction as: "Meditate on compassion, transform your being into a food offering, and let mind rest in its true nature."[52]

The offering of the body for the benefit of others is a notion that seems to have been present within Buddhism since the very early stages of its development. It is described in Mahāyāna literature as the ideal of the bodhisattva's renunciation and compassion, and as such it appears as one of the major themes of the *Jātakas*, for instance in *The Garland of the Buddha's Earlier Lives*. In one of these stories, the future Buddha offers his body to a famished tigress who is about to devour her own young. Moved by profound compassion, the bodhisattva ponders:

> Why should I search after meat from the body of another, whilst the whole of my body is available? Not only is the getting of the meat in itself a matter of chance, but I should also lose the opportunity of doing my duty. Further, this body being brute, frail, ungrateful, always impure, and a cause of suffering, should I not rejoice at its being spent for the benefit of another....And finally that wish I yearned for, "When may I have the opportunity of benefiting others with the offering of my own limbs?" I shall accomplish now, and so acquire complete wisdom....May I gain by it the power of simultaneously taking away the world's sorrow and imparting forever the world's happiness, just as the sun takes away darkness and imparts light!"[53]

One also finds this sacrifice of the body in Sūtras such as the *Sūtra of the Wise and the Foolish*[54] and the *Sūtra of All Merits*, as in the following extract:

> Son of noble family, the bodhisattvas animated by a great mental strength must consider this body, composed of the four elements, as a medicinal tree. In accordance with whatever needs of beings, they must tell them: "Take this or that."
>
> It means that, if they need a hand, give them a hand; if they need a foot, give them a foot; and likewise for an eye, flesh or blood. If they need bones, give them your bones; if they need a leg, give them one; if a head is needed, give it, and so forth.
>
> Son of noble family, for bodhisattvas animated by a great mental strength, it will become the origin of immeasurable benefits due to the accumulation of generosity.[55]

In the same vein, when Milarepa is under attack by an army of demons led by the Tseringmas, he offers them his body in an act of renunciation and generosity:

> This human body, composed of skandhas,
> Is transient, mortal and delusory.
> Since in time I must discard it,
> He who would, may take it now.
> May the offering of my body serve as a ransom
> For all mankind and sentient beings.[56]

Milarepa here is assaulted by demons who suddenly appear without any sort of invitation, in order to test his motivation, to instill doubt in him, or simply to steal his mind at the slightest sign of any slackening in his vigilance.

These examples demonstrate how the offering of one's body exemplifies the practice of compassion and the perfection of generosity (Skt. *dāna-pāramitā*). This kind of confrontation with demonic forces is a standard feature in accounts of hermit traditions the world over, particularly prominent among the early Egyptian desert anchorites. Facing frightening apparitions seems to be an unavoidable ordeal all ascetics must undergo on the path of renouncing the world to achieve liberation.[57]

Yet, despite a shared compassionate motivation, these practices of offering the body should not be considered identical with Chöd ritual. In the *Jātakas* for example, the bodhisattva *really* offers his body to the tigress out of generosity, whereas in the Chöd practice according to Machig, this offering is a mental and visualized means, taking for its goal not the perfection of generosity as such, but the cutting through of fears and attachments. As Jamgön Kongtrul explains:

> What needs to be cut through are the kleśas or mental afflictions.... The yogi, accordingly, must *voluntarily* establish contact with the

> objects that make these fundamental tendencies, fixed erroneous mental habits and afflictive emotions come to the fore.[58]

Karma Chagmé makes a clear distinction between the body offering as found in earlier Buddhist literature and the actual practice of Chöd:

> Through the strength of compassion, bodhisattvas having attained the first level [Skt. *bhūmi*] really offer their body out of compassion, like [the Buddha] offered his body to the tigress. But as long as one has not reached the first *bhūmi*, one should not do it even if one has the capacity to do so. That would be a mistake and one could even end up as a negative force [Tib. *bgegs*]. In virtue as well as in non-virtue, mental attitude and motivation are the most important. By mentally offering one's body during meditation, one accumulates meritorious activity. Among all offerings, the offering of the body is the best since one does not possess anything more precious than life and body. Through the practice of Chöd, one mentally renounces and cuts through ego-clinging only by the power of one's visualization.[59]

Therefore, in order to test his or her own realization and provoke the appearance of self-grasping, the yogi deliberately takes up residence in charnel fields, cremation grounds and other wild, fearful spots and invites to the banquet of his or her own physical remains the most ferocious demons, the most bloodthirsty spirits and the cruelest ḍākinīs, in order to "cultivate one's incapacities," as Machig calls it. This attitude is further explained by Āryadeva in *The Grand Poem*: once you have invited the demons to the solitude of fearful spots,

> If overcome with fear, you should remain absorbed in this fear,
> Just like directing the burning needle of moxibustion with sharp precision onto the flesh
> ... ...
> But if your practice is not right you will run away in panic [chased by such magical interferences].
> Don't flee but remain unwavering, solid like a door frame,
> Even if terror or panic arise.

In short, the transference combined with the transformation of the aggregates into food is clearly distinct from the offering of the body in standard Mahāyāna perspective. The voluntary and controlled application of skillful means in Chöd practice is similar to techniques belonging to the Vajrayāna. As mentioned by Jamgön Kongtrul in *The Garden of Joy*, the maṇḍala offering of one's body and the following various banquets have the purpose of improving one's post-meditation and are connected with the Mantrayāna conduct which aims to tame awareness and so forth.[60] Therefore one ought to distinguish the general practice of the offering of the body (rooted in the Indian Sūtra tradition, which served as the crucible from which the Chöd tradition sprung) from the teachings of Machig Labdrön, who systemized this compassionate attitude into a specific tradition with distinct initiations, rituals and visualizations and its own techniques such as the opening of the gates of space or the various offering banquets. In the chapter "Stay at Ragma," Milarepa alludes to transforming the aggregates into an offering of food:

> Leaving the body as a food offering
> Is the guide to subjugate ego.[61]

This, however, does not mean that he practiced the Chöd of Machig, or even that he was acquainted with it. Rather, it indicates that the Indian tradition of offering the body according to Āryadeva and Dampa represents a development of the most ancient Buddhist tradition current in eleventh-century Tibet. Chöd unquestionably has roots in India, and therefore it is clear that Machig did not create a new tradition *ex nihilo*. Rather, she acted as a catalyst, gathering together different currents which she organized into a system that came to be known as the Chöd of Mahāmudrā.

IV Gods and Demons

> Attachment to whatever phenomena,
> From the most coarse up to omniscience,
> Should be viewed as the play of Māra.
>
> —*Spoken words of the Buddha*

1 The Mad Saints

Having mastered the philosophical point of view (Tib. *lta ba*) and become proficient in the specific meditative Chöd techniques described above, the Chödpa is usually encouraged to leave behind the familiar environment and to consider adversity and negative conditions as friends while engaging on the path of action (Tib. *spyod pa*). The practitioner should voluntarily seek out situations and locations that call forth fear and emotional disturbance, so as to be able to cut through them as soon as they appear. In the terms of Āryadeva's *Grand Poem*:

> In desolate rocky mountains or among snowy peaks,
> In charnel fields and cremation grounds, in wilderness,
> In villages and in towns, in caves and lonely grottos,
> Wherever you may be, meditate on nonduality.

And a little further:

> Having moved to desolate spots,
> When magical displays of gods or demons arise,
> Separate awareness from the material body.

After realizing the non-existence of a self, Machig left behind the monastic life and her accustomed surroundings in order to roam about without destination, dropping any partiality regarding places of residence, habits or social conventions. In accordance with Dampa

Sangyé's prediction, Machig subjugated the demons and guided her disciples to realization at one hundred and eight spots throughout Tibet, Nepal and India. Following her example, all commentaries on Chöd advise the adept to meditate "at some hundred cremation grounds or charnel fields, some hundred springs and some hundred haunted places, the most fearsome possible."

This yogic conduct (Tib. *brtul shugs spyod pa*), or "chosen behavior" in Cyrus Stearns' translation, is often bewildering or even shocking in the eyes of the world. It illustrates the qualitative change of status of these yogis in their quest for realization and often earned them the epithet of "madman" (Tib. *smyon pa*).[1] In a reply to one of her spiritual sons who asked her about the practice of yogis who have attained the realization of the non-self, Machig recommended that they act

> Like a child with perfect spontaneity,
> Like a madman unconcerned with what is socially acceptable,
> Like a leper unattached to his own physical well-being,
> Or like a wild animal roaming about in lonely and desolate places.[2]

Rangjung Dorjé, the Third Karmapa, in his commentary to *The Great Collection of Precepts*, explains the Chödpa's behavior as follows:

> The activity is a chosen behavior free from mental afflictions.... Thereby, those who have realized the non-self show numerous and varied actions for the benefit of living beings and practice a path that cuts through negative thought. Those who know this path of action, however vast [and varied] their behavior may be, are devoid within of any grasping and attachment to reality, similar to a fish moving through the water, and without a trace of emotion like the wind blowing at the summits of mountains. Having thus eliminated all obstacles to their behavior and actions, and without any regard for themselves, they realize the Prajñāpāramitā.[3]

According to Khenpo Tsultrim Gyamtso, the practice of this activity is an essential element of the Chöd tradition. The yogi who has realized the non-existence of a self demonstrates this realization for the benefit of beings through chosen behavior rather than through his or her teaching. Examples of this "conduct free of all negative emotions and of illusory appearances" (*brtul shugs*) are to be found in the sacred biographies of Tibetan "mad saints" such as Drugpa Kunleg, who may insult people, get involved in fights, even kill, show eccentric and shocking sexual behavior or manifest violent emotions such as anger and so forth. And yet these yogis, with their behavior incomprehensible to the ordinary mind, are actually devoid of emotions such as desire, attachment or anger, in the same way that a wrathful mask depicts anger without itself being angry, or in the way that a fish has neither conception about nor attachment to the water in which it freely moves. Although he or she may manifest anger or desire, the yogi is not personally associated with this emotion: witness the great master from Kham who insulted and beat up those who came to visit him, dumped out on the floor all food they offered, and finally chased visitors away by throwing stones at them! On the one hand, this mad behavior was merely a skillful means to rid himself of intruders and fully concentrate on his meditation—all along there was neither anger nor insult in his mind. On the other hand, by this type of behavior the yogi eliminates for others obstacles such as demons, negative forces and other evil, and being free of desire or concern for his or her own well-being, realizes the Prajñāpāramitā.

The path of action that developed within the Chöd is based on authentic scriptural sources and appears to have been directly borrowed from the tantric Buddhist tradition of India, following in the footsteps of Padmasambhava, Yeshé Tsogyal and the mahāsiddhas. Indeed, according to Jamgön Kongtrul, this path of action in Chöd is identical to "the secret practice, the practice with consort or the group practice such as described in the Cakrasaṃvara Tantra and the Hevajra Tantra," for instance.[4] In the latter, one does come across descriptions of yogis dressed in ornaments taken from charnel fields who meditate "at night below a solitary tree or at a cremation ground,...or at some lonely spot."[5] These yogis represent models of liberation. Likewise, in the same tantra, the ultimate conduct is described as "the experience of the single taste" (Tib. *ro snyoms*) of all duality, for at the ultimate level all good or bad, positive or negative dissolve in the experience of the unique flavor, the limitless play of the clear light nature of the mind, just as all pleasant and unpleasant dream images possess one and the same "flavor" to the dreamer who becomes aware of dreaming.

The conduct associated with the experience of the single taste is shared by the Vajrayāna, the Mahāmudrā and the Great Perfection traditions. Machig confirms that this is also the view of Chöd:

> This action, the unobstructed experience of single taste
> Is the greatest of all paths of action.[6]

Thus the yogi illustrates by his or her behavior the experience of this single taste that cuts through all biased duality and transcends without restraint the relative world of social conventions and value judgments.

The biographies of the eighty-four mahāsiddhas abound in descriptions and examples of such modes of eccentric and nonconventional behavior: the Brahmin Tilopa, who renounced his caste and became a sesame oil merchant during the day and doorkeeper to prostitutes at night; Nāropa, who renounced the comfort and security offered by the monastic institution of Nālandā, where he was one of the most respected masters, in order to roam about as a vagabond for years on end in his quest for the ultimate realization; or Kukuripa, who lived on a desolate island all by himself, surrounded by some hundred female dogs.

This yogic (or self-imposed) conduct at times led to excesses. In particular it gave rise to the "perverted Chöd" doctrines (Tib. *log gcod*), as predicted by Machig. It is indeed difficult to distinguish the authentic practitioner—the yogi par excellence—from the vagabond beggar who pretends to be a Chödpa and takes advantage of popular belief. Drugpa Kunleg berates those Chöd impostors:

> Their behavior like that of a madman who, without looking inside, limits himself on the outside to cutting down haunted trees, turning haunted rocks and disturbing haunted lakes—such modes of conduct will only bring about fatigue now and great unhappiness later. It is of no use whatsoever![7]

The co-existence of both the monastic institutions and the wandering yogis undoubtedly contributes to and demonstrates the strength of the living traditions. Even if the latter group opted for a lifestyle entirely outside the institutional framework or social norms, they enjoyed a natural respect in Tibet, where "the Tibetan is at all times ready to suspend his judgment about whoever has renounced the society's conventions,"[8] as, for instance, in Milarepa's confrontation with the geshé Dhar Lho.[9] In the Tibetan tradition the yogi still represents the highest ideal of renunciation. Regarded by society at large as a sort of spiritual "investment," the yogi eventually repays the debt by sharing his or her experiences and realizations.

The life of Machig emphasizes how she "brought relief to innumerable people suffering from physical and demon-caused illnesses." Realizing the non-existence of a self, the Chödpa, following in Machig's footsteps, enters the path of action. Eventually, as mentioned by Rangjung Dorjé, he or she is able to "eliminate obstacles," annihilate negative forces (*bgegs*) and demons in others, to undo spells cast on them and to pacify inner and outer gods and demons. Āryadeva describes this practice for the sake of others in *The Grand Poem*:

If you wish to benefit someone [through the practice of Chöd],
Generate compassion as a preliminary,
Then realize how yourself, the sick person, the demon and the illness
Are all empty [devoid of inherent existence].
Then cleanse by means of mudrā and meditate upon emptiness.
The patient should then lie down facing you.
If thereby the disease is not pacified
Take the patient to a desolate spot, take refuge and generate the mind set on enlightenment.
Three times step over the sick person and follow this by meditation [on emptiness]
Free from extremes [and reference points].
Next [in the patient's name] present a maṇḍala offering
Together with the small sticks and pebbles over which you have invoked the blessing.

The gods of the upper regions should be viewed as sacred
And the nāgas of the lower regions should be subdued.
Any task you request from them, the nāgas will accomplish.
Thus befriend through rites the gods from wherever you reside
And force all nāgas into submission, making them act as your servants.

In this way the Chödpa forces all harmful beings, male and female, to bind themselves by an oath of allegiance, in order to use and direct them in activity for the sake of others. The battlefield terminology applied in the description of the Chöd ritual, during which the meditator cuts through, conquers and eliminates demons, does of course remind one of accounts of shamans entrenched in close combat with the spirit world. No doubt the mistaken equations of Chöd with the cults of possession and exorcism rituals stem in the first place from parallel language used in the observer's descriptions.[10] The Chöpa's very lifestyle on the fringe of society—dwelling in the solitude of burial grounds and haunted places, added to the mad behavior and contact with the world of darkness and mystery—was enough for credulous people to view the Chödpa in a role usually attributed to shamans and other exorcists,[11] an assimilation which also happened to medieval European shepherds. Only someone who has visited one of Tibet's charnel fields and witnessed the offering of a corpse to the vultures may be able to understand the full impact of what the Chöd tradition refers to as places that inspire terror. To the direct and unmediated teaching on impermanence is further added the dramatic character of the Chöd rite itself, reinforced by the use of instruments such as the damaru drum, the horn carved out of a human thigh bone (Tib. *rkang*

Right:
Chödpa at Pashupatinath, Kathmandu Valley. Photo: Mani Lama.

Below:
Sky-burial at Drigung Monastery. Photo: J. Edou.

gling) and the bell, all derived from the Indian tantric tradition.[12] Every one of these elements contributed to the efficacy of the rite and gave Chöd practitioners their particular position within the Buddhist tradition of Tibet. But the spiritual tendencies by which this line of mad saints—most of them lay practitioners who had little patience with social mores or convention—favored a path of realization through active confrontation with the world of illusion and with their own emotions also kept Chödpas away from libraries and printing houses and the conservative power of the monasteries. The oral transmission, accordingly, gave rise to a cluster of more or less independent lineages, extremely hard to trace back at present and proving most elusive in any attempt towards a coherent and definitive synthesis.

2 Cutting through Gods and Demons

The Tibetan expression *lha 'dre* is generally translated as "gods and demons," whereas "god-demon" is much closer to the single entity thus evoked in Tibetan. Popular tradition shows a tendency to consider the beneficent and pleasant as a god, and the harmful and frightening as a demon, but Machig seriously warns against this kind of superstition. The nature of these god-demons is unstable and unpredictable, and any god, however pleasant or beneficent, can transform into a demon, just as what at first glance appears demonic might in the long run turn out to be beneficial.

In the context of eleventh-century Tibet, when the Chöd teachings crystallized into a separate movement, the Tibetan's daily world was inhabited by obscure forces—beneficial gods and malignant demons, mischievous ḍākinīs (some of them cannibals), invisible harmful spirits hidden in rocks, trees or rivers—always ready to catch hold of those lacking sufficient protection. This shadowy world beyond the reach of reason is, within traditional societies, considered *more real* than material reality, and this is no doubt the reason why Buddhism needed more than the great philosophers of India in order to gain a foothold in Tibet. Only powerful siddhas of the miracle-worker type were able to subjugate this world of the imaginary and to transform it into an environment of protectors of the teaching. This is what Guru Rinpoché did at Samyé and what Milarepa achieved in his celebrated combat with the five Tseringmas.

Machig herself at the Tree of Serlag defeated the armies of the nāga king and bound him with the firm vow to protect her teachings.[13] It may well be due more to her role as a miracle worker than to the profundity of her teachings that Machig eventually assumed a prominent place at the heart of popular tradition, where positive and negative forces are in constant confrontation and where any event in daily life is easily viewed as either demonic trickery or the blessing of a god. Machig herself is not always free of this attitude. The night after uniting with Thöpa Bhadra, she tells her benefactress Lhamo Drön:

> I've been deceived by the vulgar prophecies of some malevolent demon.
> When a man and a woman unite, they are flirting with the demon of adverse conditions.[14]

In the course of a private audience some years ago, His Holiness the Dalai Lama addressed this topic with the following remarks:

> Buddhism does not accept a creator god, yet most Tibetans, not unlike what used to be the case in China and Japan, worship one deity or another while firmly believing in the reality of this deity—with a faith even stronger than Christians' belief in their God. From a Buddhist point of view this is of course totally wrong. The faith of these people is based on superstitious beliefs and they know nothing about Buddhas and bodhisattvas. They put their faith in divine intercessors, in all sorts of [mundane] deities such as local gods, beneficent or malignant spirits. They also conceive of hell as an actual place, and for them liberation or nirvāṇa, too, is situated somewhere up there....[15]

And, no doubt, some cashed in on those beliefs, which makes Patrul Rinpoché, in *The Words of My Perfect Teacher (Kun bzang bla ma'i zhal lung)*, lash out against those fake Chödpas who, in these times of spiritual degeneracy, try to cut through the outer demons without any understanding of the real meaning of Chöd, which is concerned with the elimination of the demons within:

> People today who claim to be practitioners of Chö do not understand any of this, and persist in thinking of spirits as something outside themselves. They believe in demons, and keep on perceiving them all the time; in everything that happens they see some ghost or *gyalgong*. They have no peace of mind themselves, and are always bewildering other with their lies, delivered with much assertive blustering: "There's a ghost up there! And down there a spirit! That's a ghost! That's a demon! That's a *tsen*! I can see it... Ha!—I've got it, I've killed it! Watch out, there's one lying in wait for you! I've chased it away. There—it looked back!"[16]

The concept of the god-demon extends far beyond the limited framework of creatures usually called gods or demons by popular traditions and standard classifications. Machig herself describes six kinds of gods and demons:[17]

(1) The gods and demons that are but simple labels (*kun brtags*) or conventional designations, like those mentioned above, obscure forces such as beneficial gods and malignant demons, mischievous ḍākinīs, invisible harmful spirits hidden in rocks, trees or rivers, etc.

(2) The gods and demons according to their essential nature,[18] such as the gods liberated from the world and the mundane gods. The supramundane Vajradhara (rDo rje 'chang), Yum Chenmo or Amitābha ('Od dpag med) are gods who reside in the Pure Lands: they are liberated from saṃsāra and the laws of karma, but at all times remain in the world. By contrast, the mundane gods belong to either the formless world, the world of form, or the world of desire.[19] The latter are unstable and act in beneficial or malignant ways according to circumstances, including one's own attitude towards them. The eight kinds of *btsan* demons and the Lord of Death (gShin rje) belong to this category.

(3) The supernatural or extraordinary gods and demons:[20] this category covers extraordinary interventions or events, from telepathic powers to miraculous phenomena such as rains of flowers or wondrous harvests as well as frightening apparitions and other calamities. Such occurrences are ascribed to a supernatural origin, either divine or demonic, according to circumstances.

(4) The co-emergent or natural gods and demons are the "divine" realization of the five wisdoms or the "demonic" appearances of the five poisons born from clinging to the reality of a self. In the words of Machig:

> Since time immemorial, the self-knowing wisdom—the unborn and pure dharmakāya—and the emotions born from an ego have both been co-emergent and natural, and furthermore, since knowledge and ignorance are inseparably interconnected, one therefore calls them [respectively] the co-emergent gods and demons.[21]

Here the term co-emergent or natural (Tib. *lhan skyes*) refers to a specific equation: the wisdom that since beginningless time is none other than the dharmakāya or truth body of the Buddhas, and the ignorance that holds on to a self—these two are undifferentiated, simply two aspects of the same thing. When the Buddha nature is free from adventitious impurities, it is the dharmakāya. Covered by these impurities, it is ignorance. Furthermore, since neither wisdom nor ignorance are produced by causes or conditions, they are viewed as co-emergent or natural. The Chödpa, having understood and separated wisdom and ignorance, will apply this wisdom as a remedy to cut through ignorance, the erroneous notion of a self.

(5) The infallible karmic gods and demons:[22] these may appear as the product of collective karma such as the seasons (where summer is divine and winter demonic), the cycle of day and night, of birth and death, or youth and old age. But they also exist on an individual level, such as one's family background or social status at birth, one's physical and mental characteristics, etc. They are the karmic retribution of one's past actions, but are often interpreted in terms of good fortune or bad luck, of blessings or catastrophe, of gods or demons. This still holds true in Tibetan popular belief where everything is evaluated in terms of "tashi" (*bkra shis*) or "ta mi shi" (*bkra mi shis*), auspicious or inauspicious. There again, Machig insists, this kind of dualistic distinction between positive and negative, happiness and unhappiness, good fortune and bad luck, is not based on anything real; it is simply the result of the inescapable play of cause and effect within the infinity of possibilities.

(6) The ultimate gods and demons:[23] the mundane deities are unable to offer genuine protection; only a Buddha who has attained unsurpassable enlightenment provides ultimate refuge from the suffering of saṃsāra. In this sense a Buddha is considered an ultimate god. Likewise, since it is extremely difficult to liberate oneself from cyclic existence and from rebirth in the hell realms in particular, these are considered ultimate demons.

Machig concludes this classification with the remark that, generally speaking, these names have been given by the ignorant, and the Chödpa should under no circumstances allow him- or herself to be misled by the infinite play of these appearances. Chödpas must train themselves to integrate all of these divine or demonic apparitions in their Chöd practice while remaining in perfect equanimity with whatever appears. Doing so, this duality of either positive or negative will spontaneously dissolve and become self-liberated, for all of these gods and demons are but mere illusions devoid of inherent existence, the unlimited display of the clear light nature of the mind. Indeed, from the viewpoint of Chöd, one should

> Abandon the notion of permanence and reality.
> Wander alone in desolate valleys, without concern for your
> body or life.

> Work for the benefit of others and offer your body to feed the demons...
> Since at the level of pure and ultimate truth, neither gods nor demons exist,
> You should understand that even the stains of karma, once ripened,
> Are unable to affect the natural purity of the suchness of all phenomena.[24]

3 The Four Demons of Chöd

These demons must be understood in the context of the emptiness of inherent existence of both the ego and phenomena. If all phenomena are devoid of inherent existence on the ultimate level, for as long as ignorance has an ascendancy over mind and phenomena continue to appear as having an existence separate from the mind that perceives them, they must be viewed as demons. Here, too, the example of the dream allows us to understand by analogy the nature of these demons. So long as the dreamer is under the sway of the dream, those demons out to devour him or the sweet fairy gently protecting him are real. But as soon as he wakes up, these images instantly lose their reality and hence also their impact. From the Madhyamaka point of view, the nature of these apparitions is neither true nor mistaken, but it is devoid of all assertion or negation, beyond all conceptualization.

Western tradition generally associates demons with monstrous beings or with the Beast, but Machig goes out of her way to tell us that "those huge, black and frightening ones" are not the real demons. In a spiritual sense the real demons are everything that hinders and interferes with the attainment of liberation. This is the way they are described in the śāstras, and accordingly, there is no demon more huge than the erroneous holding on to a self. When one cuts through this demon of attachment to the reality of a self, that alone eliminates all other demons without exception.[25] In *The Great Collection*, Machig summarizes as follows the Chöd view of demons:

> The origin of all demons is in mind itself.
> When awareness holds on and embraces any outer object,
> It is in the hold of a demon.
> Likewise, mind is stained when a [mental image]
> Is wrongly taken to be a real object.[26]

In this way, all outer or inner objects grasped by mind as if they were real which thereby generate desire, aversion, or ignorance, should be viewed as demons because they prevent the realization of the clear light emptiness nature of mind, Mahāmudrā.

Traditionally, Chöd defines four kinds of demons that need to be cut through, the first three of which derive from clinging to ego, and the fourth being ego-clinging itself.[27] In Chöd terminology the term *snyems*, literally "arrogance" or "pride," in fact is to be understood in the sense of "the erroneous grasping to the reality of a self." Therefore, the demon of ego-grasping (*snyems byed*) is the cause of clinging to the reality of tangible and intangible phenomena, and these are also considered to be demons.

(1) The tangible demons (thogs bcas bdud) are the perceptions of the five senses such as forms, sounds, odors, etc. In Machig's words:

> Since mistaken grasping to reality comes from material objects,
> I have explained them as tangible demons.[28]

These objects may be pleasant, unpleasant or neutral, generating attachment, aversion or ignorance. Hence, as long as the adept has not realized their illusory and adventitious nature, outer phenomena are demons. Once this illusory nature has been purified and the adept realizes the emptiness of these phenomena—like the dreamer becoming aware that he or she is dreaming—mind can no longer be harmed by those demons produced by the sense faculties. And as forms, sounds, etc. do not really exist, the same holds true for the desire or aversion they produce: these are but simple appearances devoid of any reality on their own, and from which one has to free oneself. Āryadeva enumerates three kinds of remedies to cut through the tangible demons:

> Depending on whether your experience is excellent, medium, or ordinary,
> Remain in spontaneous absorption free of thought, similar to a dense forest;
> Meditate with your concentration aimed at these [demons], as if you were endowed with supernatural powers;
> Or, like [using] a sharp axe, by analysis and reasoning firmly establish [their non-existence].[29]

The ordinary Chödpa applies reasoning in order to establish the nonexistence of these demons, and dwells in the nature of mind beyond all conceptualization, the Sūtra level. When his or her capacities have increased, the Chödpa will be able to directly comprehend their illusory nature, which will enable him or her to transform these apparitions as if endowed with supernatural powers. This is considered the

Vajrayāna approach, the path of transformation of appearances. Finally, through excellent Mahāmudrā practice, these demonic apparitions will spontaneously liberate themselves in the emptiness clarity of mind.

(2) The intangible demons (thogs med bdud) cannot be perceived by the senses. They are the positive or negative thoughts that arise in the mind. Āryadeva says of them:

> What are known as the intangible demons
> Consist of magical manifestations of gods and demons, and arrogance.

And Machig:

> The intangible demons...are the emotions such as suffering and so forth,
> The fear of invisible demons or the waiting for imaginary gods,
> As well as all expectation or rejection regarding mental objects.
> Since they all derive from arrogance, the faulty grasping onto a self (*snyems bya*),
> They are the demons of the mistaken attachment to reality.[30]

When they are frightening they are called demons; when they are positive or pleasant they are called gods. They are the conditions that leave the mind under the sway of emotions and karma. Included within this group are spirits, phantoms, zombies, and so forth. Some are purely imaginary while others possess some sort of relative level of existence. The mind that dualistically clings to these gods and demons, faults and qualities, has itself no inherent existence and must be recognized as emptiness. So one does not need to eliminate these feelings, perceptions or concepts, or even prevent their appearance. One should simply allow the mind to remain in its natural calmness and clarity. When one abandons dualistic grasping to subject-object, body and mind are no longer restless and naturally become calm, just like waves on the surface of the ocean calm down and dissolve by themselves (*rang sar*). This is the natural way to free oneself of the intangible demons.

(3) The demon of exaltation (dga' brod bdud) or of intense joy is born from attachment to blissful meditational experiences.

> The exaltation towards ordinary phenomena
> And the exaltation of the supreme result
> Are born from erroneous grasping to the reality of the self.
> If one becomes attached to the reality [of this joy], it turns into a demon.
> If it appears spontaneously without any attachment in one's mind,
> It is then called the armor of the dharmakāya devoid of all grasping.[31]

Attachment to the reality of this joy or exaltation is at the root of the eight worldly dharmas, the concerns for gain and loss, praise and defamation, etc.[32] By finding satisfaction in experiences or powers that may manifest as a result of meditation (the clear vision of the yidam, prophetic dreams, the ability to impose one's will on others, etc.), one easily develops arrogance and pride. In this sense, exaltation is one of the greatest obstacles to the attainment of enlightenment and should be considered a demon. The best remedy to counter it consists of realizing that everything appearing in one's mind, qualities as well as faults, has not the slightest inherent existence, being similar to an illusion or a dream image. One thus remains absorbed in the realization that both the perceiving mind and the perceived objects are not other than emptiness, beyond all conceptualization.

(4) The demon of arrogance (snyems byed kyi bdud) is the demonic force at the root of the three others and hence the one that must definitely be cut through. Here, arrogance is synonymous with attachment to the self, which is why this demon is also referred to as "the demon of

ego."[33] It is the very origin of suffering and of transmigratory wandering in the cycle of existences, the demon directly preventing the attainment of enlightenment. Mind under the sway of afflictive emotions tends to grasp at a self where there is none, and to consider as real an "I" and "mine." When one holds onto an "I" one also grasps at an "other," and this fundamental duality gives birth to attachment and aversion. This mistaken viewpoint is the basic ignorance of emptiness in regard to the existence of a self. Here, too, the remedy is to remain in the serene nature of the mind, free from all conceptualization about reality and non-reality. To summarize,

> As long as there is an ego, there are demons.
> When there is no more ego, there are no more demons either!
> If there is no ego, there is no more object to cut through,
> Nor is there any more fear or terror.
> Free from all extremes, co-emergent wisdom[34]
> Gives birth to the understanding of [the nature of] all phenomena.
> This is referred to as the fruit of liberation from the four demons.[35]

The Chöd adept starts off by cutting through the holding onto a self, the fourth demon which dominates ignorant mind. In the biography, Machig does go through such an experience and instantly her entire spiritual orientation undergoes a tremendous change.[36] However, as a direct result of this experience and the qualities of realization it evokes, the demon of exaltation appears. Since it is impossible to prevent the arising of this joy and of these qualities, the sole protection available is to use them (*lam du 'khyer*, "to carry them onto the path"), fully aware that they have no more reality than a dream image or an illusion created by a magician. In other words, following the *Biography of Machig*:

> I am the yoginī who has realized the meaning of the
> Prajñāpāramitā.
> The inner demons are the internal emptiness,
> The outer demons are the external emptiness,
> The inner and outer demons are the emptiness of both [internal
> and external].
> The demons above are the emptiness of the great,
> The demons below are the emptiness of the ultimate.
> Tangible demons are the emptiness of collected [phenomena],
> Intangible demons are the emptiness of uncollected [phenomena].
> All demons of exaltation are the emptiness of that without
> beginning or end,
> All demons of arrogance are the emptiness of suchness [Skt. *tathatā*,
> Tib. *de bzhin nyid*].[37]

Although the tangible demons such as the belief in the reality of the four elements are the most obvious ones, they can only be eliminated by a bodhisattva of the first bhūmi, whereas certain intangible demons such as sickness, suffering, attachment or aversion can be eliminated by ordinary beings. Machig concludes:

> In this way, the two kinds of demons, the tangible and intangible,
> Constitute what must be abandoned;
> The two demons of exaltation and grasping to a self [arrogance]
> Are the means by which one abandons them.[38]

While the Chöd tradition establishes a definite distinction between the four demons, all are related to the fourth one, the demon of arrogance, the mistaken conception of a self. As soon as one cuts off the demon of ego, all the other demons are simultaneously eliminated. Buddhahood is no different from this state.[39]

In short, Machig defines the authentic Chöd as the practice consisting of cutting thoughts where they are, as they appear in the mind. Finally, when there are no more discursive thoughts nor subject-object notions, ultimately there is nothing left to be cut through:

> To utilize one's own incompetence and limitations is explained as the meaning of Chöd.
> When one realizes that all comes from mind, there is not the slightest object left to be cut through.
> When one realizes the emptiness of mind itself, there is no more duality left between what cuts through and what must be cut through.
> When one experiences this nonduality, one cuts without having to cut all the demons, like a thief in an empty house.[40]

4 The Level of Final Accomplishment

> The definitive sign of realization in Chöd is to be free from fear.
> The level of final accomplishment in the practice is the spontaneous pacification of magical interferences [by gods and demons].

Āryadeva in his *Grand Poem* uses the technical terms "the definitive sign of realization" (*chod tshad*) and "the level of final accomplishment" (*tshar tshad*). Machig associates these expressions with two other terms, "the symptoms" (*lhong*) and "magical displays or interferences" (*cho 'phrul*). Together, these represent four levels of realization in Chöd practice. When her disciple Chökyi Sengé inquired whether these four levels appear in progressive order or simultaneously, whether they are associated two by two or are independent, Machig explained the entire process of realization according to the Chöd system.[41]

To start with, what is referred to as "symptom" (*lhong*) is synonymous with "sign" or "characteristic."[42] In Chöd terminology, when the practitioner offers his or her body as food to gods and demons in frightening places and practices the Chöd samādhi uniting emptiness and compassion, the splendor of the yogi's meditative absorption in the essence of reality is unbearable to those beings. As Āryadeva says:

> When you are thus meditating on nondual *pāramitā*,
> The local gods and demons can't stand it, and in despair
> Cause magical interferences of all kinds,
> Real, imaginary or in dreams.[43]

So the gods and demons create obstacles and set about disturbing the yogi's practice. For the yogi, these manifest physically or mentally as uncomfortable or unpleasant states, and this discomfort is described as the first symptom of realization in practice.

If the yogi perseveres in meditation practice, these minor discomforts and disturbances gradually transform into visions, hallucinations, mirages, or dreams produced by beings attempting to interfere with any realization. These magical appearances or interferences (*cho 'phrul*) can be caused by all sorts of creatures: karmic debtors, negative subterranean or celestial negative forces such as Rāhu or Yama, the Lord of Death (gShin rje).[44] As for the outer miraculous occurrences, they may manifest in the form of earthquakes, floods, avalanches, forest fires and other natural catastrophes. They may also affect the objects of the senses—form, sound, taste—or mental states, both in waking and in dreams.

Machig's *Quintessence of Cutting through Demonic Objects* (*sNying tshom*) defines four kinds of miraculous occurrences in progressive order, from the coarsest to the most subtle: (1) the tangible with embodied form, (2) the verbal (*skad gdon*), (3) visions of destruction created by demons, and (4) those caused by dreams.

Machig insists that all of these magical manifestations of gods and demons derive from mind itself, and that the means to eliminate them, for those of excellent meditative capacity, is "to liberate them in their own place," according to the higher view of Mahāmudrā:[45]

> In dealing with these, [if your meditative capacity] is excellent,
> Remain absorbed in the true nature [of mind].
> Whatever miraculous displays of gods and demons appear,

> Recognize them as the miraculous display of your own mind,
> And do not concentrate your awareness on these monsters.
> Remain at ease, serene in the very nature of this recognition.
> When you are absorbed in a natural, serene state,[46]
> These miraculous displays will be naturally pacified.
> And once appeased in the essence of phenomena,
> They will next appear to you as friendly.

Those of medium capacity should separate body and consciousness, then allow mind to remain in empty space: then these miraculous occurrences will dissolve into emptiness.

A meditator of lesser capacity should apply the teachings of transforming the body into an offering of food to gods and demons while the mind remains naturally absorbed in its own nature. When the yogi's realization of emptiness increases, he or she is no longer affected by miraculous displays. On the contrary, they gradually lose their power over the mind, and the gods or demons themselves will start to pay attention to the yogi's words, eventually coming under the spell of his or her spoken advice. Supernatural powers and qualities appear in the yogi, but the real sign of coming realization takes the form of an intense joy: this experience is the third level of realization, called the "level of final accomplishment" (*tshar tshad*).

This level of accomplishment also varies according to the capacity of the meditator. For those of lesser capacity, the outer level is to remain serene and calm when facing miraculous interferences of gods and demons; the inner level is when the gods and demons show their confidence in the meditator and reward him or her with supernatural siddhis; the secret level is the ongoing sensation of well-being or bliss, achieved when sickness as well as negative forces and thoughts have been totally eliminated or pacified; and the ultimate level of accomplishment is to be animated by love and compassion, to have internalized the realization of the impermanence of all phenomena, and, henceforth, to apply oneself to Dharma practice with full confidence. For meditators of superior capacity, the outer level is to subjugate fears and harmful magical interferences by the splendor or charisma (*zil gnon*) of realization; the inner level is to remain without arrogance, i.e., without any conception of a self, when faced by whatever evil may appear, be it illness, frustration, or demons; the secret level is to view adversity and obstacles as friends; and the ultimate level is the actualization of immaculate dharmatā, the empty nature of self.

In this process, gods and demons become conscious of their karma and of their negative mental inclinations. They will receive the yogi's instructions and in this way will be set on the path to enlightenment. In exchange they must vow not to harm anyone and to protect the yogi's teachings. At this stage, the meditator has cut through all mental confusion and dualistic notions of good and bad. Experiencing directly the truth of suchness of phenomena and the very nature of nonself, he or she realizes the dharmakāya, while also establishing others, such as the lord of the soil (*sa bdag*) and local gods and demons, on the path of liberation. This is called the definitive sign (*chod tshad*) in the realization of Chöd. Again, the outer sign of this realization consists in no longer being subject to fear or terror when faced with the magical interferences of divine or demonic forces; the inner sign is the insight that illness and negative emotions are none other than karmic retribution; the secret sign is to be free from confusion when faced with any thought that appears, whether good, evil, or indifferent; and the definitive sign is to have cut through the erroneous holding on to a self, regardless of what sense objects or gratification may appear.

One should not attach undue importance to any such classification: in actual experience things may well differ according to the individual, for instance the order in which one experiences these levels. Some might not experience one or another of these levels, yet realize the remaining three. Every combination is possible depending on individual karma and tendencies, as well as on specific confrontations with different gods or demons. In addition, the texts provide numerous other explanations and systems of classification. Machig summarizes the result of Chöd practice as follows:

> Once tangible and intangible demons as well as those of exaltation and of grasping to a self are pacified, as the temporary result, one's body will be free of illness, one's mind free of suffering. The ultimate result is the realization of Buddhahood, the very nature of the three kāyas.[47]

In the light of these four levels of realization, it is of interest to reread the second chapter of *The Hundred Thousand Songs of Milarepa*, entitled "The Voyage to Lashi." Here Milarepa is attacked by Bharo, a powerful demon of Nepal, and his armies, who create all sorts of terrifying apparitions. At first, Milarepa addresses them as follows:

> Through mirages and illusions,
> You pernicious male and female devils
> Can create these fantastic terrors.

Although they are unable to distract Milarepa from his meditation, these demons refuse to be subjugated. Milarepa next teaches them the law of cause and effect and sings for them the song of "The Seven Adornments":

> I, the Yogi who desires to remain in solitude,
> Meditate on the Voidness of Mind.
> Awed by the power of my concentration,
> You jealous demons are forced to practice magic.
> For the yogi, demonic conjurations
> Are beauty and adornment.

At this point most of the demons are convinced by the yogi's spoken word: they stop interfering and request him to teach them Dharma. In the end they vow allegiance to him and take the commitment to serve him. Between the lines we can distinguish the four levels of realization of Chöd, from the first symptoms to the signs of realization where the demons submit to the yogi and set out on the path to enlightenment.[48]

We also find these different levels of realization all through the life of Machig, starting from her first experiences at the Tree of Serlag, where she subjugates the armies of the nāga king, up to the conclusion of her life story, where it is said:

> Machig studied and realized the concise, medium and extensive words of the Buddha. She perfectly studied the chapter on demons, in particular teachings such as:
>
> > Attachment to any phenomenon whatsoever,
> > From coarse form to omniscience,
> > Should be understood as the play of a demon....
>
> Having obtained liberation through these teachings, she gained the extraordinary experience of naturally eliminating the four demons....

To summarize, the Chöd tradition fits into the universe of popular Tibetan demonology. As we have seen, this demonology is a veritable science in which each entity is listed and classified according to its powers and has its experimental verification within the living transmission. Machig's Chöd tradition is a dramatization and a synthesis that utilizes all the resources of the mental sphere, combining into a single doctrine the ultimate teachings of Mahāmudrā, tantric visualization techniques, and the vast pantheon of primordial forces, local gods and demons that inhabit the imagination of the Tibetan people. This appears to be the main function of Chöd: to serve as a link between the highest metaphysical vision and the popular religion. Its closeness to the world of positive and negative forces explains why the Chödpa, while remaining outside religious institutions, was so popular among Tibetans and often called upon to deal with diseases, spirit possessions, exorcisms, and so forth, roles normally filled in Central Asian cultures by shamans.

Wandering Chödpa in front of the Jokhang in Lhasa. Photo: J. Edou.

V Transmission

The opening of the gates of Dharma
Is not an initiation of a deity transmitted to the body;
It is an initiation of the ultimate meaning transmitted to the mind.

—*Machig Labdrön*

1 The Three Chöd Traditions of Machig

Among the various Chöd traditions that came into being in India and Tibet, such as *The Elimination of Confusion* according to Padmasambhava's Recovered Treasures, Nāropa's *Single Taste*, the visions of Mahāsiddha Thangtong Gyalpo (1361-1485),[1] or the Chöd of Götsangpa (1189-1258),[2] Machig's Chöd tradition constitutes an original and specific system, both from a philosophical point of view and in terms of the methods of realization. By comparing the lineage transmissions she received with those she passed on to her disciples, it becomes possible to determine her role in the codification of the teachings.

The first main transmission to become part of her spiritual inheritance is definitely the one which came down from Dampa Sangyé, directly or through Sönam Lama.[3] While Dampa did not grant her any actual empowerment, he transmitted to her the precepts from the Indian mahāsiddha tradition, as well as the Chöd precepts connected with the Prajñāpāramitā. This latter tradition, obtained from Āryadeva the Brahmin, is referred to as the oral transmission lineage and is also known as the Sūtra tradition.

The second transmission, the Vajrayāna Chöd, directly revealed to her by Tārā through visionary experiences, does not seem to have existed as such prior to Machig, although some sources do mention a Vajrayāna Chöd transmission going back to mahāsiddhas such as Luhipa and Saraha. Machig is considered to be an emanation of the

Great Mother Yum Chenmo, the Perfection of Wisdom, a wisdom ḍākinī—itself a guarantee of the authenticity of her revelations.[4]

The third transmission originated with Machig herself and consists of a corpus of teachings born from the previous two, combined with her own meditative experience.

It remains an arduous task to systematize these major currents, defined variously according to different authors and schools. *The Concise Life Story* classifies them under two distinct headings:[5] (1) Machig's general teaching, subsumed under the term "Chöd of Mahāmudrā" and covering the separation of body and consciousness, the offering of the body, and the use of *PHAT*;[6] and (2) Machig's specific teachings—her three Chöd traditions as laid out in her great systematic treatises, *The Grand Exposition according to Sūtra*, *The Grand Exposition according to Tantra*, and *The Grand Exposition according to [Combined] Sūtra and Tantra*;[7] her treatise on the two stages of Vajrayāna meditation, the *Appendices*;[8] and the teachings given in a non-systematic way to individual disciples according to circumstances, which cover all her remaining teachings.[9]

The authors of almost all great commentaries offer lists of Chöd lineages,[10] among which that given in the *Concise Life Story* is the most complete. It summarizes the Mahāmudrā Chöd tradition as eight pairs and sixteen branches (only seven pairs and fourteen branches of which are mentioned):

(1) the male lineages (*pha brgyud*) and the female lineages (*ma brgyud*)
(2) the terrestrial and celestial teachings
(3) the Indian and Tibetan teachings
(4) the great systematic treatises and the various non-systematic teachings
(5) the Sūtra and Tantra traditions
(6) the unified and the comprehensive traditions
(7) the Oral Transmission (*bka' ma*) and the Recovered Treasure (*gter ma*) traditions.[11]

(1) The male and female lineages. These vary from one author to the next. According to Karma Chagmé, the male lineage is the Chöd of Dampa, also called the Chöd of Means, whereas the female lineage is the one Tārā gave to Machig, and is known as the Chöd of Knowledge. He also mentions a third one: the son lineage (*sras brgyud*), also called the experience lineage (*nyams brgyud*), which Machig passed on to her son Gyalwa Döndrup.

Still, according to Karma Chagmé, one should distinguish these male and female lineages from the male and female Chöd. The male Chöd (*pho gcod*) was transmitted from Dampa to Mara Serpo, by him to Machig, and by her to her disciples. The female Chöd (*mo gcod*) was the tradition Machig passed on to her four spiritual daughters.

(2) The terrestrial and celestial teachings. The latter are all the Dharma teachings in the texts that are said to have fallen from heaven onto the house of the Indian Dharmarāja;[12] all Recovered Treasure teachings (*gter ma*) are the terrestrial ones. Karma Chagmé points out that most teachings of the second intermediary cycle, such as the various Perfection of Wisdom texts, are terrestrial Dharma, having been recovered from earlier hiding places. The same holds true for most Chöd teachings as well.

(3) The Indian and Tibetan teachings. The four great currents of the Indian tradition refer to the four treatises (of Padmasambhava, Nāropa, etc.) already mentioned.[13] What came forth from Machig's mind in her role as an emanation of Yum Chenmo are known as the Tibetan teachings.

(4) The great systematic treatises and the various non-systematic teachings. These are Machig's specific teachings mentioned earlier.

(5) and (6) The Sūtra, Tantra and Unified traditions will be treated in detail below. The comprehensive tradition is not further mentioned by Karma Chagmé and does not seem to constitute an actual system.

(7) The Oral Transmission and the Recovered Treasure traditions. The Recovered Chöd (*gter gcod*) tradition includes the teachings hidden by Padmasambhava and discovered by Rinchen Lingpa, Sangyé Lingpa, and others. Machig and her descendants such as Gangpa Mugsang and others also hid teachings at places like Chimpug near Samyé and in Lhasa's Plain of Sorrows[14] to be discovered later by tertöns such as Kunpang Tsöndrü Sengé and others.[15] Some sources even indicate that Machig personally hid certain terma teachings in the Amdo region. The Oral Transmission tradition (*bka' ma*) is the so-called long lineage of canonical scriptures transmitted without interruption from master to disciple.[16]

The Sūtra Tradition

This tradition is based on the *Heart Sūtra* and taught in Āryadeva's *Grand Poem*, in Dampa Sangyé's *Set of Six Fragments on Chöd* (*gCod brul tsho drug pa*)[17] and in Machig's *Great Collection*.[18] Known as the lineage of instructions of the ultimate meaning of the Buddha's word, it comprises three main transmission lineages:

(1) the male lineage of means (Tib. *thabs*)
Buddha Śākyamuni
Mañjuśrī
Nāgārjuna and Āryadeva
the Brahmin Āryadeva
Kyo Sakya Yeshé
Sönam Lama and Khubön
Machig Labdrön

(2) the female lineage of wisdom (Tib. *shes rab*)
Yum Chenmo (dharmakāya)
Ārya Tārā (sambhogakāya)
Ḍākinī Sukhasiddhī (nirmāṇakāya)
the Brahmin Āryadeva
Dampa Sangyé
Sönam Lama
Machig Labdrön

(3) the nondual lineage (Tib. *gnyis med*)
Yum Chenmo
Buddha Śākyamuni
Ārya Tārā
Mañjuśrī
the two Āryadevas
Dampa Sangyé
Sönam Lama
Machig Labdrön

The means lineage emphasizes the gradual meditation methods such as love and compassion and the accumulation of merit according to relative truth. The wisdom lineage presents Chöd under the aspect of absolute truth and the accumulation of wisdom (Skt. *prajñā*, Tib. *shes rab*). The nondual lineage unites these approaches.[19]

The Transmission History adds to these a fourth lineage, originating with Machig herself—the experience lineage of the non-systematic teachings of Machig born from her realization. It also appears under the name of "the tradition of liberation" since it agrees with the oral teachings of the Buddha.[20]

According to *The Concise Life Story*, this Sūtra tradition was taught by Machig in *The Grand Exposition according to Sūtra* (*mDo'i rnam bshad chen mo*) as well as in other texts classified under the specific non-systematic teachings.[21] This text distinguishes four Sūtra transmissions received by Machig:

CHÖD LINEAGES
To Machig Labdrön

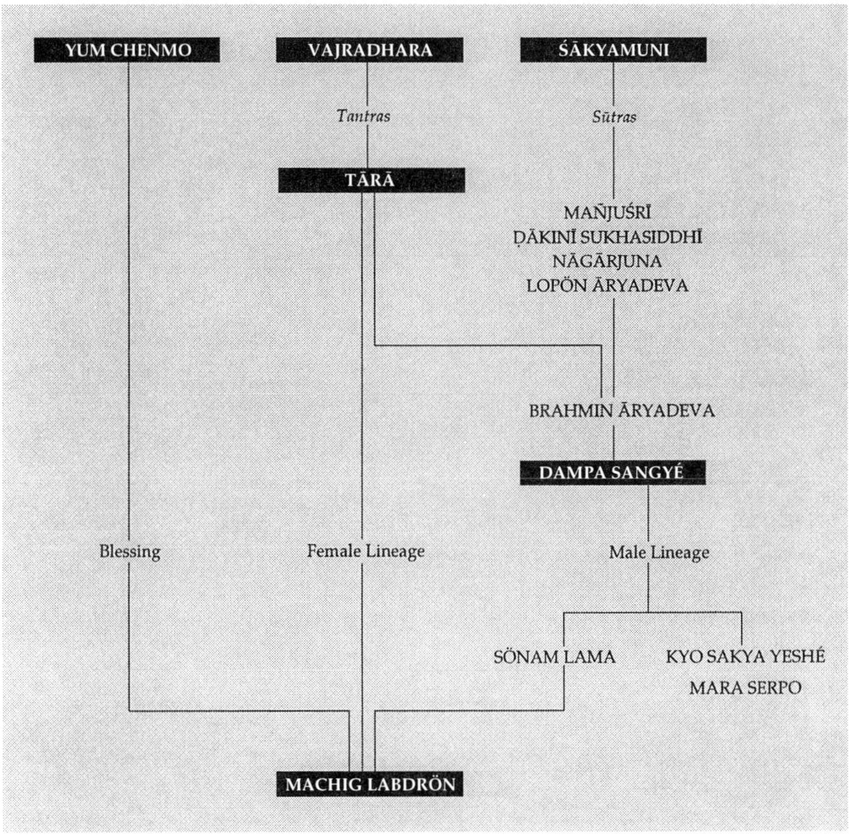

(1) the lineage that establishes foremost the emptiness of perceived outer phenomena, identical with the lineage of means, including, among others, Nāgārjuna, both Āryadevas, and Dampa

(2) the lineage that focuses on the emptiness of the inner perceiving consciousness, passed on from the Buddha to Maitreya, Asaṅga, Vasubandhu, and Dampa

(3) the lineage that unites perceived objects and perceiving consciousness, transmitted from the Buddha to Mañjuśrī, Birawa, Ḍākinī Sukhasiddhī, Āryadeva the Brahmin, and Dampa

(4) the lineage of offerings and of the maṇḍala practice according to the Sūtras, including the Buddha, Tārā, Mañjuśrī, Birawa, Ḍākinī Sukhasiddhī, Āryadeva, Dampa and Sönam Lama.[22]

It is generally agreed that Machig gave this Sūtra tradition to all her spiritual sons and daughters, with only Gyalwa Döndrup receiving also the extraordinary instructions which, according to Karma Chagmé, became known as the son lineage of experience (Tib. *nyams*).[23]

Machig's eldest son Drupa, or Gyalwa Döndrup. He is considered the main holder of the Sūtra tradition of Chöd. Drawing by Dolpopa Tenzin Norbu.

The Tantra Tradition

Following Machig's own statement, the Chöd tradition according to the Tantras follows "foremost the Mother Tantras of Highest Yoga."[24] At the request of her companion Thöpa Bhadra, Machig transcribed these Vajrayāna teachings in *The Grand Exposition according to Tantra* (*sNgags kyi rnam bshad chen mo*), so far an elusive text which may no longer exist.

All Highest Yoga Tantra methods of realization (Skt. *sādhana*, Tib. *sgrub thabs*) include the two stages of generation of the deity (*bskyed rim*) and completion (*rdzogs rim*). Generally speaking, the generation stage consists of the visualization of the deity and its maṇḍala palace, in the course of which the practitioner identifies him- or herself with the deity. In most Chöd manuals, the meditator begins by visualizing him- or herself in the aspect of Vajravārāhī (rDo rje phag mo) or as the Wrathful Black Lady (Khros ma nag mo) before performing the transference of consciousness. Although different methods exist for practicing this kind of visualization, Chöd applies the instantaneous generation technique, in which the meditator appears instantaneously as the deity, as opposed to gradual visualization of each part. The generation stage is not touched upon in the textual sources, as it is considered to be already known by the Chöd practitioner. Some lamas comment that normally one would require solid experience in the Vārāhī generation stage prior to engaging in the Tantra tradition of Chöd.

Once in self-generation as the deity, the Chödpa performs, according to the techniques previously described, the transference of consciousness which is related to the completion stage. By presenting the coarse body as a food offering, the yogi practices the perfection of generosity and renounces attachment to the body, but finally mind and wind (Skt. *prāṇa*, Tib. *rlung*) must be united, for this is the very foundation of the completion stage as explained in the main Highest Yoga Tantra treatises. Here again, the Chöd texts do not dwell at any length on this technique, as the yogi would already know it. Tāranātha implies as much when he recommends that after the stage of absorption in nonduality, the meditator apply one of the appropriate visualizations of the channels (Skt. *nāḍī*, Tib. *rtsa*) and winds.[25] There exist a vast variety of sādhanas and rituals within Highest Yoga Tantra, but the techniques to make the winds enter the central channel are essentially identical.

Although Machig received numerous visionary initiations from deities as well as numerous instructions from Dampa, the Vajrayāna Chöd tradition covers primarily the precepts and initiations she received from Ārya Tārā through direct inspiration. Accordingly, most commentators summarize its transmission lineage as follows:

Vajradhara (rDo rje 'chang)—the truth body (dharmakāya) of the Buddhas
Ārya Tārā—the subtle bliss body (sambhogakāya)
Machig Labdrön—the emanation body (nirmāṇakāya)

Often, however, Yum Chenmo takes Vajradhara's place as the dharmakāya, which is the way Tārā explains it to Machig.[26]

Tārā transmitted to Machig Labdrön three main tantras, each with its own generation and completion stages:

(1) The Great Uḍumvara Tantra (*U dum wa ra*). The corresponding sādhana originally only centered on Vajradhara, but following her vision, Machig composed an extended sādhana of the ten gurus of the oral transmission, coming from Yum Chenmo down to herself. According to Jamgön Kongtrul this tradition has been transmitted through a cycle called "the hundred initiations of the transformation of the lamas."[27]

(2) The Great Tantra known as Taming the Five Poisons [and] the Nāgas (*Dug lnga klu 'dul ba*). Originally this sādhana was exclusively centered on the five primordial Buddhas. Machig composed a sādhana of the Buddhas of the ten directions, including Mañjuśrī, Avalokiteśvara and Vajrapāṇi, the Buddhas of the past and future, as well as the five primordial Buddhas. From this tantra is derived the cycle of the hundred initiations of the transformation of the Buddhas in the ten directions.

(3) The Great Tantra known as The Quintessence that Dispels the Darkness of Ignorance (*Thugs bcud ma rig mun sel*). Included in this tantra are the ten-deity maṇḍala practice of Vajradhātu's Ruling Lady (Vajradhātvīśvarī, rDo rje dbyings kyi dbang phyug ma) and the five-deity maṇḍala practice of Vārāhī (Phag mo). Machig merely transcribed these two sādhanas in their original form. This Mother Tantra included the cycle called the hundred initiations of the transformation of the ḍākinīs.[28]

To these initiations and teachings Machig added the other Vajrayāna transmissions she received on different occasions, as related in *The*

Marvelous Life. The Concise Life Story enumerates these teachings under the heading "the specific non-systematic teachings." They include:

(1) the Mahāmāyā practice
(2) the essential instructions on mind
(3) the profound path of guru yoga
(4) the consciousness transference called "Entry into the Supreme Path"
(5) the three cycles of visualization on the Protectors of the Three Families (Mañjuśrī, Avalokiteśvara and Vajrapāṇi)
(6) the three cycles on compassion, the Avalokiteśvara meditation and so forth.[29]

Having bestowed on Machig these different transmissions and their accompanying empowerments, Tārā further tells her to preserve the tradition of the two stages in meditation on the Tantras, for "within ten generations, this Vajrayāna tradition will pervade all the extent of space." However, according to *The Concise Life Story*, she also warns her about the future extinction of this tradition. In the colophon of *The Marvelous Life*, the editor stresses that this tradition has reached the compiler Namkha Gyaltsen intact but that it will degenerate after him.[30] Jamgön Kongtrul confirms this version when he explains that the Vajrayāna Chöd is composed, among others, of

> the hundred initiations on the transformation of the gurus, the hundred initiations on the transformation of the Buddhas, the hundred initiations on the transformation of the ḍākinīs, which together make up the three hundred Chöd initiations; there are also the hundred initiations of the hundred ganacakra (*tshogs*) rites and the eighty Chöd initiations and so forth,

but,

> most of these transmissions have disappeared at present.[31]

Finally, Tārā tells Machig to unite the point of view of the heart of the Prajñāpāramitā and the exceptional means of the four mudrās, a set of yogic techniques to make the winds enter the central channel.[32]

Most sources are of the opinion that Machig transmitted these teachings to her son Thönyön Samdrup. This is the transmission obtained, eight generations later, by Namkha Gyaltsen, the compiler of *The Marvelous Life*. According to him, the hundred ganacakras and the hundred initiations had become a separate lineage starting with Thönyön Samdrup.[33]

The Combined Sūtra and Tantra Tradition

In *The Garden of Joy*, Jamgön Kongtrul summarizes the combined tradition of Sūtra and Tantra as follows:

> What is known as the Mahāmudrā Chöd conforms to the intention of the middle cycle [of the Buddha's teaching] and the practice of the Mantra Vehicle's yogic behavior[34] which consists in searching out what is unpleasant, throwing oneself entirely into adversity, realizing that gods and demons are in the mind, and understanding the equality of self and others.[35]

Accordingly this tradition unites into a single doctrine the non-differentiated Sūtra and Tantra traditions and Machig's meditative experiences. Karma Chagmé subsumes them all under the heading of the seed syllable *PHAT*: "*PHA* represents the Perfection of Wisdom, whereas the retroflex *TA* has the meaning of the Great Mantra Vehicle. By combining them in the power-word *PHAT*, one unites the sum total of Sūtra and Tantra." He goes on to say that the essence of the Sūtra tradition is contained in the red banquet, in the course of which one offers one's body, flesh and blood out of compassion for all beings, and in particular for the most needy among the gods and demons, thereby accumulating the six perfections. In contrast, the Tantra tradition is contained in the multicolored banquet which consists of the offering of one's body in the form of an offering ritual (Skt. *ganacakra*, Tib. *tshogs*), such as is described and practiced in the Highest Yoga Tantra.

According to *Transforming the Aggregates*, this combined tradition includes the following elements:[36]

(1) the Tantra tradition as described above as well as the long life cycle and the four kinds of burnt offerings (Skt. *homa*, Tib. *sbyin sreg*)[37]

(2) the instructions of the oral transmission which include the four initiations of meditative stabilization (Skt. *samādhi*, Tib. *ting nge 'dzin*) according to the Prajñāpāramitā, the five kinds of ganacakra offerings and the sacrificial cake initiation (Tib. *gtor ma*)

(3) the non-differentiated meaning of combined Sūtra and Tantra traditions, through the single initiation of the transformation of the Buddhas in the ten directions, as well as the Chöd of Machig, based on her own meditative experiences.

This non-differentiated tradition was explained by Machig in *The Grand Exposition of Combined Sūtra and Tantra* (*Zung 'jug gi rnam bshad chen mo*), as well as in teachings known under the general heading "the specific non-systematic teachings," such as the oral instructions called "the Nectar of Mind," the sealed instructions on the secret of Chöd's yogic exercises, the "*HUNG* cycle" and its commentaries according to the Pacification of Suffering,[38] the "Precious Torch," the "Torch of Secret Wisdom," and so forth.[39]

2 Machig's Lineage Descendants

Following her success in the debate with the Indian ācāryas, Machig's teaching was propagated in India. In Tibet, her sons, daughters and main disciples became the holders of a spiritual heritage that soon branched off into different lineages as it spread throughout the country. Sources vary and often contradict one another here, yet commentators generally agree that Machig gave the Sūtra tradition to her son Gyalwa Döndrup, the Tantra tradition to her son Thönyön Samdrup, and the Combined tradition to her spiritual son Khugom Chökyi Sengé.[40]

(1) The Sūtra tradition. Starting from Gyalwa Döndrup,[41] the Sūtra tradition was transmitted through two lineages of explanation (*bshad brgyud*):

Nyenchung Lotsāwa
Salchen Özer
Dorjé Gyaltsen
Chöying Dorjé
Tsöndrü Sengé

and

Sangyé Nangzhig
Dorjé Gyaltsen
Nyima Sengé

and one practice lineage (*sgrub brgyud*):

Khambu Yagleg (Gyalwa Döndrup's son)
Rinchen Sengé, and so forth.

According to Karma Chagmé, Gyalwa Döndrup was the principal holder of the son transmission of Machig's experiences.[42]

(2) The Tantra tradition. Thönyön Samdrup was without doubt Machig's favorite son and disciple. Apart from the Tantra transmission, she bequeathed to him the Combined Sūtra and Tantra tradition and numerous other Chöd precepts. In the cave at Zhampo-gang,

CHÖD LINEAGES
From Machig Labdrön

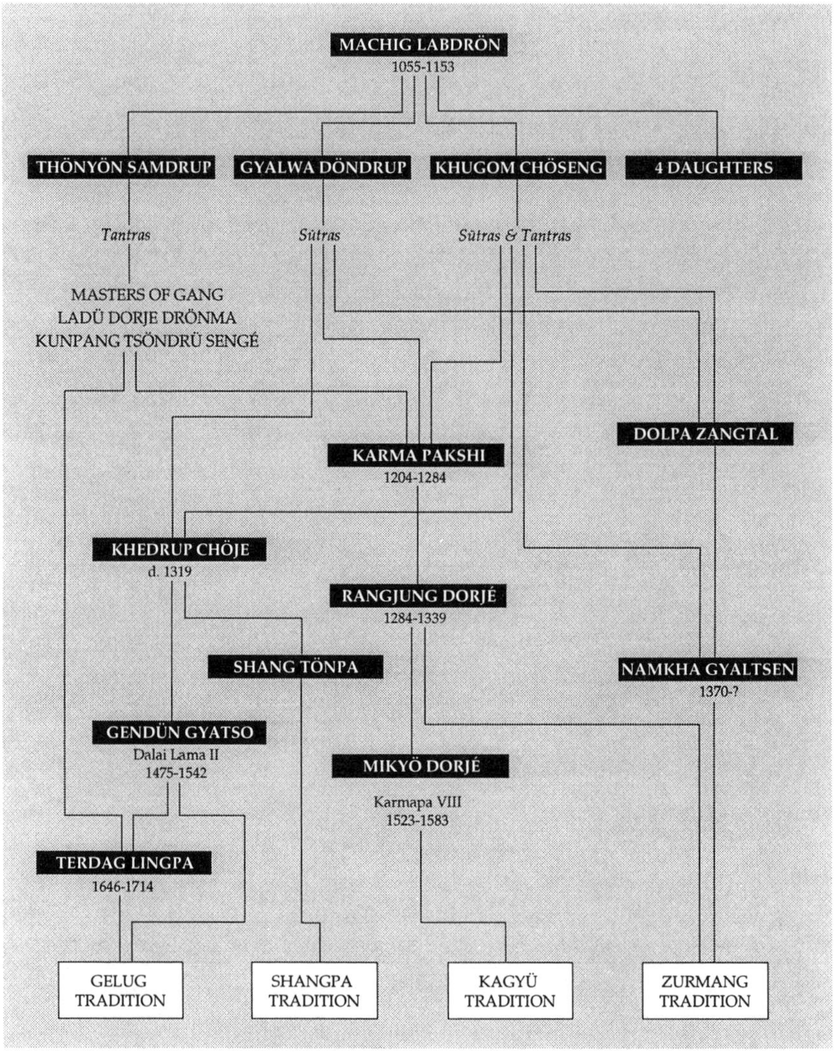

Machig transmitted to him *The Grand Exposition according to Tantra*. There, too, he practiced meditation in the company of Gangpa Mugsang, who also received from him Machig's Vajrayāna instructions.[43] The lineage continued via:

Gangpa Lhundrup
Sangyé Tensung
Dorjé Dzinpa

and so forth, finally to

Namkha Gyaltsen, the compiler of *The Marvelous Life*.

This lineage of the ultimate meaning (*don brgyud*) is also known as the Masters of Gang (Gangs) lineage, after the place that appears to have been an important practice and transmission center of Chöd. In accordance with Tārā's prediction, this Vajrayāna tradition combining generation and completion stages seems to have deteriorated soon after Namkha Gyaltsen.[44]

(3) The Combined tradition of Sūtra and Tantra. Although Thönyön Samdrup also received the Combined Sūtra and Tantra transmission, Machig mainly passed it on to her spiritual son Khugom Chökyi Sengé[45] and to her four spiritual daughters in Lhotrag, where she resided for a nine-month period. This tradition is summarized in Machig's *Grand Exposition of Combined Sūtra and Tantra*, which incorporates, apart from Machig's meditative experiences, the profound path of the four ḍākinī initiations according to the Mother Tantra, the Mahāmāyā sādhana, the guru yoga called "The Profound Activity" (*Zab las ma*), the three cycles of visualizations of the Protectors of the Three Families (*rigs gsum mgon po*) and especially the instructions on the Avalokiteśvara meditation, as well as others.

Khamnyön indicates that this combined tradition of Khugom Chökyi Sengé was widely disseminated, in particular thanks to the first Karmapas, whereas the Vajrayāna transmission known as "The Very Essence of the Profound Meaning" was passed on from Dönyö Dorjé to Terdag Lingpa Gyurmé Dorjé (1646-1714) and finally to Khamnyön's own two spiritual masters.[46]

The Second Karmapa, Karma Pakshi (1203-1284), received Machig's transmission as well as the tradition called "the Union of the Oral Transmission and Recovered Treasures" (*bka' gter zung 'jug*), which includes among others the Recovered Treasure texts of Ladü Dorjé

Drönma discovered by Kunpang Tsöndrü Sengé.[47] Ever since Karma Pakshi these teachings have been perpetuated within the Karma Kagyü school.

The Third Karmapa, Rangjung Dorjé (1284-1338), became one of the first commentators on Chöd, composing a commentary, *The Synopsis*, to Machig's *Great Collection of [Chöd] Precepts*, and a compilation of rituals and commentaries to the Chöd precept (*bka' gcod*), *A Precious Garland [Compiled] from the Collected Chöd [Teachings]* (*gCod tshogs las rin po che'i 'phreng ba*, usually referred to under the abbreviated title *Tshogs las*), and a refutation of perverted Chöd (*log gcod*).

Mikyö Dorjé, the Eighth Karmapa (1507-1554) and Karma Chagmé (1525-1583) received these transmissions. Thanks to the authority of their commentaries, this combined transmission is the best known and most widely practiced today.

The Zurmang tradition—named after the monastery that was among the most active in transmitting, practicing and explaining the Chöd of Machig—united this early transmission of Rangjung Dorjé and the Sūtra tradition of Gyalwa Döndrup, Dolpa Zangtal and Cherbu the Chinese.[48]

Although the Chöd of Machig mostly remained outside the four Tibetan schools, the Kagyü school seems to have played a dominant role in the preservation of these teachings. In Tibet, only three monasteries were fully devoted to Chöd: Kyabché Gompa, Gyuné Gompa and Chagchöd,[49] all three of them Kagyü. At the Shukseb Nunnery near Lhasa, more than one hundred nuns still follow the tradition of the *Laughter of the Ḍākinīs* (*mKha' 'gro'i gad rgyungs*), a practice from the famous Recovered Treasure of Jigmé Lingpa, *Longchenpa's Essential Drop* (*Klong chen snying thig*).

Within the Gelugpa school, the Chöd tradition developed through a combination of two main currents: (1) the visions of Tsongkhapa (1357-1419), known as the short lineage (*nye brgyud*); and (2) the long lineage (*ring brgyud*) going back all the way to Machig Labdrön, as received by Khedrup Chöjé (died 1319) of Samding and transmitted by him to the Second Dalai Lama, Gendün Gyatso (1475-1542).[50] The Fifth Dalai Lama received this long lineage from Chöying Rangdröl (1604-1669), as well as the Vajrayāna transmission from Terdag Lingpa.

Chöd continued to exist within the Gelugpa school, at Drepung and Ganden for instance, but as a marginal phenomenon, practiced most often outside the monastic framework. A violent debate, in fact, was waged over it at the beginning of this century, ending sometime in the thirties with an outright ban of this practice within Gelugpa monastic precincts. This controversy was mainly instigated by Tongpön Rinpoché, who feared that the Chöd might turn the monks away from their studies. Even so, many among them apparently continued to practice it in secret.[51]

Machig's Chöd tradition was also maintained within the other Buddhist schools of Tibet. Tāranātha, one of the most eminent masters of the Jonangpa school, seems to have played an important role in the exegesis of Chöd. He wrote several commentaries and composed, among others, a ritual around the Opening of the Gates of Space.[52] Likewise, the Shangpa masters, spiritual descendants of Khyungpo Naljor, are already quoted in the early Chöd lineages, among them Sangyé Tönpa (thirteenth century), Khedrup Chöjé and Shang Tönpa in the long lineage coming down from Machig and Khugom Chökyi Sengé.[53]

Strangely enough, the Sakya school seems to be the only Tibetan school that never received the Chöd transmission of Machig, although, as noted by Janet Gyatso,[54] the practice of the accumulations of the Kusali is quite close to the techniques of transforming the aggregates into an offering, as previously described.[55]

The Nyingma Chöd tradition is primarily based on the Recovered Treasure texts of Padmasambhava contained in the cycle *The Elimination of Confusion*. Machig does not play any central role in this transmission, but the Nyingma tradition still considers her to be an emanation of Guru Rinpoché's consort Yeshé Tsogyal, who, together with Guru Rinpoché, is considered to be the source of the Recovered Treasure tradition. Padmasambhava gave Yeshé Tsogyal the following prophecy:

> Between now and the end of time
> You will have five incarnations—
> Thirty times will you labor to lengthen the Buddha's teaching.
> In particular, in the region of Dwag [po]
> You will be known as Lab, manifest as a woman
> Endowed with all of Tārā's signs.
>
> Great Lady, listen to the essence of my instructions:
> You will develop the Chöd teachings,
> One of the teachings most beneficial for beings.
> At that time, Ācārya Salé will be Master Thöpa
> And with him for your consort, you'll open the secret gates....
>
> At that time, I, Padmasambhava,
> Will be an Indian by name of Dampa.
> I'll elaborate the teachings on the Pacification of Suffering
> In the border region of Latö.[56]

This Recovered Treasure tradition of Padmasambhava developed from the tertön Dawa Gyaltsen (gTer ston Zla ba rgyal mtshan) of whom it was said that he "adopted the yogic conduct of a Chödpa, meaning the manner of a madman."[57] Likewise the tradition of *Longchenpa's Essential Drop* (*Klong chen snying thig*), the famous Recovered Treasure of Jigmé Lingpa, contains a Chöd practice called *The Laughter of the Ḍākinīs*, and *The Words of My Perfect Teacher (Kun bzang bla ma'i zhal lung)* of Patrul Rinpoché also includes, within the maṇḍala offering, a practice of the accumulations of the kusali.[58] The above-mentioned titles constitute the main Chöd practices within the Nyingma school, but others do exist, such as those based on Terdag Lingpa's tradition. As mentioned before, the latter received Machig's Tantra tradition of Chöd from Dönyö Dorjé and also composed a commentary to the *Treatise of the Single Seat* (*gDan thog gcig ma*), as well as an initiation rite for Opening the Gates of the Dharma.[59]

Finally, the Bön tradition as well possesses its Chöd cycles, some of them coming from the hearing transmission (*snyan brgyud*), others from the Recovered Treasure traditions, but Machig does not appear in any of the lineages of either of these two traditions. According to Tenzin Namdak, all the Bön traditions of Chöd follow the highest tantras. The old Bön distinguishes three types of Chöd practice, peaceful, extended and powerful, and the new Bön added a fourth one, the wrathful.[60] Each of these four types is practiced with a different deity and constitutes a system of its own. Janet Gyatso is probably right in stating that an in-depth study of the Bön Chöd cycles may well clarify much on the Chöd tradition in general.[61]

6 Biographies of Machig

1 The Marvelous and the Imaginary

Quite surprisingly, the biography presented here in translation is called a *lo rgyus* in Tibetan, a historical account or chronicle of Machig, rather than a *rnam thar*, hagiography, as one would expect. Although on the very last page[1] the text is referred to as "the *rnam thar*," there is no trace of such a designation in the title or subtitle of the work, whereas *The Concise Life Story*—definitely the source of the version translated here—does use this expression for the general title of the work.[2] Structurally and stylistically, this text can be clearly identified with the classical hagiographies of the mahāsiddhas of India and Tibet. Indeed, the six stages that seem to define a typical *rnam thar* structure according to Nathan Katz[3] fit perfectly with the Labdrön account:

(1) birth in a particular caste: Machig is the daughter of a local governor.
(2) unusual accomplishments during early career: she is masterful in recitation and exegesis of the Prajñāpāramitā.
(3) a turning point involving renunciation of previous vocation: the experience of Machig at the Tree of Serlag and her abandoning the monastic life, honors, status, etc.
(4) initiation into Vajrayāna practice, usually by a ḍākinī: at the Tree of Serlag Machig receives empowerments of different deities and ḍākinīs; later, she even receives initiation directly from Tārā.
(5) meeting the guru: Dampa Sangyé and/or Sönam Lama.
(6) attainment of the highest siddhi and the working of miracles: in Machig's case, particularly miraculous cures.

Tāranātha, one of the most respected historians of Tibet, does not mention either Dampa Sangyé or Machig Labdrön in his *Collected Works*,[4] but in a general way he discounts the historical value of such early hagiographies:

> In general, the sacred biographies of the early yogi-translators, not especially outstanding for their [chronological] order, do not appear to be based on sources much superior to bazaar talk.[5]

This statement does not refer directly to Machig Labdrön since she does not belong to the standard yogi-translator category, as does her contemporary Marpa, for example. Still, such an observation from a Tibetan historian calls for some caution regarding the historical value of this type of literature.

The primary goal of hagiographers (in contrast to historians) is not the presentation of a straightforward factual account. As implied by the very term "complete liberation" (*rnam thar*), sacred biographies contain the tale of the spiritual progress of the adept and the way he or she becomes free of illusions and particular social and historical conditioning. This inner de-conditioning, which leads from the ordinary worldly state to the awakened state of the Buddhas, is often catalyzed by outer events; thus, in hagiographies spiritual experiences may be recorded as tangible miracles. It may also happen that outer events are presented as inner experiences, for from a Mādhyamika perspective, there is no longer any definite distinction between inner and outer, the play of phenomena being the limitless play of illusion. Thus viewed, every interpretation of these hagiographies necessarily runs the risk of reducing meditative experiences to the level of ordinary facts—or vice versa—and thereby missing the intended meaning. Only readers acquainted with these inner experiences will be able to break the code.

Hagiographies thus tend to present exemplary models with didactic intent and initiatory value as they evoke in operation the landmark signs to enlightenment. Against the framework of biographical facts, they will include edifying, often archetypical episodes such as wanderings in the wilderness, miraculous cures, teachings related to the spiritual transmission, and finally the initiations received and meditative experiences encountered that punctuate the yogi's spiritual path en route to enlightenment.[6] These last two points, initiations and spiritual experiences, as well as the philosophical view of emptiness clearly distinguish the Indo-Tibetan *rnam thar* from the Western hermit tradition, as it is described in *The Golden Legend*, for instance.[7]

While the hagiography's supernatural dimension may be somewhat related to classical tales of magic, its main feature seems to be the accomplishment of a providential plan with the continuous intervention of the divine through visions, dreams and predictions. This divine intervention links heaven and earth and explains the supernatural power of the yogi. In Machig's case, this mythic potency even precedes her birth, for the text starts off with the account of her previous life as an Indian paṇḍita. Likewise the divine intervenes when her birth is revealed to her mother by a prophetic dream, a ḍākinī announces her forthcoming encounter with Bhadra, and Tārā appears in a vision to reveal Machig's true nature.

One consequence of this continuous divine intervention is to undercut the dramatic drive of the narrative. It limits the psychological freedom and the personal motivation of the protagonist, ascribing a providential, fantastic element to fate and choices. Just as history fades away behind a screen of wondrous tales, the psychological personality too—considered illusory and conditioned, hence caught in sorrow—gives way to a universal model of liberation from ignorance and ego. As a further substitute for personal anguish or psychological choice, there is confidence in the blessing of the deity. Machig no longer controls her actions, and hence has no functional role or choice: when she wonders whether she should unite with Thöpa Bhadra, her doubts are instantly eliminated by the appearance of a ḍākinī who confirms the need for this union.

It is interesting to note that the author here uses the expression *tshul bstan*, "to demonstrate or show a mode or way of acting," when expressing Machig's "showing" signs of weariness for human existence. This expression occurs regularly in *rnam thar*[8] to illustrate that the siddha does not act according to momentary whims, but instead follows a well-defined plan to guide beings to liberation. In fact it is almost surprising that the author only uses it three times in the entire biography, the first when Machig, in the guise of the Indian paṇḍita, demonstrates the transference of consciousness in order to take birth in Tibet.

This familiarity between the adept and the divine world which overrides profane time and space is typical of the spiritual world of Vajrayāna, the path of universal purity (*dag pa rab 'byams*). Although based on the view of the emptiness of all phenomena, Vajrayāna can be defined as a return to the relative world of appearances, with which the yogi must now train him- or herself to play, while progressively replacing ordinary consciousness with the awakened consciousness of pure vision. By this profound pure vision the yogi will make the pure Buddha fields appear and may even directly perceive or converse with the deity.[9] *The Concise Life Story* contains the following anecdote:

> One day, after receiving an initiation from Machig, Thönyön Samdrup experienced a series of visions. He asked her about the nature of these visions, and also whether the pure Buddha fields were right here or not. Machig replied: "Son of the Prajñā lineage, it is like this, keep it in mind. This vision of the pure Buddha lands is due to the fact that you are freed from the obscuring veils of the delusions. Once freed from the veil of these delusions, one sees the Buddha lands anywhere, just as the moon's reflection appears in any water container. Son of noble descent, I myself, wherever I reside, at all times am surrounded by a divine assembly."[10]

From a Mahāyāna perspective the nature of the deity is emptiness devoid of inherent existence, and in the texts it is often described as having the nature of a rainbow, the inseparable union of clarity and emptiness. How then can we understand the nature of these visions that appear throughout Machig's life? The biography presents them as providential interventions but they usually are the fruit of the yogi's meditation, of the purification of the veil of emotional afflictions, as Machig puts it. Once such mastery in meditation has been obtained the yogi may address questions to the deity in the course of daily practice, especially when faced with dangerous situations or a fundamental dilemma, his or her own or that of others who need assistance. Occasionally the replies will appear in dream and here the yogi learns how to distinguish the meaningful prophetic dreams (the "great dreams" in C. G. Jung's parlance) from ordinary ones that are interferences or simply reflect past events. To quote an example from a present-day yogi, the Venerable Lobsang Tenzin:

> Following Tsong-kha-pa's advice, I made the decision to complete meditation on the generation stage first. After I had made this decision, I dreamt of an old lady offering me very delicious food, something which looked like melted butter and chang (Tibetan beer) in a triangular cup. The offering was exceptionally delicious and I drank it all. Then I told her that even if it was all melted butter I would be able to drink the whole lot. Thus, I felt very hopeful that if I practised my potential would surely ripen, so I made the firm resolution to practise genuinely.[11]

Fortuitous as these dreams and visions may be at first, they will tend to manifest more frequently as meditative power increases and the practitioner's mind is purified, until such time as he or she obtains full mastery in meditation and becomes, like Guru Ratna in our text, "a mahāsiddha of Cakrasaṃvara, and one able to emanate the manifest maṇḍala palace of the deity."[12] Once again the hagiographical text draws no clear distinction between outer events and inner experience.

The life of Machig teaches us precious little about the political situation in eleventh-century Tibet. Its primary function lies in asserting the exemplary efficacy or educational authenticity of the teachings (when Machig must justify her system in front of the Indian ācāryas, for example), rather than in any aesthetic pursuit like developing narrative suspense. In fact, the tale itself lacks any sort of narrative flow: the reader is forced through continual leaps, without much transition, from all-encompassing generalities to the most insignificant detail. Equally common are radical changes in style, some of which may be attributable to later emendations.

Of course, these observations hold true for numerous *rnam thar*. Still, the narrative technique used in Machig's is strikingly different from that found in Milarepa's *rnam thar*, where all the resources of literary technique are skillfully applied so as to serve the unfolding of the plot and to outline more sharply the psychological ambivalence of the protagonist, without in any way diminishing the marvelous character of the work. This is the reason why Milarepa's biography is rightfully appreciated as both a model in this literary genre and one of the sublime masterpieces of all hagiographic literature. One possible deeper reason for this difference might be connected to the fact that Machig is considered an emanation of the ḍākinī of primordial wisdom and hence accomplishes a divine master plan whereby she demonstrates the path to enlightenment. Milarepa, on the contrary, accomplishes everything, including the ultimate goal, in only one lifetime and may therefore be portrayed in a profoundly human way, subject to doubts and failures. When the master Bhirājā alluded to his realization as being the result of meritorious activity in previous lifetimes, Milarepa strongly denied the allegations, insisting that he achieved realization by his own effort and perseverance in this lifetime alone.

The example of Milarepa may well be the exception to the rule. Generally speaking, the narrative system of hagiographies seems to follow a set pattern to illustrate the pursuit of liberation: endless wonders replace history, the spiritual takes over from the psychological, solitude overrules social interaction, and the imaginary has precedence over reality. All these characteristics build up a myth, which no doubt explains why this type of literature is so widespread in Tibetan popular culture.

2 The Ḍākinī of Primordial Wisdom

Machig viewed herself as a woman and realized yoginī; historical accounts raised her to the rank of a non-human ḍākinī of primordial wisdom. *The Marvelous Life* tends to emphasize the divine nature of Machig, but she remains a complex figure and, more than anything else, it is this double nature, relative and absolute, human and divine, that lends the biography its rich and paradoxical character, situating the entire tale in the domain of mystery. Machig herself comments upon this double nature in an address to her disciples:

> Likewise I, Labdrön, an ordinary [woman], I am the palace (*pho brang*) where the five Buddhas and their consorts meet and remain, together with their entourage, the male and female guardians and the ḍākinīs.[13]

What is a ḍākinī? The Tibetan equivalent of this Sanskrit term is "khandroma" (*mkha' 'gro ma*), which Herbert V. Guenther felicitously translates as "cypher of transcendence,"[14] but could more literally be translated as "celestial messenger" or "sky-goer" in line with the etymological explanation given by the Venerable Tenga Rinpoché:

> The wisdom-bliss free of desire is the essence of all desirable qualities. This feminine wisdom, the ḍākinī, appears and disappears (*'gro*) without hindrance in limitless space (*mkha'*).[15]

H. H. the Dalai Lama further comments on the term:

> The meaning of the Tibetan term *mkha' 'gro ma* is literally "she who flies" or "moves through space." This implies actual qualities, but these are not necessarily spiritual. Ḍākinīs are human beings—not birds!—who, due to certain personal powers or qualities, are able to fly: such is the ordinary or negative definition of *mkha' 'gro ma*.
>
> At the highest level, *mkha'* signifies not "empty space," but śunyata, emptiness or inner space, the ultimate truth, whereas *'gro* represents the mind absorbed in this inner space or śūnyatā.[16]

And finally David Snellgrove's explanation:

> There is frequent reference to them in the tantric texts [of India], where they appear as the partners of the yogins, flocking around them when they visit the great places of pilgrimage. Their pres-

> ence was essential to the performance of the psycho-sexual rites and their activities generally are so gruesome and obscene as to earn them quite properly the name of witch. They enter Tibetan mythology in a rather more gentle aspect, and ceasing altogether to be beings of flesh and blood, they become the bestowers of mystic doctrines and bringers of divine offerings. They become the individual symbols of divine wisdom with which the meditator must mystically unite....[17]

This latter description provides a general idea of the evolution of the ḍākinī from India, where she appears in destructive, bloodthirsty and sometimes cannibalistic forms, to Tibet, where she gradually became more beneficent and assumed new roles: teacher who transmitted instructions, partner for certain tantric practices, deity of meditation (*yi dam*) and yoginī, often considered an emanation of wisdom like Machig. This evolution is illustrated in the present biography: the ḍākinī first mentioned is the arrogant mistress of a cremation ground near Bodhgaya in India, who is subsequently subjugated by Arthasiddhi Bhadra. But it is a beneficent ḍākinī who allows him to transfer his life principle to Tibet, and it is other peaceful ḍākinīs who announce Machig's birth to her mother, transmit certain empowerments to Machig herself, come to welcome her on behalf of Thöpa Bhadra, and assist her son during his solitary retreat.

Mahāyāna Buddhism associates the feminine principle with emptiness, the very source of liberation, the Prajñāpāramitā, matrix of the realization of all the Buddhas. She is called the Great Mother, Yum Chenmo, and also the Wisdom Ḍākinī. In the tantric tradition, in order to realize or to actualize this feminine wisdom principle, it must be united with the male principle of skillful means or great bliss. This union of bliss and emptiness (*bde stong*) is symbolically represented by sexual union, meaning the nondual experience of ecstasy and the inseparability of the two principles. Hence, in the pure vision of the adept this feminine principle, whether coarse or subtle in appearance, whether in the guise of an ordinary woman or of a deity, remains the manifestation of emptiness, i.e., the wisdom ḍākinī.[18]

The figure of Machig herself, as described in her biography, evokes the multiple aspects of the ḍākinī: sometimes she appears as a well-behaved and studious young girl, sometimes as a divine being endowed with all the signs of a wisdom ḍākinī; later she appears as a powerful mahāsiddha who subjugates demons and achieves miraculous cures, as a fully realized yoginī, and as a tantric partner involved in karmamudrā practice. In this latter case, the feminine consort (*rig ma*) is called "knowledge woman," for it is due to her cooperation that the co-emergent awareness-bliss, which experiences the essence of reality, appears. In some instances feminine consorts are spiritual emanations, in others they are actual physical partners,[19] but in either case they are considered ḍākinīs. The masculine word *ḍāka* has the same Sanskrit etymology as *ḍākinī*, "sky-goer," but in Tibetan texts, instead of its equivalent, *mkha' 'gro*, one most often finds the term *dpa' bo*, "hero" or "warrior." Even though ḍākas should theoretically assume the parallel functions of tantric partners and celestial messengers for female practitioners, in the Tibetan tradition their roles do not cover as wide a range of activity, status and power as those of the ḍākinī. In the popular tradition, the term *mkha' 'gro ma* is highly respectful and is often given to women teachers, recognized incarnations and accomplished yoginīs as an equivalent to lama (*bla ma*), tulku (*sprul sku*) or even rinpoché (*rin po che*), which seem to be applied mostly to male teachers.

A Biography of Machig gives a quite different version of Machig's meeting with Thöpa Bhadra, whom it calls Thöpa Bharé and describes as a local master, *slob dpon*, of the Echung area. She converts him with spiritual songs of realization (*mgur*) and displays of her magical powers, and he finally becomes filled with faith and devotion. The whole section gives the impression that she takes him as her consort or tantric partner—ḍāka—even though the text is not explicit on that point.[20] If, as we tend to think, this text is a more unadorned version of Machig's life, where she is presented as a more down-to-earth woman and practitioner, this would indicate that the status of female practitioners has changed in the course of history and that our version has been gradually polished to give Machig an appearance more acceptable to the stronger patriarchal ideology that developed in Tibet in later times.

Vajrayāna literature defines two kinds of ḍākinīs: (1) The mundane ḍākinīs (*'jig rten gyi mkha' 'gro*), who may be either bloodthirsty and ferocious, like the protector ḍākinīs of burning grounds, or sweet fairies, celestial messengers who assist the yogi in meditation. These mundane ḍākinīs are often ancient local deities associated with a spring or a mountain[21] who have been put under oath by great miracle-workers and have served as protectors of the teaching. (2) The supramundane ḍākinīs include the wisdom ḍākinīs (*ye shes mkha' 'gro*), the source of spontaneous activity of the Buddhas that dispels obstacles. According to Machig, the five ḍākinīs of the maṇḍala outwardly possess the nature of the five Buddha bodies, inwardly are the five wisdom ḍākinīs, and secretly represent the five Buddha wisdoms.[22] As Machig explains to her son:

> From an outer point of view, I am the mother of the Buddhas.
> From an inner point of view I am Ārya Tārā, and
> From a secret point of view I am Vajravārāhī
> Surrounded by the four ḍākinīs.
> I, the ordinary woman Labdrön,
> In this maṇḍala of the wisdom ḍākinī and of the five deities,
> Am Vārāhi (Phag mo), the aggregate of consciousness.
> The aggregate of form is the Buddha ḍākinī,
> Of feelings is the Ratna (Jewel) ḍākinī,
> Of perceptions is the Padma (Lotus) ḍākinī,
> Of compositional factors is the Karma (Action) ḍākinī.[23]

In the course of a private audience, H. H. the Dalai Lama gave the following explanation of ḍākinīs, whom he called "the female guardians of the Tantras":

> There are three kinds of ḍākinīs: (1) The ultimate ḍākinīs who are the wisdom that realizes śūnyatā, emptiness. This wisdom is the most subtle level of awareness, the clear light transformed into wisdom that realizes emptiness.
>
> (2) In order to allow for the birth of this ḍākinī, one must eliminate the gross forms of consciousness by means of the inner heat (*gtum mo*) practice that is a particular form of bliss. This bliss is the means of eliminating coarse consciousnesses; therefore, the inner heat represents another meaning of ḍākinī.
>
> (3) In order to develop this inner heat, under certain circumstances and conditions, one should rely on a female consort as one's assistant, and this is a third meaning of ḍākinī. These consorts differ according to their physical characteristics and their spiritual qualities. According to their level of spiritual realization, these ḍākinīs are called "field-born," "mantra-born" and "co-emergent" or "innate." There are different interpretations of their specific characteristics.

H. H. the Dalai Lama gives one interpretation in his introduction to *Tantra in Tibet*:

> [1] field-born sky-goers [*zhing skyes mkha' 'gro*] are born with bodies of flesh and blood; [2] innate [or co-emergent] [*lhan skyes*] sky-goers have attained realization of the stage of completion [*rdzogs rim*] in Highest Yoga Tantra; [3] mantra-born sky-goers [*sngags skyes*] have not yet generated the stage of completion but are abiding in realization of the stage of generation [*bskyed rim*]. According to another interpretation, [1] field-born sky-goers have attained

> the subjective clear light [the third of five levels in the stage of completion]; [2] the innate sky-goers have lesser realization but are still within the stage of completion; [3] and mantra-born sky-goers are said to abide on the stage of generation.[24]

Khenpo Tsultrim Gyamtso has given another interpretation of these three kinds of consort ḍākinīs (and ḍākas) in the form of a spontaneous spiritual song:

> Between ḍākas and ḍākinīs there are [obvious] differences
> In the way their bodies look in apparent reality;
> But for clear light mahāmudrā
> In essence, there is not an atom of difference!
>
> Those intelligent and fortunate ones
> Who have entered into the Vajrayāna
> And attained the power of mantras
> Are renowned as mantra-born ḍākinīs.
>
> By attending a realized teacher
> And by the power of recognizing the uncontrived state
> They realize directly the true nature [of the mind].
> These are called co-emergent ḍākinīs.
>
> By dwelling in the fields of the twenty-four
> Sacred places of body, speech and mind,
> They accomplish the benefit of others.
> These are called field-born ḍākinīs.[25]

On a relative level, Machig is a young woman, exemplary in her behavior. Through her understanding of the Prajñāpāramitā and her direct experience of non-self, she becomes a mahāsiddha whose teaching created a considerable stir. Already at birth she bears the signs of a ḍākinī, but, like most great predestined teachers of the past, male or female, she still has to actualize this divine nature through study, meditation and action, by receiving teachings and empowerments that bring about a maturation such that Tārā finally can reveal her true nature to her. On the level of absolute truth, Machig is a non-human ḍākinī, a mind emanation of Yum Chenmo. According to certain prophecies the mind emanation, among the multitude of Yum Chenmo emanations, has to pacify beings in four sacred places: (1) the spheres of the thirty-three gods and the pure land of Tuṣita (dGa' ldan), (2) Bodhgaya in India, (3) Tibet and (4) the region of Uḍḍiyāṇa (O rgyan) in the west. Accordingly, prior to her Indian incarnation in Bodhgaya as Arthasiddhi Bhadra, Machig manifests herself among the gods. Later, she appears in a third incarnation as Machig Labdrön in Tibet. Regarding her fourth and last task, she declares in front of the grand assembly at Zangri during her debate with the Indian ācāryas:

> At the age of ninety-nine, I'll set out for the west, to the region of Uḍḍiyāṇa. After having accomplished the benefit of beings there, I'll leave for the city of the rākṣasas.[26]

To sum up, the ḍākinī covers the entire variety of possible manifestations of the feminine principle, from the vile sorceress to the most profound deity, from the most ordinary woman to the most powerful ḍākinī. This wealth of multiple facets makes it difficult to encompass the ḍākinī within a single definition, but in the evocative universe of the Vajrayāna tradition, she represents the natural play of the manifestation of phenomena, the spontaneous, luminous, empty dance of wisdom, the unique source of all accomplishments.

3 The Tradition of *The Grand Exposition*

The five main Tibetan texts used in this study of Machig's life fall under two categories: the three condensed historical accounts and the two biographies.[27] The historical accounts include:

(1) *The Blue Annals,* by Gö Lotsāwa, composed at the end of the fifteenth century, four centuries after Machig's death
(2) *Dharma History: A Banquet for the Learned,* by Pawo Tsuglag Trengwa, the Second Nehnang Pawo Rinpoché, written ca. 1550
(3) *The Transmission History of the Pacification and Chöd,* by the nineteenth-century Khamnyön, which contains a short history on the Chöd tradition.

The biographies include:[28]

(1) the most extensive account, called *A Concise Life Story of Machig Labdrön, Derived from An Exposition of Transforming the Aggregates into an Offering of Food* (*The Concise Life Story*), by Kunpang Tsöndrü Sengé[29]
(2) the first two chapters, here translated as *The Marvelous Life,* of the ten chapters of *An Exposition of Transforming the Aggregates into an Offering of Food, Illuminating the Meaning of Chöd* (*Transforming the Aggregates*),[30] under the following headings:
   I. A concise life story of Machig
   II. Machig's achievements and transmission lineages
   III. Explanation of the Chöd tradition
   IV. About gods and demons, and the levels of Chöd
   V. The stages in the transformation of the aggregates into food offerings
   VI. The signs of death, definitions of the aggregates and explanation of the winds (*prāṇa*)
   VII. The ten precepts of Chöd and the measure of accomplishment
   VIII. The modes of appearance of magical interferences
   IX. Machig's predictions about the world
   X. Predictions about Chöd and conclusion.[31]

Only the first two chapters seem to be authored by Namkha Gyaltsen (Nam mkha' rgyal mtshan), and the rest was compiled by Jampa Sönam (Byams pa bsod nams). The full text is presented as a compilation of Machig's answers to questions raised by her sons, daughters and disciples. The text is attributed to Machig in person (hence to be considered an autobiography) and is said to have been transcribed after her own words, as expressed in the homage of Jampa Sönam at the start of the book:

I offer homage to Ma, the non-human wisdom ḍākinī.
This *Exposition of Transforming the Aggregates into an Offering of Food*
I have transcribed from the very words of Machig.

According to *The Concise Life Story*,[32] Machig, when fifty-six or fifty-seven years old, composed four major treatises known under the generic title of *The Grand Exposition* (*rNam bshad chen mo*):

(1) *The Grand Exposition according to Sūtra*, at Sakarlog, requested by Khugom Chökyi Sengé and five other disciples who wrote it down.
(2) *The Grand Exposition according to Tantra*, at the cave of Shampogang, requested by her son Thönyön Samdrup. The text was transmitted by eight of her disciples, including her four spiritual daughters and Khugom Chökyi Sengé.
(3) *The Grand Exposition according to Sūtra and Tantra Combined*, in Lhodrag, requested by Khugom Chökyi Sengé, and copied out by twelve people.
(4) *The Grand Exposition of Transforming the Aggregates into an Offering*, at Zangri, through the request of Thönyön Samdrup.

One of the difficulties in identifying these texts lies in the fact that most sources use the generic title *The Grand Exposition* without specifying whether it refers to all four treatises or to only one of them. No version of these four original texts has so far become available. A reference to Machig's *Grand Exposition of Transforming the Aggregates into an Offering* is found in the *Labrang Karchag*, but whether it refers to Machig's original version remains mere speculation since the text is not available.[33] However, the colophon following chapter ten of our main source, *Transforming the Aggregates*, describes a lineage for the *Grand Exposition*:

Machig Labdrön
Thönyön Samdrup, her son,
Gangpa Mugsang
Gangpa Lhundrup
Sangyé Tensung
Nyamé Dorjé Dzinpa
Gangpa Rinchen Gyaltsen
Lama Dorjé
Namkha Gyaltsen, the compiler of the *Marvelous Life*,
Tashi Gyaltsen
Nyima Gyaltsen
Mönchöd Tsöndrü Sengé.[34]

According to the *Transmission History*, Namkha Gyaltsen compiled a collection of texts named *The Grand Exposition* (*rNam bshad chen mo*) which included a biography of Machig, but not Machig's Vajrayāna tradition.[35] According to Khetsun Sangpo's *Biographical Dictionary*, he was born 1370, and a text by the Third Karmapa, Rangjung Dorjé (1284-1339), is included in his *Grand Exposition*.[36]

The colophon of *Transforming the Aggregates* states that the editor, Jampa Sönam, took the first two chapters (translated here; referred to as *The Marvelous Life*) from Namkha Gyaltsen's *Grand Exposition* in full together with their colophon. The remaining eight chapters he may have combined and edited with other sources he received, such as a hearing transmission (*rlung*) for an extensive Machig biography called *The Grand Exposition of Transforming the Aggregates into an Offering of Food, Illuminating the Meaning of Chöd*.[37]

The second main source consulted, *The Concise Life Story*, belongs to the Recovered Treasure tradition. This version, appearing in a manuscript in cursive script, contains many expressions in eastern Tibetan dialect. Comparing the two texts shows that *The Concise Life Story* is undoubtedly the direct source from which *Transforming the Aggregates* was condensed after the correction of numerous spelling mistakes. The sequence is closely followed, with entire sections adopted word-for-word, but *Transforming the Aggregates* eliminates some over-marvelous or over-lengthy descriptions, as well as technical explanations of transmissions, titles of texts and lists of names.

In the colophon the name of the author appears as "the one called the renunciate, the beggar Tsöndrü Sengé" (*kun spangs brtson 'grus seng ge*). *The Blue Annals* identifies him as Sangyé Tönpa and presents a biography of him which is identical with Sangyé Tönpa's in the *Transmission History*. The latter work does not mention any Tsöndrü Sengé in this context but it does, however, mention a Kunpang Tsöndrü Sengé in the context of the Chöd lineage received by the Karmapas:[38]

> Yeshé Gyaltsen, after whom the Lineage Transmission and Recovered Treasure traditions became united (*bka' gter zung 'jug*)
> Ladü Dorjé Drönma
> Kunpang Tsöndrü Sengé
> Nyima Gyaltsen
> Mönchöd Tsöndrü Sengé
> Drupchen Kunga Sengé
> Karma Pakshi (1204-1284).

The *Transmission History* does mention the Recovered Teachings (*gter chos*) of Tsöndrü Sengé and further refers to a "well-known terma cycle of Tsöndrü Sengé from Nyemo Rigongwa."[39]

In the colophon to *The Concise Life Story*, Tsöndrü Sengé does not specify having discovered this text and nowhere is he mentioned as a tertön. Instead he states that he composed this text himself on the basis of Machig's *Grand Exposition of Transforming the Aggregates into an Offering of Food* (*gZan skyur gyi rnam bshad chen mo*), as well as on four other sources, among them the *Twenty-One Vows* and the *Great Chöd Chronicles*.[40] He also received oral commentary on Machig's life from his lama and used an "extraordinary biography of Machig by her next incarnation, Dorjé Drönma, who personally hid it as a terma."[41] While Tsöndrü Sengé does not make any claim to its recovery, he nonetheless assembled and combined all these sources without, in his own account, necessarily respecting the chronological order of the events, nor the relative importance of the various episodes in the sources. Thus, though based on Dorjé Drönma's Recovered Treasure, Tsöndrü Sengé's composition is not itself a terma in the strict sense of the word, though it bears the specific terminal punctuation characteristic of texts of that genre.

According to the *Transmission History*, Kunpang Tsöndrü Sengé lived before Karma Pakshi (1204-1284); the colophon mentions the composition date as the Water-Horse year. The year 1162 can be eliminated as it was less than ten years after Machig's demise, and so can 1282 (just two years prior to Karma Pakshi's death), which leaves 1222 as the most likely date of *The Concise Life Story*'s composition, but this date should be taken with caution since the lineages given in the various sources don't always match and are often contradictory.

According to the sources available and keeping in mind the bibliographical contradictions noticed above, Machig Labdrön composed four treatises called *Grand Exposition* (*according to Sūtra; according to Tantras; according to Sūtra and Tantra Combined;* and *of Transforming the Aggregates into an Offering of Food*). These included her autobiography and were written down by her direct disciples. Around 1222, Kunpang Tsöndrü Sengé collected various versions of Machig's biography, including her *Grand Exposition of Transforming the Aggregates into an Offering of Food* and a Revealed Treasure of Ladü Dorjé Drönma (considered a reincarnation of Machig),[42] in a single text called *The Concise Life Story*.

Then, around the turn of the fifteenth century, Namkha Gyaltsen (supposedly born in 1370) would have received one or more of Machig's four *Grand Expositions*. He would have revised and corrected Machig's original biographical material to which he added some explanations and notes of his own[43] as well as commentaries, under the generic title *The Grand Exposition*. At this point we don't know if he had access to Kunpang Tsöndrü Sengé's *Concise Life Story* or not. Finally, in the nineteenth century, the editor Jampa Sönam based his biography of Machig on Kunpang Tsöndrü Sengé's *Concise Life Story* and included in his own compilation Namkha Gyaltsen's two biographical chapters, as well as parts of the eight other chapters which he combined with other sources into a single version.

In the absence of any original versions of Machig's four treatises, we could consider *The Concise Life Story* to be the most ancient biography of Machig that can be traced.[44] It is based on her *Grand Exposition of Transforming the Aggregates into an Offering of Food* and supposedly was written seventy years after her death. It would therefore have been the source for later accounts such as *The Blue Annals* and other historical chronicles but, as will be noted in the next chapter, the latter accounts do not always faithfully follow it. There is therefore every reason to believe that other versions of Machig's biography were in circulation. Khamnyön says as much in his *Transmission History*, unfortunately without quoting any by title.[45]

4 Comparative Study of the Tibetan Sources

From the five texts mentioned, it is possible to draw a general outline of the life of Machig Labdrön as accepted by all sources, although on numerous points important disagreements become apparent, including mutually exclusive versions of events.

Most sources agree on 1055 as Machig's birthdate: a Sheep year following a Wood Horse year during which, on the fifteenth of the tenth month according to our text, she entered her mother's womb. Although Namkhai Norbu has it that Machig was born in a Bönpo family, none of our sources confirms this assertion.[46]

Regarding the episodes of her youth there are noticeable variant readings, but it seems certain that she received her name Labdrön on the occasion of a large festival. According to the *Transmission History* her mother, Bumcham, experienced prophetic dreams in which "a shining light lit up her entire body, the whole house, then the entire region of Lab," as a result of which the inhabitants decided to call the little girl Labdrön, "the Shining Light of Lab."

It is the name Machig Labdrön that allows one to distinguish this Machig from many other Machigs, a common name for yoginīs throughout the Dharma history of Tibet. As mentioned earlier, Roerich was misled by the single name of Machig and went on to identify Machig Zhama with Labdrön, an obvious error. Snellgrove, together with most Western commentators, followed suit in this confusion between the two lady yoginīs.[47]

The dates given for Machig Zhama are 1062-1150. Considered an incarnation of Princess Wen Cheng, the royal spouse of Songtsen Gampo, she became the disciple and later the consort of Ma Lotsāwa. She received the transmission of "The Path and Its Fruit" (*lam 'bras*) and her lineage became known as the lineage of Zhama (*lam 'bras zhwa ma lugs*).[48] She went to seek out Dampa Sangyé after having fallen victim to an incurable venereal disease, and he explained to her how this disease was the karmic result of having broken her Vajrayāna vows (*samaya*) by practicing as a consort with different yogis. Within the *lam 'bras* chapter of the *Blue Annals*,[49] there is no mention of Chöd; hence it is a definite error of Roerich's, cleared up once and for all in the present biography by Dampa's explanation.[50] He clearly distinguishes Zhama of Latö in the *lam 'bras* lineage from Labdrön, who is associated with the Chöd of the Four Demons. The *Blue Annals*[51] quotes a story similar to the one told by Dampa while he was residing at Dratang, also involving four ḍākinī disciples, but referring to a different group that included Labdrön and Zhama, but not the other two, Dröchungma and Drönema.

The biography translated here situates Machig's birthplace at E'i Gangwa in the region of Lab, which in the other sources is known under the alternative spellings of gYe'i Labs[52] or Khe'u Gang.[53] The *Transmission History* has "E'i Damzö in the region of Mé,"[54] but later notes that marvelous signs appeared "in the entire region of Lab."[55] Jamyang Kyentsé Wangpo, in his *Guide*,[56] mentions the region of E Yul, to the east of Tsétang, south of the Tsangpo River. Even though he does not specifically state that this is the area where Machig was born, many oral sources have confirmed it.

At a very early stage Machig showed signs of a predilection for the Prajñāpāramitā, which would remain her philosophical resource throughout her life. While still young she was able to read all three versions—the extensive, medium and abbreviated ones. And her capacities for reciting, understanding and meditating soon surpassed those of her teachers, the first of whom was Geshe Atön (A ston, according to *Transforming the Aggregates*) or Wöntön (dBon ston, according to the *Transmission History*). But her two main teachers were Trapa Ngönshé (Grwa pa mngon shes), born 1012, who gave her all the basic teachings, and the renunciate master Sönam Lama, "the teacher from Kyo" (sKyo ston bsod nams bla ma), who, throughout her life, she considered her root guru.

On Machig's youth, *A Biography of Machig* differs from all other sources. From her early years until the age of fifteen when she finally left her family, she argued with her parents, who wanted her to marry. "But I am hopeless as a housewife. I cannot work properly with my hands. Who wants a wife that is unable to work?" Machig states that she wants to dedicate her life to Dharma but her mother tells her, "Everyone will eventually die, whether great or humble, so what do you expect?...The path of Dharma is extremely difficult, especially for a woman." Finally her mother grabs her by the hair and seizes a precious turquoise given to Machig by her elder brother, saying, "I have worked [from early morning] with dew as my shoes until [late at night] with stars as my hat to get that. Anyway, Dharma practitioners don't need possessions. You can go now." Machig then leaves her home and family for good and goes to study with Trapa Ngönshé.[57]

All versions agree that she met Sönam Lama, who became her root guru. During her initiation by Sönam Lama, Machig rose up into space and went straight through the wall of the temple.[58]

Suddenly finding herself at the foot of the Tree of Serlag, Machig instantaneously switched from one world to another, dropping altogether the image of the young, talented, studious and well-respected nun. That experience was the sign that Machig had obtained the necessary spiritual conditions to move away from the monastic institutions and to enter the great family of the wandering realized yogis (*smyon pa*) living outside all social norms, as the siddhas of India. It also became the event that elevated her to the status of the shaman in popular imagination.

Here too the *Marvelous Life* characteristically presents the inner experiences as quasi-historical outer events. Thus, in her battle against the ferocious nāgas at the Tree of Serlag, Machig's outer behavior echoes the activity of the great miracle-workers who pacified the demons of Tibet; from a purely Buddhist or inner point of view,[59] she experiences emptiness. While the biography favors the outer events, the *Transmission History* specifies that "her mind was absorbed in the suchness (*dharmatā*) of phenomena" even while she "offered her body as food to the demons." This is also the first explicit reference to Chöd practice.

When Machig unites with the Indian yogi Thöpa Bhadra, thereby fulfilling the prophecy-command of several ḍākinīs, they unite wisdom, the feminine principle of emptiness, with skillful means, the masculine principle of great bliss. Machig here takes on the part of a human ḍākinī, the consort of Thöpa. Machig defines this karmamudrā practice as follows:

> The yogi who has reached the level of utilizing emptiness on the path (*lam du 'khyer*) and who has mastered the yogic techniques of channels, winds and drops [respectively *nāḍī, prāṇa,* and *bindu*], with the assistance of great joy, may immensely increase his physical power. This is called the great seal of action, karmamahāmudrā.[60]

Later, when Machig went to live with Thöpa Bhadra, they first travelled to Kongpo and then to neighboring Dakpo. The text informs us that they spent one year at Nyangpo and some time in Langtang, Penyul region. All the sources agree that they were subject to much slander from the people of Ü and Tsang. This episode seems to be an integral part of the popular tradition that claims she broke her vows of celibacy in order to unite with Bhadra.

The *Marvelous Life* stands quite alone in claiming that Machig never received monastic ordination. After her union with Bhadra, Sönam Lama tells her, "There is no fault, since you did not take the [monastic] vows."[61] By contrast, the *Transmission History*[62] tells of the ḍākinī who in a dream suggests she unite with Bhadra, at which Machig exclaims, "But I am a nun!" Similarly upon her return Lama Trapa Ngönshé reassures her, "You took the vows with me, so now I reinstall you in your previous status. Don't feel discouraged regarding this union, for it will be greatly beneficial in the future." The *Blue Annals* and *The Banquet* likewise mention Machig's monastic ordination from Trapa Ngönshé.

Surprisingly, Khamnyön, author of the *Transmission History*, quotes as one of his main sources the *Grand Exposition* (*of Transforming the Aggregates?*),[63] yet moves away from it on this crucial point in saying that she broke her vows. At first sight, it suggests that the original version of the *Grand Exposition*—if this is indeed the most ancient biography of Machig—has been corrected at a later stage by editors eager to preserve an ideal image of Machig. This interpretation, however, is damaged by the fact that Tsöndrü Sengé, who refers to the *Grand Exposition* as one of the sources for his *Concise Life Story*, as well as the author of *A Biography of Machig*,[64] both insist that she had *not* taken any monastic vows. The only alternative endowed with any plausibility would be to view Machig as living within a monastic setting wearing the burgundy robes (and maybe even keeping her hair short), but without having taken monastic vows. Even today this is still the custom for children studying in a monastery, and occasionally for young adults too; thus people might have taken her to be a nun where in fact she was not. In the absence, however, of a copy of Namkha Gyaltsen's *Grand Exposition*, it is impossible to reach a definite conclusion and to know whether *The Grand Exposition* or *The Marvelous Life* has been tampered with.

According to the biography, Machig had three children: Drupa, who after his initiation by Machig at the age of forty-two received the name Gyalwa Döndrup, usually considered the main lineage holder for the Sūtra tradition; Drupsé, on whom Machig bestowed the name Thönyön Samdrup, "Crazy Son of Thöpa Whose Intentions are Fulfilled," who was to become the main lineage holder of her Vajrayāna teachings; and Drupchungma, "Little Realization," nicknamed Ladüma.

Khamnyön[65] points out that, depending on the source followed, Machig had either three, four or five children. According to Karma Pakshi, Rangjung Dorjé and Karma Chagmé, she had three sons and two daughters; others claim she had only three or four children. Still, Khamnyön concludes, Gyalwa Döndrup (Drupa), Thönyön Samdrup and the girl Ladüma were the most renowned.

Two versions seem to dominate the account of Machig's sons, those offered by *The Concise Life Story* and by the *Banquet*.[66] The latter does not mention her union with Thöpa Bhadra, but refers to her male descendants in the same wording as the *Blue Annals*.[67] Recorded there is an anecdote about her son Drupché or Drupé (Gyalwa Döndrup). One day he stole a goat from a magician, but fearing the latter's powers, sought refuge at his mother's place. She delivered him from the spell cast on him by making him eat offerings prepared by the magician. As a result, the spell turned back on its perpetrator. It is at this point that the son, then aged forty-two, started to practice his mother's teachings and attained liberation. Living the life of a solitary hermit (*zhig po*), he composed numerous poems, one of which has remained famous:

> Mother, who in the beginning created my body,
> Mother, who later gave me food and drink,
> Mother, who finally made me recognize the nature of my mind,
> Mother of great kindness, in front of you I bow down.

He had three children, each of whom also became a lineage holder of Machig's tradition; he himself passed away at the age of eighty-nine.[68]

Our *Marvelous Life* version pays but scant attention to the life of Gyalwa Döndrup, who is only mentioned in passing, but goes into great detail about Thönyön Samdrup's cure from insanity, which was followed by his solitary retreat at the Zhampo-gang cave. In contrast, the *Banquet* does not even mention Machig's son Thönyön Samdrup, but describes briefly the life of another Thönyön Samdrup, grandson of Gyalwa Döndrup (also mentioned at the end of *The Marvelous Life*). He was nicknamed "the Snowman of Zhampo-gang," where he meditated after having been cured of leprosy. He was the father of Lentogma, also known as Dorjé Drönma, who according to all prophecies was the incarnation of Machig. *The Concise Life Story* stands alone in describing in detail the descendants of Machig; its account is summarized in the last lines of the *Marvelous Life*.[69]

Machig remains a controversial figure throughout each of the biographies. Having possibly broken her nun's vows in order to marry Bhadra, she was rejected by the people of Central Tibet. Her final test occurred when she had to justify her teachings in front of the three ācāryas who had come from India specifically to judge the validity of her teaching. She finally triumphed over her detractors when she recalled her previous lives and explained the Chöd of Mahāmudrā "to five hundred thousand five hundred and seventy-three people." Once the ācāryas had verified the truth of her assertions about the body left in the Potari cave in India, they conceded their defeat and requested her to come and settle in India as a teacher.[70] The *Transmission History*[71] concludes Machig's life story with the following summary, a standard feature of all versions of her biography:

> Bodhgaya being the center of the world (*'dzam bu'i gling*), all the Dharma teachings originated in India. This tradition of Labdrönma originated at Zangri Kangmar, the center of Tibet. This Tibetan Dharma teaching is the only one that later was propagated in India. It consists of methods to put into practice the meaning of the Prajñāpāramitā. It split into different lineages...so that all might gain confidence in this authentic system that cuts through demons.

The date of her death remains uncertain. The *Blue Annals*,[72] like the *Banquet*, asserts that she died at the age of ninety-five; *The Concise Life Story*, *Transforming the Aggregates* and *A Biography of Machig* agree on the age of ninety-nine—the age she also predicted in her debate with the Indian ācāryas. According to the latter sources, she would have passed away in 1153, since Tibetans count the years starting from the new year following the birth, not from the actual birth date. *The Concise Life Story*,[73] however, tells us that she died in a Fire Monkey year, an obvious error, since the closest Fire Monkey years are 1116 and 1176.[74]

Having passed on her last instructions to the people close to her, Machig disappeared like a rainbow in the vast expanse of suchness, without leaving any physical remains.[75]

Even with the variations in her biographies, Machig remains an extraordinary personality. Controversial during her lifetime, by the age of fifty she had overcome all obstacles and until her death at an advanced age she continued to be tremendously active in the propagation of the Chöd of Mahāmudrā. She became widely recognized as an emanation of Tārā and as an incarnation of Yeshé Tsogyal. In the popular imagination her immense prestige did not wane for the next eight centuries.

The memory of Machig still survives at Zangri, the Copper Mountain, on the right bank of the Tsangpo, about thirty kilometers downstream from Tsétang. A small monastery, recently reconstructed, overlooks the valley, with (in 1986) only two Gelugpa monks in charge, neither of them very knowledgeable about the historical antecedents of the spot. They do, however, look after some relics and a thanka painting of Machig. The meditation cave within its precincts still houses a beautiful life-sized statue of her. It is of uncertain age, but already mentioned in Khyentsé's *Guide*,[76] composed at the close of the nineteenth century.

Although she foretold that she would not again take birth in this world as the primordial wisdom ḍākinī, numerous women (and men) have been considered her emanations ever since. They perpetuate the memory of Machig, the ideal of feminine wisdom manifesting in various forms adapted to the capacities of different beings.

PART TWO:

THE MARVELOUS LIFE OF MACHIG LABDRÖN

Chapters I and II of

An Exposition of Transforming the Aggregates into an Offering of Food, Illuminating the Meaning of Chöd

Phung po gzan skyur gyi rnam bshad gcod kyi don gsal byed

Statue of Machig Labdrön from the Tashilhunpo Monastery, Shigatse. Photo: J. Edou.

VII Machig's Previous Life, Her Birth and Early Years

To the guru, yidam deity and assembly of ḍākinīs, I offer homage with full prostrations.
To your feet, Great Mother, non-human ḍākinī of primordial wisdom, I bow down.
I have composed this treatise of transforming the aggregates into a food offering, in accordance with Machig's spoken words.
But first there follows a short historical account of Machig herself.

1 The Previous Life

Machig was a wisdom ḍākinī, Vajraḍākima, belonging to the Mind group of emanations of Yum Chenmo, she who gives birth to all the Buddhas of the three times. Animated by the intention to work for the benefit of sentient beings, Machig took birth as the princely son of King Śrīṣura Ārya of Kapila in India. The child was given the name Pranidhāna Siddhi.

He learned writing and reading, as well as all the branches of learning, without need for much instruction, since he understood and memorized everything by merely hearing or seeing it just once. By the age of five he already possessed limitless knowledge in every domain and everyone considered him to be a miraculous emanation of the Buddha.

Then, at the age of ten he took monastic ordination from Paṇḍita Piti Bhadra, receiving the ordination name of Arthasiddhi Bhadra. For three years he remained with his guru, studying grammar and logic, the vehicle of the Pāramitās, the Vinaya scriptures on monastic discipline, and Abhidharma; and in these collections his scholarly achievement soon surpassed that of his guru. The master, fully aware of his capacities, next taught him the four classes of Tantra, and in these he became an outstanding scholar.

Next, in his teacher's presence, he made some excellent corrections in the Piṭakas, and even in the set of Tantras he had some clarifications to offer. Moreover, he presented Piti Bhadra with the insights arisen in his own mind. The guru was most pleased and spoke: "Arthasiddhi Bhadra, I am no longer entitled to act as your guru. At present you should go and see Guru Ratna in Tamradvīpa in the north. He is a mahāsiddha of Cakrasaṃvara, and is able to emanate the manifest maṇḍala palace of the deity.[1] He is an absolute master in all the scriptural divisions of the Piṭakas and wears as an ornament all the excellent qualities without exception. With him you'll cut through all remaining doubts and practice the unexcelled Anuttāra[2] within the Secret Mantra vehicle. Once you attain realization therein, you'll be of immense benefit for numerous sentient beings!"

So the next day Arthasiddhi set out and when they met, Guru Ratna recognized him as a worthy receptacle for the teachings. In the sky above he emanated the maṇḍala palace of Cakrasaṃvara as the sixty-four deities and then granted the four empowerments, complete in every detail.

Eventually, Arthasiddhi obtained the supreme siddhi[3] and could thus travel through the Buddha's pure lands absolutely unhindered.

For three years he remained close to the guru, successfully cutting through his doubts on all the dharma teachings of both Sūtra and Tantra. Moreover, he gained complete mastery of the generation and completion stages within Highest Yoga Tantra and attained realization. At this point the guru told him: "You should now proceed to Bodhgaya, the Vajra-Throne, tame the tīrthikas there and bring them into the training. There is no one other than you able to enter into debate with them."

So at the age of sixteen, he set out for Bodhgaya and in the course of a series of encounters, he defeated the tīrthikas, a hundred thousand of them, who all entered the Buddhist tradition.

For four years he remained at Bodhgaya, till one day the majestic Lady Tārā spoke: "You should soon leave for Tibet and act for the benefit of beings there. So intensify your meditation practice!"

Having thought this over, he decided: "I'll lead the life of a hermit, roaming from one sacred spot to the next."

He travelled north and arrived at a cremation ground,[4] but as soon as he had lain down to sleep, the ḍākinī of that charnel field appeared, dressed in bone ornaments and holding aloft a chopper and khaṭvāṅga.[5] She spoke to him: "Hey you! Can't you find any other place to sleep besides this cremation ground of mine?" And with these words she conjured forth all sorts of strange magical apparitions. But he overpowered her by his meditative stabilization [Skt. *samādhi*], so that she ended up offering him her life essence and bound herself by oath to actively protect the Dharma.

At dawn he experienced a direct vision of Nairātmyā, Lady No Self, as the fifteen deities, and she spoke: "Yogin, proceed to Potari and speed up your practice, for soon you'll have to travel to Tibet!" Then she dissolved like a rainbow and was gone.

He wondered, "I am still so young and she tells me to successfully conclude my practice. By what practice will I successfully reach the goal? And those wild Tibetans are bound to be difficult to tame. I have not the slightest idea how I should achieve that!"

Hardly had such thoughts occurred to him when, at the first sign of light at dawn, there arrived Mahāmāyā, Grand Illusion Goddess, as the five deities, telling him, "Move to Bhadra Cave in Potari and there practice the meditation of Kālikā, the Black Lady, and entourage.[6] Yogin, since you'll soon have to tame wandering beings in Tibet, quickly develop your perseverance!" With these words she dissolved into light and vanished.

After daybreak, the ḍākinī of the cremation ground told him, "I'll act as your guide."

Having thus befriended the ḍākinī, he travelled with the power of swift-footedness and without any trouble reached Bhadra Cave, where he practiced the Majestic Lady Kālikā as the five deities. Within two weeks the common siddhis appeared, and one month later he experienced a direct vision of his yidam's five deities, who granted him the complete empowerment into the maṇḍala palace of Jñānaguhya [Wisdom Secret]. The latter gave numerous prophetic commands, such as "You must go forth and tame the beings of Tibet," then dissolved into light which melted into his heart.

About a month later the majestic Lady Tārā appeared and gave him a prophecy concerning his forthcoming activity in Tibet, then she too dissolved into his heart.

On the third day of the ascending moon, the Lord Amitāyus [Boundless Life] granted him further predictions as well as numerous ritual authorizations and blessings.

Likewise, on the eighth, Avalokiteśvara [Lord of Compassion] bestowed blessings with more prophecies.

On the tenth, Padmavajra appeared together with an assembly of ḍākinīs and questioned him on many points of Dharma; there was not a single question he couldn't answer. Padmavajra then revealed to him the secret maṇḍala of Haya[grīva] and Vārāhī, bestowed the corresponding empowerments, and made prophecies about his future activity in Tibet. All the ḍākinīs presented offerings to him, with the request to leave for Tibet.

From the tenth to the fourteenth the ḍākinīs each in turn exhorted him to leave soon.

Finally, at the first signs of dawn on the full-moon day, a most wrathful dark-blue ḍākinī adorned with bone ornaments and carrying khaṭvāṅga and chopper told him, "Yogin, prepare yourself to move to Tibet. Since I must kill you, quickly dissolve your consciousness into my heart!" Raising her chopper, she demonstrated the act of killing him.[7] As instructed, he dissolved his consciousness into the heart of the ḍākinī and she blessed his bodily remains so that they would not deteriorate. He was just twenty years old.

Next, with the wrathful ḍākinī of the cremation ground now acting as his guide, he safely reached E'i Gangwa in the region of Labchi in Tibet and he entered the womb of his future mother. All this took place on the full-moon day, the fifteenth of the fifth month in the year of the Horse.

2 The Birth of Machig

The following concerns her birthplace and parentage. Just below the lower valley known as Tamshö of E'i Gangwa, in the region of Labchi, was the tiny town called Tsomer. The chieftain Chökyi Dawa [Moon of Dharma] was variously known as Learned Nomad, the Chief, the Headman or the Elder. His wife, the daughter of a wealthy family, was known as Bumcham [Lady Hundred Thousand]. Both were of high birth, attractive, well-off and peaceful. They were extremely kind to both their subjects and immediate entourage of servants. In all their acts they behaved in accordance with the Dharma and used all of their goods in the service of religion. Strongly devoted to the Three Rare and Precious Ones, they acted towards the sangha community with a strong sense of caring. They definitely ranked as bodhisattvas whose speech was Dharma-inspired. Their body, speech and mind was totally attuned to the Dharma and they encouraged others to act likewise. They were the noble beings par excellence of the entire Tamshö region, where they ruled over some five hundred hamlets.

On the full-moon night when the previous Arthasiddhi Bhadra entered the womb of Lady Bumcham, just after midnight, she had the following dream: Four white ḍākinīs appeared to her, each carrying a white flask, and they bathed her from head to toe, then dissolved into light. Then, red, yellow and green ḍākinīs, seven of each color, presented her with offerings and said, "Homage to you, Mother. Please be a mother to us." Once more a ḍākinī appeared, this one night-blue and wrathful in appearance, wearing bone ornaments and holding a chopper. She was surrounded by a fourfold entourage of light sky-blue ḍākinīs, all of them carrying choppers and skullcups. They stood around her, one in front, one behind, one on her right and one on her left. The dark-blue ḍākinī, standing one cubit above the ground, struck her chopper at Bumcham's heart, telling her, "This heart of yours, obscured by ignorance, I'll pull it out and I'll eat it," and from Bumcham's opened breast she tore out the heart. Blood came spurting out and entered the skullcup of the ḍākinī in front, then all of them drank from it. Next, the ḍākinī blew on a white, clockwise-turning conch shell, and the sound resounded throughout the universe. She then placed the conch shell, which at its center bore the white letter *A* blazing with the light of five colors, in the hollow of Bumcham's heart, telling her, "I'll give you this to replace your heart." From the ḍākinī's heart there now radiated a five-colored light that dissolved into the crown of Bumcham's head. Next, the light of the four light-blue ḍākinīs pervaded her entire body. After that, they dissolved into light that melted into the central night-blue ḍākinī, who, in turn, dissolved into the middle of a light that filled all of space.

Not once during the entire dream did the young woman experience any alarm or unpleasantness. Even as her heart was being torn out, she felt no pain. On the contrary, her dream was pervaded with joy, a state of mental and physical well-being, clear cognition and lucidity. Never before had she experienced such bliss in a dream, and this feeling of well-being persisted even after she woke up.

The next day, after sunrise, a village woman called Amen arrived at their place to report an auspicious dream she had had concerning the chief's family.

"Come in," they told her and she entered their main private shrine room.

"I had a most extraordinary dream. In your family, merit has been generated for many generations without break. But now one is about to come whose meritorious activity will be equal to space!"

Thus she spoke. Lady Bumcham, upon hearing this, pondered, "Yesterday evening, I too had an extraordinary dream experience and now my body and mind, as well as all of the visual world, are still filled with such joy and peace. And now I am really curious to listen to this dream of Amen's."

When the family had been called together, they gave her a fine reception and asked her to recount her vision of the previous night.

"Yesterday around dawn, this mansion of yours suddenly became three times its normal height and the golden pinnacle grew three times in size as well. At its tip, high up, a golden umbrella with triple rims was slowly rotating. There were mirrors hanging from it in each of the four directions, like so many moons. They were gently moved by the breeze and their brightness lit up the entire region. As this light spread through the four directions, four young women appeared who announced, 'We are ḍākinīs.' Then each blew a white conch shell in such a way that the sound could be heard on every one of the four continents. At the four corners of the house were large silken banners, each fluttering in the wind in its own direction. Numerous butterlamps had been lit and the entire region shone brightly under their blaze. Then, from the sky, a ray of red light entered the mansion. As I was at the time on a hillslope behind the house, when this red light appeared I inquired from one of the women blowing conches, 'What's going on here?' 'We're preparing the residence of the Mother,' she replied. From the shrine room there resounded the soft music of many instruments and I wondered, 'What are they doing in there? And what mother is she talking about? Maybe I'll find out if I go and have a look inside,' but just as I rose, I woke up...."

Many others too had excellent dreams, among them their own daughter Bummé who had just turned sixteen. That same night she had seen a white light descending from the sky onto her mother and lighting up the whole house. Then a girl of about eight appeared, holding a vajra. She inquired, "How are you, my sister?"

"Where do you come from?" I asked and she said, "I've come from Potari."

"Potari? Where's that?"

"In India."

"But who are you?"

"Don't you know me? I'm Tārā!"

As Bummé was pondering whether this could be true or not, she tried to reach out to hold her, but the little girl fled into her mother's lap where she dissolved. At that moment Bummé woke up.

Many other excellent omens such as this one occurred. Bumcham herself, though already forty-eight years of age, noticed how her wrinkles disappeared, how her complexion became youthful again, and how she gained a fresh splendor, to the point that people started to say, "Of all people, Jomo Bumcham has always accumulated positive merits in matters of Dharma activity. This is now the ensuing blessing. She has grown youthful again, to the extent that it is impossible to distinguish between mother and daughter!"

Bumcham herself felt light and happy. During this period she had innumerable clear visions and, at night, she could clearly see objects and places, just as if a lamp had been lit and there were no darkness at all. At times she could read others' thoughts, bad or good, so much so that she became known for her clairvoyant dreams.

Then, starting from the twenty-eighth of the second month of the following year, the year of the Sheep, within her womb Bumcham sensed the syllables *A* and *HA RI NI SA* being recited.[8]

On the morning of the third day of the following month, there was a voice calling out that said, "Mother, I need white cotton cloth, purified with incense and myrrh, and sprinkled with perfume." Bumcham prepared the baby's clothes accordingly.

Finally, on the full-moon day of the third month of the Sheep Year, at the first light of dawn, the child was born.

The entire house was filled with sweet perfume, incense and rainbow light, while celestial music resounded from space and flowers rained down. All the inhabitants of the region presented offerings to the clan-gods of the family. They later claimed that while doing so, they saw rainbows and a rain of flowers and heard melodies resounding from the sky.

Just after birth, amidst rainbow light, the child assumed a dancing posture with one leg outstretched and one leg bent, and then addressed her mother, "Mother, are you all right?" after which the little girl recited the syllable *A* like a mantra.

On the child's tongue one could clearly see a red syllable *HRI* ablaze with light.[9] Her forehead was adorned with a bright third eye, shining forth with five lights of different colors arrayed like a rainbow, each as thin as a horse-hair. At the crown of her head shone a white light the size of a fingertip, marked with the white syllable *A*.[10]

Sister Bummé wrapped the child in the cotton cloth and took her on her lap. After a little while, the syllable *HRI* melted into the child's tongue and was no longer visible. Bummé mixed some clarified butter and barley sugar, and gave it to the child, but the little one didn't want to eat any of it and spat it out right away. With her three eyes she gazed into space without blinking. Moment by moment, the light on the crown of her head started to mingle with the fivefold light from the eye in her forehead, eventually dissolving within it.

Next, slightly drawing in her chin, she looked straight at her sister with a fixed stare, clicked her tongue a couple of times, and finally accepted the piece of butter. Having now taken on the appearance of a normal child, she looked at her mother and smiled. As for the mother, she did not suffer from the birth and her happiness and joy only increased.

In the morning when Bummé saw the child staring straight ahead, she called out to her mother, "Mother, the child is looking at me with her three eyes! Isn't that marvelous?"

But hearing the father coming, Bumcham said, "Bummé, we must hide the girl!"

The mother wrapped the child in the cotton cloth and placed her in a dark spot behind the door. The father entered the shrine room, and Bummé told him, "Lord of the Family, Mother has given birth to a strange girl with three eyes. We've gotten rid of her...."

But the father replied, "Whatever she is, bring her here!"

And so Bummé fetched the little girl and brought her to her father. Having carefully examined her, he said, "In the middle of the girl's central eye there is a white syllable *A*, as fine as a hair, and she also has all the other signs of a ḍākinī. Look after this girl with the utmost care! And, Bummé, don't take her outdoors, don't take her into town. Keep this girl's existence a secret!"[11]

The little girl grew up quickly, surrounded with excellent care and affection. At the age of three she already showed much diligence in performing prostrations in front of the divine images of the shrine room. She could recite the Six-Syllable [mantra of Avalokiteśvara], the *TARE* [mantra of Ārya Tārā], the *HRI* and *A* syllables, as well as the *GATE* [the Prajñāpāramitā mantra] and the *HA RI NI SA* [mantra of

Vajrayoginī]. By the age of five her mother had taught her the alphabet, and just by being shown it once, she was able to memorize it.

There was a monk called Jowo Dampa who, as the family's priest, was reciting texts for them. They asked him to teach the child how to trace letters and their combined forms.

By the age of eight she could draw letters on paper,[12] and daily she would recite twice the *Eight Thousand Lines* [of the Perfection of Wisdom]. One day the monk said to her mother, "Jomo, this daughter of yours is no ordinary individual, but seems to be a kind of ḍākinī. I am unable to contain her intelligence. Her wisdom is like a wild running forest fire, consuming everything. You should name her Sherab Drönmé, Shining Light of Knowledge."

And so the mother gave her the name Dröntsema, Little Light.

The rumor spread, however, that Jomo Bumcham had a daughter with three eyes, and now everyone wanted to see her. Those who saw the little girl were all strongly attracted to her, full of admiration, so that her renown increased even more. All the inhabitants of the region agreed: "This Little Light of *A* is really an emanation of the Buddhas," and they came to offer her prostrations, requesting her blessings.

As for Bummé, she requested monastic ordination from Geshé Atön, who gave her the ordination name Töntso Rinchen Bum, "Hundred-Thousand Jewels [from the] Ocean [-like] Teacher." She became the foremost among his learned disciples.

3 Labdrön

Having heard about Machig, the governor of the district one day organized a great festival to which he invited Chökyi Dawa and Jomo Bumcham, requesting them to bring along their young daughter. He sent out a messenger who led the little girl and her parents, together with an entourage of twenty-two, into the presence of the ruler.

Upon their arrival he gave an excellent reception in honor of Machig, and then asked Bumcham to come and introduce her daughter to him. As she approached the governor, Bumcham became so shy that she couldn't reply to any of his questions. Her voice started to tremble, so the child answered for her. The numerous paṇḍitas, geshés and courtiers were impressed by her self-assurance, and when they saw that she had three eyes, they understood she was no ordinary person.

"Do you also know how to read?" the ruler asked her. Dröntsé replied that, yes, she knew letters, and proceeded to recite in three different modes the *Condensed Perfection of Wisdom* [Skt. *Sañcaya-gātha-prajñā-pāramitā-sūtra*], a copy of which was lying there. All acknowledged her reading ability and her expertise in recitation. And when the paṇḍitas further inquired whether she also understood the meaning, she explained the passage she had just read. Now all were convinced that she was not just an ordinary being. "She is definitely an emanation of the wisdom ḍākinī," they exclaimed.

The ruler next asked her to come nearer, as he wished to examine her. He attentively observed her and when he noticed the eye in her forehead, with the syllable *A* in its center, as well as the full range of other ḍākinī signs, he was most impressed and asked her, "What's your name?"

She told him, "I am called Rinchen Drönmé [Precious Light] or Dröntsé, or also Adrön."

"Since your name is Drönmé and since you took birth in Labchi, from now on we'll call you Labdrön, the Shining Light of Lab! It will be most auspicious in the future."

All those present, the paṇḍitas, monks and chief statesmen and a crowd of three hundred thousand inhabitants, agreed this was most excellent and henceforth she was known by all as Labdrön, the Shining Light of Lab. Everyone in the crowd wanted to see her with their own eyes and all were filled with joy, confidence and devotion for her.

Finally, the ruler had Labdrön dressed in new clothes and boots, keeping the old ones [as objects for worship]. To her parents he offered three horses and some thirty valuable presents. He urged all of them, parents and servants alike, to take good care of little Labdrön and not to let her go about just anywhere, so that she would not meet evil people who might have a negative influence on her.

"Please keep a close watch over her, for she will be of immense benefit to one and all in the Land of Snows," he said.

Upon their return to Tsomer, for a period of five years, mother and daughter daily studied and recited the Perfection of Wisdom in its extensive, medium and abbreviated versions while staying in the shrine room. At the age of ten, Labdrön was able to read four volumes a day, and eight by the time she reached the age of thirteen. That same year, her mother passed away and her sister Töntso Rinchen Bum looked after her. She took her to meet Geshé Atön, who said, "Bummé, your little sister possesses all the signs of a ḍākinī. I would like her to read a text for me."

Thereupon Machig read the *Perfection of Wisdom in Eight Thousand Lines* [Skt. *Aṣṭa-sāhasrikā-prajñā-pāramitā-sūtra*] in less time than is needed to grind one measure of barley. The geshé was visibly pleased: "Amazing! She knows how to modulate her recitation in eight different modes! She'll become the foremost of my disciples! I want to teach her the meaning."

Together with her sister Bummé she stayed for a period of three years at the geshé's place and he taught them the Prajñāpāramitā, the six perfections, the ten bodhisattva bhūmis and the five paths.[13] Yet in matters of exegesis, soon no one could match her ability, neither her teachers nor the other disciples, nor the geshés, including Geshé Atön himself.

One day he addressed her as follows: "I'm no longer able to act as your teacher. At Dratang in Yoru, at the monastery of Dobtrang, there is one called Clairvoyant Monk, a true authority, looking after numerous monks. Among his many qualities, his understanding is vast and his realization is profound. With him you will be able to cut through any remaining doubts. Under him you will achieve true mastery. That's where you should go."

And so, at the age of sixteen, accompanied by her sister, Machig set out to meet Lama Trapa, the Clairvoyant Monk.

"Bummé, is that your younger sister, the one so talented at reading?"

"Yes it is," Bummé replied.

"I would like to see how she compares with our *chöné*.[14] We call him 'Perfection in Six Indian Modes,' for in one day he can complete the recitation, in six different modes, of four volumes of the [*Perfection of Wisdom in One*] *Hundred Thousand* [*Lines*] [Skt. *Śata-sāhasrikā-prajñā-pāramitā-sūtra*]."[15]

And so one day, the chöné and Machig started to read the texts. The chöné completed four volumes, and Labdrön in the same amount of time completed twelve volumes, each of which she recited in the eight different modes.

Trapa exclaimed, "This is absolutely marvelous! This lady not only surpasses our chöné by two extra modes, but as far as purity of recitation goes, she is without equal! Is there any chance for this young lady to stay here to recite texts?"

Bummé objected, "Adrön and I should practice meditation in order to reach the Khecari realm of the Sky-Goers."[16]

But Labdrön interrupted her, "As far as I'm concerned, I will stay here, since I should accomplish my task for the benefit of all beings. But if that is what you want, you should start to practice right away and you will enter the bliss of the Ḍāka Realm. Once I have completed my task for beings here, I will meet you there."

Thereupon Töntso Rinchen Bum spent the next three years in meditation, then left for the ḍākinī realm without leaving behind any bodily remains.

Lama Trapa clearly saw that Labdrön was a worthy vessel and accordingly he passed on to her reading transmissions and explanations on the meaning of many sūtras, including the *Hundred Thousand*, the *Twenty-Five Thousand* and the *Eight Thousand* [-line] versions of the Prajñāpāramitā. Soon she also mastered the commentaries, all the way from the short commentary on the *Twenty Thousand*, to the extensive commentary on the *Hundred Thousand*, to such an extent that she knew how to explain their meanings down to the last syllable. A genuine realization was born in her and she presented her insight as an offering to the lama.

He was extremely pleased. "Jomo, now that you have perfectly absorbed the meanings of all three versions of the Perfection of Wisdom, and gained mastery in the sūtras, I have difficulty matching your realization."

As a sign of his admiration he had a ceremonial hat made for her of dark-red brocade lined with white, shaped like a ten-petalled lotus. It had silken ribbons of equal length, five in the back, five to the right and five to the left, each set made of five different colors. He offered new clothes and a pair of small boots. He then requested her to sit on a throne, three cushions high and covered with a newly woven carpet.

Then Lama Trapa made this formal request: "Please remain here for four years to recite texts for us."

Looking straight ahead without blinking, she put on the ceremonial hat. With the blue and red ribbons reaching down to her waist she looked truly magnificent.

"Our young ācārya looks splendid in that little hat!" he exclaimed and, henceforth everybody started to call her Jomo Shachung, Lady Little Hat, which is how she came to be known.

As a leading figure, Machig showed dignified restraint in her actions, was always clean and neat, and was endowed with a natural gentleness and nobility in body, speech and mind. To be conscientious and meticulous came effortlessly to her. She was happy in the monastic community, and going to the village did not appeal to her at all: for her the secluded life of the monastery was pure delight. To her lama and the sangha she was most devoted, respectful and totally sincere.

So she promised to act as the lama's *chöné* and recite texts for a four-year period, and the entire community rejoiced since they were inspired by genuine faith in Young Ācārya. Thus her renown increased.

4 Dampa Sangyé

At that time the rumor went around that one Indian *atsāra*[17] had arrived at the Conquerors' Temple. He was said to be endowed with supernatural perception. He was inquiring as to the whereabouts of an Indian paṇḍita who formerly had meditated at the Bhadra Cave in Potari and supposedly had now taken birth in Tibet under the name of Labdrön.

One night Machig dreamed of a white ḍākinī who told her, "A black atsāra has arrived here, all the way from India. Tomorrow he'll come to see you."

She inquired, "This atsāra, who is it?"

"He is called Dampa."

The next day she awoke with the first rays of the sun and wondered, "Dreams are usually misleading. Still, could it be true?"

As she walked outside the gate, at the outer stone post she suddenly stood face to face with the atsāra. Immediately she started to greet him respectfully with full prostration, but he wouldn't let her and instead touched her forehead to his.[18]

"Dampa Rinpoché, how wonderful that you have come to Tibet!" she said, to which he replied, "It is much more amazing that you, Lady Labdrön Wisdom Ḍākinī, have come to Tibet for the sake of living beings. It fills me with joy!"

Labdrön later inquired of him, "How am I to act for the sake of living beings?"

[He replied in verse:]

> Turn away from all negative aims and eradicate all resistance.[19]
> Cultivate what seems impossible to you.
> Cut through entanglements[20] and recognize your desires.
> Wander in desolate places that inspire fear.
> Understand that all beings are similar to empty space.[21]
> While in the wilderness, look for the Buddha within yourself
> And your teaching will be like a sun illuminating space!"

Dampa also made several predictions to her, then went on his way. Labdrön went back and resumed her recitation task.

Around that time it happened that one day Sönam Dragpa, a descendant of Kyozur Paṇchen Śākya, arrived. He was vastly learned in both the outer Tripiṭaka Sūtras and the four inner Tantras. He was also endowed with magical powers. Formerly in charge of the training of several hundred monks, he had recently tired of all involvement in worldly affairs, of teaching and of dealing with an entourage and monks. He now wandered about by himself, spending most of his time in solitary retreat. He was known as Kyotön, Renunciate Master, or simply Sönam Lama, Meritorious Lama. One day he said to Machig, "Young Ācārya, you seem very learned indeed in the Prajñāpāramitā texts, but do you really know their meaning?"

"Yes, I do," she replied.

"So please explain it to me."

She gave him a detailed explanation and commentary on the ten bodhisattva stages and the five paths, showing the way to reach the final fruit of Buddhahood.

"You indeed appear to know well how to explain the meaning, but you have not yet integrated it totally in your mindstream."

"How does one do this?" she inquired.

"Everything you've said so far is what we call understanding. Your explanation of the ultimate nature of all phenomena is completely correct. But now you need to integrate this knowledge in your mindstream, and as soon as you succeed, the former mind enslaved by partial fixations will be replaced by a new state of mind free from all grasping at the reality of phenomena. Then, liberated from attachment to reality, you will be totally free of the conception of subject and object, equally divorced from all mental states related to action and agent. This understanding of nonduality is a great fire which destroys the darkness of ignorant clinging to a self. The essence of all teachings is to thoroughly examine the nature of your mind.[22] So you should do it!"

With these words Sönam Lama went on his way. Labdrön took up her recitation again, reflecting on the meaning of the lama's instructions. While reading the chapter on demons, she understood what he meant and an exceptional realization, such as she had never experienced before, arose in her. Free from any conceptualization, she eliminated the demon of ego-clinging and self-centeredness. This insight of realizing the non-existence of a self was like the sun dissipating darkness: the erroneous belief in the existence of a self was forever silenced.[23]

Machig's realization was confirmed by numerous signs. Whereas previously she would only wear fine clothes, ornate and in brilliant colors, she now dressed in beggar's rags and the patched pieces of cloth she came across here and there—a sign that she had cut through all attachment to clothes.

Previously she used to only seek the company of friends, teachers, other disciples, and monks, but now she could be seen among lepers and beggars—a sign that she had cut through all partiality regarding the company she kept.

She would never before have stayed anywhere but in a monastery or hermitage, but now she slept just about anywhere, on the side of the road or in the house of a leper—a sign that she had cut all attachment to her surroundings.

In the past, except for the occasional trip to her family at E'i Gang or to her monastery at Dratang in Yoru, she would never go anywhere. Now, without aim, she wandered all over the country—a sign that she had rid herself of all partiality regarding places.

Whereas before she had restricted herself to healthy and pure food such as the three whites and the three sweets,[24] now, with the exception of meat, she ate anything, even from the hands of a leper or beggar—a sign that she had definitely cut through all attachment to food.

Formerly she had enjoyed praise and compliments, but now she was utterly unaffected by slander, blame or abuse. Even when facing suffering, she remained serene, without attraction or aversion towards those near or far away, utterly fearless in the equanimity of the expanse of dharmatā.[25]

5 The Initiation

She was twenty when she completed her years as *chöné* at Lama Trapa's monastery. She requested an empowerment from him, but he replied, "It is impossible for me to grant you an initiation. You should address your request to Sönam Lama since you have a connection with him through aspirations made in previous lives. Therefore through his empowerment, you will attain the siddhis without hindrances." With this advice, he presented her with seven measures of the most excellent yak meat and a beautiful roll of red satin, and sent her off.

Machig first visited her family in the Apo region. She requested her brother Sakya Gyaltsen[26] to provide her with thirty loads of barley, which she added to the meat and the roll of cloth. Carrying all these with her, she arrived in the presence of Kyotön Sönam Lama, to whom she repeated the prediction of Lama Trapa. Seeing that she was a worthy vessel, the master agreed to her request for initiation.

In the temple of E'i Gangwa[27] he gave [the young woman and four other yogis, Ngagpas Lokya Lhakyab, Ja Trompa, Jinglha Zao and Zhangtön Özerpal][28] the following initiations: the mind initiation by which one realizes the meaning of the four initiations through profound samādhi, according to the Sūtra tradition of Dampa's lineage;[29] a blessing transmission known as Opening the Gates of Space";[30] and the empowerment of Mahāmāyā, the Grand Illusion Tantra, also from Dampa's transmission lineage.

During the invocation of the wisdom beings[31] of the last initiation, just as the stars had become perfectly visible in the sky, Labdrön's body rose about one cubit above the ground. She displayed the twenty-four dance postures of the peaceful deities and sang in Sanskrit, the language of the gods, with the voice [of Brahmā][32] endowed with sixty excellent qualities; and meanwhile her mind experienced the vajra-like meditative stabilization [Skt. *vajropāma-samādhi*],[33] absorbed in the limitless essence of reality. Next, without being in any way hindered by the clay walls of the temple, she floated straight through them, rose in the air and disappeared.

The place where she landed was known as the Tree of Serlag, at the foot of which there was a spring called Höpo Namkhol [Sky-Boiler the Resplendent], the residence of the nāga king Dragpo Dakyong [Wrathful Moon Protector].[34] This place was so terrifying that no one could even bear to look at it. She immediately overpowered the nāga king by her samādhi, and as he couldn't stand this, he called for help to all the other nāgas in the region. From everywhere they assembled into an immense army, showing an entire array of terrifying magical powers. Machig instantly transformed her body into a food offering for demons.[35] Unable to destroy her, the demons were forced to surrender and offered her their life essence in order to survive. The nāga king Wrathful Moon Protector and the others took the oath to never again harm living beings and to protect Machig's teachings.

Around midnight, the five deities of the Mahāmāyā maṇḍala with their consorts appeared to her in a vision and conferred on her the four initiations, complete in every detail. Later, the five manifestations of the Wrathful Lady granted her the full four initiations. They said: "So that you may gather under your power humans and non-humans of the visible world and accomplish the task of establishing them in highest enlightenment, quickly now exert yourself!"

After this, Cakrasaṃvara's divine assembly together with ocean-like multitudes of ḍākinīs gave her numerous ritual permissions as well as prophecies.[36]

Then the Great Mother Yum Chenmo appeared, surrounded by the Buddhas of the ten directions, and blessed her: "Yoginī, wander about in desolate places and generate the vast mind of enlightenment for the happiness of all living beings."

Finally, at dawn, the majestic Lady Tārā appeared and transmitted to her the one hundred empowerments from the *Quintessence That Dispels the Darkness of Ignorance*[37] and gave her many predictions: "Yoginī, you and an emanation of Buddhakapāla, the yogin Thöpa Bhadraya who will soon be arriving in Tibet, will unite as means and wisdom,[38] then achieve the aims of beings at one hundred and eight desolate places and springs. Your teaching will become like the sun rising in the sky and you will reach the level of no return."[39] Dissolving like a rainbow, she vanished.

Early that morning, the other disciples eventually found Machig at the foot of the Serlag Tree. They returned to the monastery and she went up to the lama, wearing only one piece of cloth:

> Naked, with no delusions, with no clothes,
> Not embarrassed, I offer salutations of no shame with full
> prostration.
> To you who truly clears away the obscurations,
> The lama supreme, I offer my homage with full prostrations.
> To you, guide to the heavenly abodes, I salute bowing down.
> To you, protector from evil rebirths, I bow down in salutation.

Her companions pointed out that the evening before she had failed to obtain the main part of the empowerment, but the lama intervened: "What the rest of you have received is merely the initiation of the ritual substances, but Machig has obtained the empowerment into the ultimate nature of reality!"

Later that morning, she nevertheless requested the formal bestowal of the main section of the initiation, presenting the lama with a maṇḍala offering of the universe:

> On this maṇḍala offering ornamented with outer appearances,
> Sprinkled with the water of the four elements,
> I present all living beings of the six realms
> Together with the inexhaustible precious treasures of the universe.
> To the authentic source of refuge, the rare and precious Triple Gem,
> And to the lama, yidam,[40] and ḍākinī,
> I offer the maṇḍala of outer appearance.
> Please accept it with your blessings.

For the Secret Empowerment, she offered another maṇḍala:

> On this maṇḍala offering of inner aggregates
> Sprinkled with the water of the co-emergent and spontaneously
> arisen wisdom,
> I present the eight consciousnesses
> Together with the precious treasure of their basic ground.[41]
> To the authentic source of refuge, the rare and precious Triple Gem,
> And to the lama, yidam, and ḍākinī,
> I offer the maṇḍala of the inner aggregates.
> Please accept it with your blessings.

For the Word Empowerment:

> On this maṇḍala offering of secret dharmatā,
> Sprinkled with the water of self-aware clear light,[42]
> I present unobstructed meditation experiences,
> Together with the bliss treasure of clarity-emptiness.[43]
> To the authentic source of refuge, the rare and precious Triple Gem,
> And to the lama, yidam, and ḍākinī,
> I offer the maṇḍala of secret dharmatā.
> Please accept it with your blessings.[44]

Having received these maṇḍalas, the lama passed on to her the four empowerments, complete in every detail, together with an excellent explanation of the corresponding instructions. Machig understood the complete deep meaning of the initiations and developed an exceptional and unshakeable faith in the lama.

Next, from Lama Shamarpa she received the five treatises of Maitreya.[45] She further requested from him numerous other teachings, including the cycles on generating the mind set on enlightenment [*bodhicitta*], and the cycles on sound transformation, all of which she perfectly mastered.

From Lama Betön she received numerous teachings on the Great Perfection, and the signs of realization manifested in her practice.[46]

Lama Yartingpa transmitted to her the Mahāmudrā instructions through symbols, the Six Yogas of Nāropa,[47] the cycle of teachings of Vārāhī and the six branch applications of the Wheel of Time [Kālacakra]. She also requested various teachings on the three cycles of *dohā*[48] and on the Kriya Tantra.[49] All of these she mastered.

Later, at the feet of Lama Trapa she refined her understanding of the five treatises of Maitreya and he suggested that she set out for Central Tibet.

Upon her arrival in Lhasa, she made vast ceremonial offerings to the Jowo[50] and numerous miraculous signs appeared: the sky was filled with rainbows, the sound of celestial music and a rain of flowers. All those who witnessed these wonders developed deep faith in her and requested teachings. Then she went back to her monastery at Dratang.

At that time Dampa Sangyé resided at Nyipug [Sun Cave] in Penyul. A local guardian ḍākinī announced to him the presence of the Shining Light of Lab at Dratang and he set out to meet her. At the time she was on a pilgrimage to sacred places of the region. When she saw Dampa, she offered prostrations to him and requested instructions through which she might liberate all beings.

Dampa Rinpoché replied:

> I pay homage to you, practitioner of the Tantras,
> Incarnation of the Great Mother Yum Chenmo
> Who holds the four aspects of knowledge.
> You are a ḍākinī who has opened the three gates of liberation.
> You have annihilated the army of demons.
> In front of you, Labdrön
> All the gods and I bow down.
> I rejoice in your virtuous activity!
>
> Through the power of your compassion and qualities,
> You lead sentient beings of this degenerate age to maturation and liberation.
> Yet, for the benefit of generations to come,
> I will give you the oral instructions which you have requested.

To three of his women disciples, Khargoma, Chötso and Labdrön, Dampa gave oral instructions covering the precepts on Prajñāpāramitā practice using both Sūtra and Tantra techniques. They included the oral instruction of the profound meaning, the four empowerments of meditative stabilization, an initiation of the ultimate meaning transmitted to the mind and called the Level of Heat;[51] and the direct transmission known as Opening the Gates of Space, which is oral instructions on consciousness transference. He gave these in their entirety, not leaving out anything. Furthermore, to Labdrön alone he gave (1) the cycle of the Pacification; (2) the instructions on the *Six Minor Treatises on Chöd*[52] practice; (3) the *HUNG* cycle of the Pacification, the explicit commentary cycle[53] and the *PHAT* cycle, these latter three constituting one collection; (4) the Dharma teaching given through the symbol of the blue utpala lotus; (5) Mahāmāyā, the Great Illusion, practice; (6) the Two-faced Lady [a form of Vajravārāhī]; (7) the Profound Path, a guru yoga related to the lamas of the oral transmission;[54] (8) the instructions on the transference of consciousness and entering a corpse, from the treatise called *Entering the Most Excellent Path: Vital*

Point from Where to Draw [Inseparable] Wind-Mind;[55] (9) the most essential instructions on the tiny drop (*thig le*), on how to combine in a single practice the purification of illusory body, dream [yoga] and intermediate state;[56] and (10) the oral instructions of the precepts under seal of truth on cutting through confusion, including the eight instructions on cutting through visual suggestions caused by the great charnel field guardian goddess, while not moving from one's seat.[57]

Having received these in their entirety, she mastered them. In the end she offered Dampa Rinpoché the following hymn of praise:

> Saintly Father, Pa Dampa, omniscient, one who comprehends all,
> Supreme spiritual son of all the Buddhas,
> To you, emanation body,[58] I bow down.

Labdrön thereafter remained in Central Tibet for three years. She then moved to Latö and for six months stayed in her native country.

Here is what Dampa said while at Dratang:

> Thereupon the great wisdom ḍākinī—the supreme mother giving birth to all the Buddhas of the three times, the secret knowledge-wisdom who is the source of all wisdom ḍākinīs,[59] Vajravārāhī, consort of Cakrasaṃvara, Nairātmyā [Lady No-Self], leader of the sky-goers of the great secret [*mahā-guhya-ḍākinī*]—manifested in a wrathful bluish black body,[60] the unchangeable expanse of all phenomena [*dharmadhātu*], and brought all the ḍākinīs under her power. Having become the supreme Lady of Great Wisdom [Mahāprajñā], Vajra Lady subjugating demons, she resides in the ḍākinī realm Active in Space [Khecari]. Still, due to previous karma and prayers, and her motivation to benefit all beings, she took birth in the town of Kapila in India as the princely son of Rāja Śrīṣura Ārya, and received the name Pranidhāna Siddhi [Prayer Fulfilled]. Her coming to Tibet to tame beings was prophesied by the Buddha in the eighty-second chapter of the *Sūtra Distinguishing the Essence from the Residues:*[61]
>
> > In the degenerate age of increasing strife,
> > Up north in the Land of Snows,
> > An emanation of the Mother of the Victorious [Buddhas]
> > Called Shining Light [Drönma] will appear.
>
> Also in the *Root Tantra of Mañjuśrī, "King of Tantras"* (Skt. *Mañjuśrī-mūla-tantra-rāja*),[62] there occurs this passage:
>
> > When my teaching is on the decline,
> > In the northern region known as the Land of Snows,
> > A mind emanation of the Great Mother of Wisdom
> > Will appear as the Shining Light of Lab [Labkyi Drönma].
> > She will teach the meaning of the unborn Prajñāpāramitā.

> Wandering through towns and villages, in mountainous regions,
> And in charnel fields, her teachings will flourish.
>
> Then this Indian paṇḍita Arthasiddhi Bhadra, who was prophesied by the Buddha, thought that it was the right time to discipline beings in Tibet. Seeing that four heretical ḍākinīs had been born there and were terrifying the country through their malignant powers, he decided it was time to subjugate them and manifested as four wisdom ḍākinīs.
>
> The first one, Machig Zhama from Latö, will tame beings by means of the teaching on Path and Its Fruit. The second one, Zangcham Drönchungma from Dringtsam, will tame them by means of the Great Perfection. The third one, Shelza Drönnema from Nyanam, will discipline them by means of combining the four teachings of Mahāmudrā through symbols.[63] The fourth one, Labdrön from the middle valley of Lab, is the main emanation among them. Her doctrine is known as "Cutting Through the Four Demons, a practice to cut attachment to the aggregates by offering one's flesh and blood as food [for the demons]."[64]
>
> The four heretical ḍākinīs to be subjugated are White Barwa from Parpu, Chemo Namkha from Tölung, Shelmo Gyalcham from Tsang, and Zangmo Lhatri from Lhading. Having been disciplined, they will become peaceful wisdom ḍākinīs themselves, and each will be the source of great benefit for beings.

These were the words of Dampa Rinpoché in Dratang.

To summarize, when Labdrön was thirteen, her mother passed away and went to the ḍākinī realm Active in Space. When she was sixteen, her father passed away and took birth in India, where he soon developed the power to benefit beings. When she was twenty, her sister Töntso also went to the ḍākinī realm without leaving any bodily remains and there met with their mother, Bumcham. Her elder brother Sakya Gyaltsen became very learned in the Tripiṭaka. He advanced through the monastic hierarchy, eventually becoming abbot at one college. He also attained realization in Secret Mantra, achieving the level of bodily heat. Her younger brother Pelhö Tridé succeeded his father as ruler of the district and exerted himself in support of the Buddha's teachings. Having gathered great merit, he became very powerful. As for Machig, she went back to Lama Trapa.

Here ends the first chapter, dealing with the early life of Labdrön, from her abbreviated sacred biography.

Thangka of the Wrathful Black Lady (Khros ma nag mo). Courtesy of Hotel Annapurna, Kathmandu. Photo: Mani Lama.

VIII Her Achievements

The following is a succinct account of Machig's later efforts in training disciples and her enlightened activities.

1 The Meeting with Thöpa Bhadra

Lama Trapa had a wealthy benefactress, Lhamo Drön, who one day requested that Machig come and recite texts for her and her husband. In return she offered Machig all their goods, with the further promise that she would present her with whatever else she might desire. The lama agreed and told Machig, "Please proceed to Echung, to the house of Lhamo Drön, and act as her *chöné* for the duration of one month. During that time recite thirty times the *Prajñāpāramitā Sūtra in One Hundred Thousand Lines*. In return she has offered you all her husband's possessions."

But Machig first went to meet Sönam Lama, asking him whether she really ought to go. The lama advised her to do so because of a previous karmic connection, which would result in the benefit of beings. Since both lamas had agreed, she accepted and set out for Echung. That night a red ḍākinī with an eye in her forehead appeared and said to her, "If you unite with the Indian Thöpa Bhadra and act as means and wisdom, great benefit for beings will result, and you will achieve the stage of no return." With these words she dissolved and was gone.

At dawn, a bluish-black ḍākinī with the dress and attributes of a wrathful deity appeared and told her, "Bhadra is an emanation of Buddhakapāla. Unite means and wisdom, and practice the path of Secret Mantra. As a result, your family lineage will increase, your teachings will spread far and wide, and you yourself will eventually reach the tenth bodhisattva level." With these words she dissolved into the sky. Just as it dawned on Labdrön that the ḍākinī had gone, she awoke from her dream.

Before her departure for Echung, Machig stayed with a nun. In the middle of the night, seven white women appeared and addressed her in one voice: "Yoginī, you and the Indian paṇḍita Thöpa Bhadra are connected by former karma and prayers. Put all fear out of your mind and unite with him."

Machig thought, "These prophecies, what are they worth? Might they not be some clever demonic trick? Would the two lamas know?" But just as she decided to ask these women a question, they dissolved into nothing and were gone.

At dawn a white girl riding a white mule appeared and said to her: "One and only Mother, Wisdom Ḍākinī of the Great Secret, Great Vajra Lady Subjugating Demons, I have come to welcome you."

"Where is it that you have come from?"

In reply, the white girl came down from her mule, greeted her in full prostration, and then spoke: "I am Śaṅkapālī, Conch Protectress, and I have come because I was told to do so by Guru Thöpa Bhadra. Referring to you, he said: 'She is Yum Chenmo, the Mother of Wisdom, noble and secret consort.' These are his words."

"But what is Thöpa Bhadra's family lineage? And where is he from?"

"Lama Bhadra's home is Kosala in India. His father is the Śākya Lord Ratnasiddhi and his mother is Samatī. As for the lama himself, he is an emanation of Buddhakapāla and his name is Bhadra [or Bhatraya]. Vastly learned in both outer Tripiṭaka and inner Tantra, he is also a yogin who has attained realization through his mastery of Cakrasaṃvara. Great Mother, he has come all the way to Tibet just to meet you. At present he is in Echung and he sent me to invite you there."

With these words she mounted her mule, adding, "Please come." Then she dissolved and was gone.

Machig left early that morning and by midday she arrived at Sheldrong where the teacher Sherab Bum [Hundred Thousand Wisdom], a master in the Piṭakas, was teaching the perfections to an assembly of some three hundred monks. Upon her arrival, the geshés inquired, "Jomo, aren't you Dawa Gyaltsen's daughter Labdrön, famous for her three eyes? Is that you indeed?"

"Yes, it's me."

"Well then, rumor has it that you are a ḍākinī and also an authority on Prajñāpāramitā. Would you agree to debate with us?"

So she engaged in philosophical disputation with seven of the most famous geshés there. They could find no flaw in any of her arguments, and so all the monks present were convinced that she was indeed an emanation of Yum Chenmo, a wisdom ḍākinī, and they asked her if she would care to meet their lama. She agreed, but as she was setting out they told her to wait. It occurred to her that maybe it was not the right time for this meeting. Just then a procession of some twenty monks carrying incense and playing ceremonial greeting music came out to welcome her and led her in front of the lama. She saw him as the Red Mañjuśrī and bowed down in salutation, but he would not allow any prostrations from her.

"Are you really the famous Machig Labdrönma?" he asked, and invited her to sit on a throne with three cushions which he had had prepared for her next to his own. The lama in turn perceived Machig Labdrönma as a white ḍākinī. Later the two of them had some Dharma discussions with mutual elucidations, after which he expressed how pleased he was with her clear comprehension. When she asked him for a teaching, however, he replied that he did not have a single doctrine which she did not already know. As Labdrön insisted, in order to establish a Dharma connection between them, he finally gave her an excellent explanation of the twelve links of dependent arising, in original and reverse order. For seven days she listened with full attention. During the next seven days, she reflected upon the meanings and subtle points involved. She fully understood how all phenomena originate in dependence on one another, and how an understanding of this dependent arising of all phenomena can become a means for liberation.[1]

When she finally reached Echung, Lhamo Drön led her to the upper terrace of the house. Seated there was a yogin with bloodshot eyes, dark body color and a fixed stare, performing the initiation rite of Cakrasaṃvara.[2]

He addressed her in the language of India: "So, the noble Lady is not too tired from her journey?"

"Yogin, coming all the way from India, isn't it a bit of a folly?" Labdrön retorted, and right away she entered the private chapel and proceeded with her recitations of the [*Prajñāparamitā Sūtra in One*] *Hundred Thousand* [*Lines*]. Only from time to time would she discuss some Dharma with the paṇḍita or ask him for stories about India. But then on the evening of her seventeenth day there, on the eighth day of the lunar month, Bhadra and Labdrön entered the meditative absorption of skillful means and wisdom. Light pervaded the entire house and the benefactress Lhamo Drön, fearing that the butter lamps had set the house ablaze, ran up to have a look. All she saw was a five-colored light, similar to a rainbow, which pervaded the entire house and within this, all ablaze, were two moons in union, one white, one red. Apart from this she didn't see anyone, and frightened by it, she left the rooftop chapel and went back down to sleep.

She awoke at dawn and went back up to have a look, just as the Indian paṇḍita was leaving Jomo Labdrön's room. Not at all pleased, the hostess went back down. Later, as she brought up Machig's breakfast, she casually remarked, "Last night, the master of rituals didn't bother you, did he? As it happened, I suddenly thought that the room had caught fire from the butterlamps, and so I came up to see...."

Jomo replied with an impromptu verse:

> I've been deceived by the vulgar prophecies of some malevolent demon.
> When a man and a woman unite, they are flirting with the demon of adverse conditions.
> Even the benefactress has been embarrassed by this situation,
> And I wonder how this could possibly be of any benefit for others.

One week later, Thöpa Bhadra set out on a pilgrimage, while Machig completed her month of thirty recitations of the *Hundred Thousand Lines.* The benefactors, husband and wife, offered her many presents and she returned to Lama Trapa's place. But just before her departure, her hostess took her aside and assured her that she had not mentioned a word about Labdrön's private dealings with Bhadra, not to her husband nor to anyone else, but had maintained strict secrecy. She did not consider the two of them to be ordinary individuals, but had on the contrary developed a most exceptional faith and confidence in them.

Upon her return Labdrön confided to Lama Trapa: "I have been seduced by Thöpa Bhadra."

But the lama reassured her: "Actually that will turn out to be a fortunate thing and benefit beings. Don't be afraid or feel discouraged."

Next, carrying with her all the offerings she had received, she went to meet Sönam Lama and told him she had met Thöpa Bhadra in Echung and had been seduced by him.

"For one thing," he said, "you never took ordination as a nun.[3] Also, this Bhadra is not an ordinary person, so it is not a bad thing and your family lineage will increase. You should live with Bhadra, since, through your karmic connection, good fortune will follow. That will be of great benefit to beings. In fact, last night I had an auspicious dream about it."

Both lamas had given her the same advice and prophecy concerning Bhadra, and it had been confirmed by many other predictions as well, so she decided that, after all, this union with Bhadra might be auspicious. At the age of twenty-three she went to live with Bhadra and they moved to Central Tibet.

2 The Return to Latö

When she was twenty-four, Machig gave birth to a son. Since all the prophecies had now become fulfilled, she called him Drupa, "Fulfilled."

But soon they became an object of slander all over Ü and Tsang. "People systematically avoid us," she said and so they moved to the Dagpo region. They stayed one year at [a place called] Nyangpo, then they moved to Kongpo, and at the age of twenty-five she gave birth to a son whom they named Drupsé, who also became known as Kongpo Kyab, "Protector of Kongpo."

Then, at the age of thirty, just after they had performed a ganacakra at a place called Tradölgo on the Pass of Nga, with numerous ḍākinīs assembled, she gave birth to a daughter and they named her Drupchungma, "Little Accomplishment." Since she was born at Ngala in the gathering place of the ḍākinīs, they also called her Ladüma, "Pass Gathering Girl."

When Machig was thirty-four, they moved again and settled in the Langtang area, in the region of Penyul. One year later, the ḍākinīs made numerous predictions, and she showed signs of being weary of saṃsāric existence.[4] Leaving even her daughter behind, she returned to Latö to meet her two lamas.

From Sönam Lama she requested the heart practice of the five deities of Vārāhī. As a preliminary to the empowerment, she offered him the eight-branch prayer, in the following spontaneous verse:

> Homage with full prostration to the lamas,
> Who teach self-cognizing wisdom.
> Homage with full prostration to the yidam deities,
> Who grant the accomplishments.
> Homage with full prostration to the Buddhas,
> Most excellent in renunciation and realization.

Homage with full prostration to the authentic Dharma teachings,
Which pacify and free from all attachment.
Homage with full prostration to the sangha communities,
To whom offerings are meaningful.
Homage with full prostration to the Dharma protectors,
Who truly clear away obstacles.
To all of you I offer these prayers
Until I reach enlightenment.
To all of you all I go for refuge.
I offer you the enjoyment of the five senses.[5]
All faults and negative actions, each of them I openly confess.
I rejoice in the positive activity of all beings.
I request you to continue turning the wheel of Dharma.
I request you not to pass into nirvāṇa.
All the virtue I have gathered, I dedicate to all sentient beings.

When she offered this eight-branch prayer[6] to her lama, he was most pleased and bestowed on her the full initiation. The lama saw her as a ḍākinī and Labdrön showed signs of true stability in her generation-stage practice of the ḍākinī.[7] Practicing the Highest Yoga of Secret Mantra following the lama's instructions, she soon showed signs of realization. Finally the lama gave her the textual transmission and the practical explanations and gave her the secret name of Vajradhātvīśvarī, "Vajra Sphere Ruling Lady."[8]

To Lama Trapa she offered her understanding of the twelve links of dependent arising and he was most pleased: "These days, nobody can equal your mastery in explanation, practice and profound understanding of twelve links of dependent arising in both evolutionary and reverse order. You have become a great mahāsiddha of this doctrine."

Later, she asked him for a ritual to generate the mind set on enlightenment [*bodhicitta*], but the lama replied: "You don't need to develop bodhicitta, for you are an incomparable mahāsiddha, holder of the Dharma. You are the Great Mother Yum Chenmo who gives birth to all the Buddhas and bodhisattvas. You are Mahā [Buddha] Locanā, the Great Lady endowed with the Buddha Eyes, possessing full mastery in Sūtra and Tantra. You are Mahāmāta, the Great Mother who loves all sentient beings like an only child. You are the Hidden Treasure and the source of liberation of all phenomena. Someone like you does not need to generate the mind of [enlightenment]. In your presence, I'm like a tiny star below the moon. Still, as I have played the part of being your teacher and in order to establish a karmic link between us, I'll perform the ritual."

And so he bestowed on her the bodhicitta ritual as well as the vows of a lay practitioner. During this time she perceived him as Buddha Śākyamuni, with Mañjughoṣa to his right, Avalokiteśvara to his left, and Vajrapāṇi in front.[9] Inspired by this vision of the four deities and their entourage, she offered full prostrations with these words of praise:

> Homage with full prostration to you, omniscient protector
> Resplendent as the gold of the Jambu River.
> Homage with full prostration to you, gentle-voiced Mañjuśrī
> Endowed with excellent qualities of youth.
> Homage with full prostration to you, Avalokiteśvara,
> Embodiment of compassion.
> Homage with full prostration to you, Vajrapāṇi,
> Whose power destroys all demons.

From the lama undifferentiated from the Buddha, she received the textual transmission, and from the ritual vase held by the one-faced and two-armed Avalokiteśvara, white light flowed into her, pervading her entire body. Then five rays of light blazed from the sky-blue sword in Mañjughoṣa's right hand, penetrating her heart and killing her. From the black vajra held by Vajrapāṇi, a multitude of tiny spark-like vajras emanated, destroying all her obstacles.

Right after these experiences, she took the bodhisattva and lay practitioner vows. Finally, the lama advised her to return to Central Tibet; he predicted that on a copper mountain she would accomplish her task for the benefit of her disciples. She asked him if, before leaving for Central Tibet, she could first go to Latö to meet Dampa, and he agreed.

Machig set out for Dingri. By his supernatural perception, Dampa Sangyé knew she was on her way, so he asked everyone to welcome her, and the entire population of Dingri went out to greet her.

Upon meeting Dampa she requested a set of particularly profound instructions, but he replied, "A set of instructions more profound than what I have already given you just doesn't exist. There does exist, however, a profound Sūtrayāna path which is related to the meaning of the Perfections. One ceremoniously invites to a celestial palace the Great Mother Yum Chenmo surrounded by an assembly of her sons, the Buddhas of the ten directions, the Buddhas of the three times, past, present and future, with the eight bodhisattvas, the eight great Śrāvaka Hearers, the great kings of the four directions, the sons and daughters of the gods as well as numerous offering goddesses. Next, one presents the ganacakra and the offerings. By the blessing of this practice, the yogi dissipates all obstacles in this life and eventually attains the supreme siddhi [Buddhahood]."

Machig requested this practice from Dampa and he gave it to her. Laying out a maṇḍala together with vast offerings, he performed the ceremonial invitation with incense and music. Machig distinctly saw the Great Mother Yum Chenmo and her entourage appear in the center of the palace. They granted her blessings and prophecies. Likewise, she saw Dampa as the Red Mañjuśrī and offered him this homage:

> All appearances, every single form as it appears
> Throughout the three thousand worlds
> As a mudrā of supreme body,[10] I present to you in homage.
> Please grant me realization of the immutable body.
>
> All sounds, every voice resounding
> Throughout the three thousand worlds
> As a mudrā of supreme speech, I present to you in homage.
> Please grant me realization of the limitless speech.
>
> All mental phenomena, each thing remembered and understood
> Throughout the three thousand worlds
> As a mudrā of supreme mind, I present to you in homage.
> Please grant me realization of the mind free of confusion.

Pleased by this offering, the lama granted her the complete empowerment, and she perfectly mastered the practice [*sādhana*]. He further gave her the initiation of the blessing of the lamas of the lineage transmission,[11] as well as extraordinary and profound teachings, especially those concerning gathering [the *prāṇa* or winds] in the central channel[12] according to the practical instructions of the inner science. Finally he showed her yogic exercises and various techniques to develop and control the prāṇa.

She remained with him for one and a half months,[13] composing praises about him and Dingri. Dampa predicted that she would subjugate demons in one hundred and eight wild and fearful places—fortresses of local spirits—and gather disciples at Zangri, the Copper Mountain.

3 Zangri, the Copper Mountain

After her departure from Dingri, Machig subjugated one hundred twenty-eight harmful spirits of the snow mountains, including those of Yarlhatsé, Tanglha, Gangri Jomo Jéchen, and Genyen Khari, in the highlands. Next, descending to Lo Mön, she eventually reached Zangri

Khangmar, the Red Fortress of the Copper Mountain. She was then thirty-seven years old.

The spirit who ruled the place, Zangri Khyil [Copper Mountain Whirl, a river nāga], came to request instructions on the generation of the mind of enlightenment and vowed to protect her teachings.

A nun called Chötso [Lake of Dharma] volunteered to act as her personal servant. Chötso and two others, a rich benefactress named Dardrön [Shining Light of Dar] and an elderly man named Katrag [Fame of Ka], had heard a divination predicting that the three of them were to die within a year, and so they requested an initiation from Machig. After they had presented her with the proper offerings, Machig gave them the hundred initiations and ganacakras of the transformation of the ḍākinīs according to the Mother Tantra tradition.[14] This effectively counteracted the untimely death that had been predicted, and Machig Labdrön became famous throughout the entire region for the power of her blessing.

By the time she was forty, stories about her excellent qualities and her reputation resounded like thunder throughout all three provinces of Amdo, Ü and Kham. Her meritorious activity and discipline were extraordinary. The four great kings of the four directions came to request instruction from her, vowing to protect her teachings, and the twelve mountain goddesses[15] vowed to obey her. Five other great mountain spirits—those of Yarlhatsé, Tanglha, Odé Gunggyel, Jomo Jéchen and the nāga king Dakyong—came to request from her instructions on generating the mind of enlightenment. She gave them all the precepts of lay practitioners, and they took the oath never again to harm living beings. They also promised to extend their protection to all lineage holders of Machig's teachings. For a period of twenty-one days they listened to her instructions on refuge and bodhicitta. During all this time, seven field-protecting ḍākinīs were constantly present, and almost everyone there could see them.

Later, many came to see her: the great translator Shübu Lotsāwa accompanied by seventeen of his disciples, Lama Yartipa and twenty-four of his disciples, as well as Tölungpa and thirty-four of his disciples. They held many debates but were unable to defeat Machig in either the scripture or the meaning, and the lamas and their disciples gained faith and confidence in her. They requested instruction from her and later assured everyone that she was truly the majestic Lady Tārā in person. Her fame became boundless, and even all the geshés developed confidence in her. Two teachers in particular, both experts in the Tripiṭaka, one known as Tongdé Dagyi Wangchuk and the other as Dröldé Gyalwé Jungné, came to request instruction from her. Numerous monks did the same, and she became even more well known.

One day the mahāsiddha Pamtingpa came to see her. He asked her many questions about doctrine, and there was not a single one she could not answer. He further questioned her on her realization, her insight, and the propagation of her teaching. Most pleased, he concluded, "It is really wonderful that you, a miraculous emanation of Mahāmāyā, have come to Tibet in order to lead to happiness human and nonhuman beings of the Land of Snows. It fills me with joy, and I offer prostrations and homage to you, with utmost praise!"[16]

Still, in order to establish a Dharma connection between them, Machig asked him for a teaching. Seeing that it would be auspicious, Pamtingpa agreed. He gave her an extensive commentary on the Abhidharma, as well as the entire three cycles of the whispered transmission on Mahāmudrā known as the Stainless Mirror. She took it to heart and fully mastered each topic.

Soon Machig Labdrön became known as the Mother of the Three Worlds, holder of the extraordinary doctrine of the Chöd of Mahāmudrā, a particular set of instructions which destroys the four hundred and twenty-four kinds of diseases and the eighty thousand kinds of demonic forces [*bgegs*][17] and leads to Buddhahood. Her fame spread like a wind throughout the world.

4 Ārya Tārā

At the age of forty-one, Machig Labdrön stayed in a retreat cave in Chipug which was blessed for practice. On the fourth day of the last month of spring, in the middle of the night, the majestic Lady Tārā appeared, surrounded by numerous ḍākinīs. She bestowed on Machig the four initiations of the five primordial Buddhas according to the *Uḍumvara Tantra.*[18] During the ritual Tārā manifested successively as the consort of each of them. Then she gave the following prophecies:

> Yoginī, I give you this secret empowerment of the five Buddha families called the *Pacification of the Five Poisons and the Union of the Nāgas.*[19] You will be able to transmute the five poisons into the five wisdoms of the five primordial Buddhas. Use this powerful technique for accomplishing the benefit of all beings. Fortunate Yoginī, secretly practice these profound Vajrayāna teachings, the *Uḍumvara Tantra* and the one called *The Quintessence that Dispels the Darkness of Ignorance.*[20] Preserve in a single tradition the generation and

> completion stages[21] of these two sets of teachings, which are the very heart of Vajrayāna. Through this tradition, your lineage will reach liberation. From now on the holders of your lineage will be like a rosary of pearls and within ten generations, this Vajrayāna tradition will be perfected in the vastness space.
>
> Yoginī, I hereby bestow on you the entire domain of Secret Mantra [Skt. *guhya-mantra*], Memorization Mantra [Skt. *dhāranī-mantra*] and Knowledge Mantra [Skt. *vidhyā-mantra*][22] and enthrone you as its sovereign. In the center of the maṇḍala palace, you are the dark-blue secret ḍākinī of the Vajra Family, the Great Wisdom, the Vajra Lady who subjugates all demons, Vajradhātvīśvarī, Lady ruling over the Vajradhātu,[23] who brings all ḍākinīs under her power. Secretly with your male consort Heruka, and using your khaṭvāṅga, practice the secret yogic conduct. Introduce into this maṇḍala those fortunate sentient beings who have suitable capacities and assist them in their spiritual development and liberation.

Thereupon Machig composed a hymn of praise to each of the five Buddha families and later improvised another one in twenty-one stanzas to Tārā herself. She then addressed Tārā as follows: "You have shown me great kindness and given me the most extraordinary power of initiation and blessing. Yet I don't know if a woman like me, not particularly bright, and of feeble capacities, will be able to accomplish the benefit of beings." Just as this thought came to her, she added: "Please keep me under your protection."

Tārā smiled, then after a quick glance at the ḍākinīs of her entourage, she said: "Yoginī, do not feel discouraged! In the course of previous lives you have studied and mastered the meaning of the scriptures of Sūtra and Tantra. So today it is sufficient for me to reveal this meaning to you through mere symbols.[24] You are a mind emanation of the Great Mother Yum Chenmo: we are inseparable. You are the wisdom ḍākinī, the sovereign of the Vajradhātu and the source of the liberation of all phenomena.[25] Don't lose heart. Keep your determination."

But Machig replied: "How could I possibly be an emanation of the Great Mother, inseparable from you? And in what way am I the source of the liberation of all phenomena? And where is the residence of the Great Mother?"

Tārā answered, "Yoginī, although in your innermost heart there is clear knowledge about the past, listen carefully and I'll explain it to you. The one known as the primordial Mother Yum Chenmo is the ultimate nature of all phenomena, emptiness, the essence of reality [*dharmatā*] free from the two veils. She is the pure expanse of emptiness, the knowledge of the non-self. She is the matrix which gives birth to all the Buddhas of the three times.

"However, so as to enable all sentient beings to accumulate merit, the Great Mother appears as an object of veneration through my aspirations and prayers for the sake of all beings. And so, through the power of my wishes and compassion, from the dharmatā there appears bright light in the shape of an orange-colored bindu marked with the syllable *MUM*, ablaze with light. In turn this transforms into the Great Mother Yum Chenmo, golden in color, with one face and four hands, sitting in the vajra posture, her body beautiful with all the major and minor marks of a Buddha. Surrounded by her princely sons, the Buddhas and bodhisattvas of the ten directions, Yum Chenmo resides in the Gaṇḍavyūha sphere of the celestial pure land of Akaniṣṭha,[26] in a marvelous celestial palace.

"From my heart there radiates a greenish-black ray of light marked with the syllable *HUNG* and it enters into the Mother's heart, awakening her. Then it radiates out again, gathering the power of the Buddhas and bodhisattvas of the ten directions and it dissolves again into the Mother's heart. Instantly, she transforms into a sky-blue ḍākinī with one face and four hands. She is the sovereign of the Vajradhātu. From her body, speech, mind, qualities and activity appear innumerable manifestations. Among these, the mind emanation is the bluish-black Vajra Lady with one face and two hands who subjugates all demons. On the crown of her head is a boar's head emerging from her hair. Her splendor illuminating the three worlds, she gathers all the ḍākinīs under her power. She sets all demonic forces to work as her servants; she is the source of the liberation of all phenomena.

"Now this Vajra Lady, who subjugates all demons for the sake of all sentient beings, took numerous births in appropriate times and places. She mastered the Piṭakas and accomplished tremendous deeds for the sake of living beings. Finally she took birth in Tibet. She is no other than yourself, Shining Light of Lab."[27]

Machig replied, "O great majestic Lady, from your words a light shines in my mind and it all comes back to me now! As for all the Secret Mantra teachings that you have granted me, when I have taught and explained them, and they have become a source of benefit for beings, will they be further propagated and continue?"

"Those profound instructions of Secret Mantra's Highest Yoga Tantra are not suitable to be explained in public or practiced openly. They should be practiced secretly and taught individually to those who have the capacity to receive them and to reach liberation through their practice.

"Among these teachings combine with your transmission activity the exceptional means of the four mudrās in the way I have taught them to you, and the view of the heart of Prajñāpāramitā. Indeed the Buddha himself has predicted that the age of strife is the time for you to tame both humans and non-humans in the Land of Snows. Yoginī, your teaching will continue to spread, and you will attain the stage of no return."

From Tārā's heart innumerable rays of light radiated, pervading all the directions of space, and then melted, dissolving into Machig's heart. Thereupon Tārā, together with her entourage, dissolved into celestial light that filled all of space, and it was dawn.

5 Machig's Children

As Machig was on her way to Zangri, the Black Protector, dressed in a wide robe of black silk, and the rock-god protector Dralha Gompo came to welcome her, each surrounded by his entourage. In their company she reached the Red Fortress.

One night when Machig was forty-two, she had a dream: "As I was walking in a large flower garden, on top of a flower with a thousand petals having the nature of multicolored light, I saw Kyotön Sönam Lama. His body was white and like a rainbow. Dampa Sangyé was on the crown of his head, and crowning Dampa's head was Vajradhara. To his right was Red Mañjuśrī and to his left, Āryadeva; behind him was Sukhasiddhī, and the majestic Lady Tārā was in front. Free from inherent nature, they appeared to me in their enjoyment bodies. They granted me their blessings and the siddhis of body, speech and mind. They also bestowed numerous ritual transmissions.[28] Surrounding me, in each of the four directions, were four white ḍākinīs blowing white conch shells. Their sound reached out to the four continents. I awoke to that sound."

The next day, at noon, her youngest son and daughter arrived, accompanied by their father. Husband and wife compared their meditational insights and realizations, and they also prayed for each other. Later they improvised songs for each other's well-being. Then Thöpa Bhadra left for India.[29]

Her son Drupsé was fifteen years old then. He had received from his father the cycles of Cakrasaṃvara, Padmasambhava and

Akṣobhya, as well as the secret means of achievement for Vajravidaraṇa and the Black Hayagrīva.

Her daughter Ladüma was only ten years old, but she already knew the means of achievement of Red Mañjuśrī and Mahākarunika, the great compassionate one [Avalokiteśvara in the form of] Khasarpaṇi. She could also read the *Twenty-Five Thousand* and the *Hundred Thousand* [-line] versions of the Prajñāpāramitā.

Drupsé suffered from attacks of insanity, after which he would faint. Machig gave him a set of specific instructions called The Precious Light That Utterly Pacifies All Suffering, then had him sleep for seven days in a charnel ground. Drupsé was cured of his insanity and a most extraordinary realization was born in him. Machig then passed on to him the entire cycle of these instructions, which he fully mastered.

Shortly afterward, Machig invited Dampa Sangyé to Zangri. In preparation for Drupsé's monastic ordination, she organized a great religious festival. Machig insisted on choosing his monastic name herself. When Dampa asked her the reason, she said: "I would like this name to be an auspicious connection for the future. His father is called Thöpa, and my son has just been cured from a disease that had taken away his sanity. From you, Dampa, essence of the Buddhas of the three times, he will now receive monastic ordination. So that all his wishes may be fulfilled, we will call him Thönyön Samdrup, Crazy Son of Thöpa Whose Intentions are Fulfilled. He has all the qualities to become the holder of my lineage. I know this because I had a dream in which four white ḍākinīs were blowing white conches whose sound pervaded the four continents. He arrived the same day."

Dampa Sangyé gave Thönyön Samdrup the ritual transmission of Mañjuśrī as his personal yidam deity. He also bestowed on him the full empowerments for the fivefold Majestic Lady [Vārāhī], and the five deities of Mahāmāyā. He further gave him the full explanation of the Guru Yoga as well as the instructions called The Liberation of the Six Consciousnesses According to the Śāstras. And he predicted, "In the future, you will become the principal lineage holder of Machig's teachings, and you will accomplish the welfare of living beings on a vast scale!"

A great thanksgiving offering was presented to Dampa Rinpoché, who then returned to Latö.

From that time on Thönyön Samdrup felt a profound veneration for Dampa Rinpoché. He used to say Dampa was his father and three times day and night he would, with one-pointed concentration, pray to both Pa Dampa [Saintly Father] and Ma Chig [Unique Mother]. As a result Dampa soon became known as Pa Dampa.

Around that time, her eldest son Drupa married a daughter of the Goyak family from the region of Arawa. He soon took to the Arawa style of living, in which there is no place for Dharma.

When Machig saw that Thönyön was ready, she gave him the four empowerments of meditative stabilization, an initiation of the ultimate meaning [of Dharma directly] transmitted to the mind in the Prajñāpāramitā tradition.[30] She also gave him the complete instructions on transference of consciousness, known as the direct acquaintance [with the nature of mind] through the technique of Opening the Gates of Space, together with all the essential commentaries. She transmitted to him the complete sets of the hundred empowerments on the transformation of the buddhas of the ten directions, the hundred empowerments on the transformation of the ḍākinīs, according to the Mother Tantras, and the hundred empowerments of the tormas [ritual cakes].[31]

She taught him to train his mind by means of the generation stage, and his spiritual development greatly increased. After four months he attained stability [in the visualizations]. Then he practiced the completion stage for three months and obtained the sign of realization known as warmth. In both generation and completion practices he showed formidable abilities, and she further passed on to him the cycles of the Chöd of Mahāmudrā according to her own Dharma tradition. For these, too, he showed a remarkable predisposition and took all her instructions to heart.

When he was sixteen, Machig told him: "Go and meditate at Zhampo-gang, for that is where you have an auspicious connection." So Thönyön Samdrup went there with three companions.

One month later, early at dawn, Machig, by her supernatural powers, sailed through the air and by daybreak reached Zhampo-gang where she laid out offerings for a vast ganacakra. Her son arrived at noon and she said, "Aren't the four of you tired from the journey?"

Her son replied, "No, we're all right and we're happy that you have come to join us."

Machig then passed on to her son the grand initiation of the oral transmission's blessings, the grand initiation of the five Buddha families, and the empowerment for the secret practice of the five deities of Vārāhī. She further taught him in detail the root verses of the whispered transmission and gave him the corresponding instructions.

Thönyön Samdrup, one of Machig's sons and holder of the Tantra tradition of Chöd. Drawing by Dolpopa Tenzin Norbu.

She stayed with her son for seven days, blessing the place and the cave. Innumerable ḍākas and ḍākinīs gathered and her son saw her as Vajravārāhī. Rains of flowers, sounds of celestial music and other wondrous signs such as rainbows appeared. She ordered the local spirits of Zhampo not to cause any hindrances to her son's practice, and made them vow to assist him during his retreat. Then she entrusted a ḍākinī of the lotus family called Drimema [Stainless Lady] with the task of acting as his benefactress and looking after his needs, and the ḍākinī promised to act accordingly. Finally, Machig told Thönyön, "Remain in retreat for thirteen years. Transform your aggregates, elements and sources of perception[32] into the palace of the deity.[33] Meditate on this Buddha's pure land until it dawns in your mind, and you have attained stability in your visualization. Throughout this entire period, the benefactress will remain here and take care of your needs."

Thönyön thereupon entered the cave and sat down on a cushion of grass in the sevenfold posture of Vairocana.[34] Then the cave was walled up so that no one could see him. Together with the assembly of ḍākinīs, Machig then rose into the air and returned to Zangri.

Three months had gone in this way when Thönyön Samdrup started to feel hungry and thirsty.

"Mother told me about a benefactress who was to look after my provisions, but I haven't seen anyone so far. On the other hand, through my mother's blessing, this place is now a sacred spot. Since I am under her protection, I'll probably have to sustain myself on the food of meditative absorption, so I guess I won't die of hunger!"

While he was thinking this, suddenly a figure appeared seeming to ride the rays of the sun, a red girl of the utmost splendor who handed him a small cup and said, "Meditator, this is nectar. If you drink this, you'll be able to successfully conclude your practice."

He drank the nectar, rich with a hundred tastes, and his entire body was pervaded by intense bliss, so that all craving for ordinary food vanished. He thought, "Could this be a wisdom ḍākinī? Maybe I should tell her about the signs of warmth that have occurred in my practice?"

But she spoke: "I am merely the one who was told by Machig to look after your needs. In no way am I your spiritual teacher, so don't tell me about your meditation experiences. Hide them instead as a treasure in suchness. If doubts should again disturb you, observe and examine your mind, and with reasoning, cut through them. Achieve the absolute union of view and action, and unite multiplicity into one taste!"

Having said this, she disappeared. But she returned every three years with provisions.

Five years had gone by when Machig sent a yogin to go and see whether Thönyön was still alive.

The yogin reached the cave entrance and called out to Thönyön. In response, he heard the sound of the syllable *A*.

"It's your mother who has sent me out here to inquire after you. Aren't you hungry or thirsty? Any trouble?"

Thönyön replied, "You had a good journey? Glad to hear that my mother is in good health. I am sustaining myself with the food of meditative absorption and no longer crave ordinary food, so how could I feel hungry? Wearing the robes of inner heat, all desire for clothing has subsided as well. Having all appearances for company, I have no longing for friends. Wherever I look, I enjoy the view of Buddhas and pure lands, so I have no longing to be anywhere else."

The yogin returned and told Machig what he had learned and she rejoiced in the great qualities of her son.

6 The Indian Ācāryas

By that time, the number of Machig's disciples had become as vast as space. All confided in her—from Amdo, Kham and Central Tibet came great lamas under their banners and their followers, geshés and simple monks, kings and nobles, ministers and queens and even wild Mongols, nuns and lay people, both male and female, lepers and beggars, some fortunate in every respect, some victims of every conceivable misfortune. So she was constantly surrounded by an entourage of some five thousand people of every rank and origin. They even came to visit her from Nepal in large numbers, and the reputation of her incredible personal discipline and Dharma expertise eventually reached India.

At Bodhgaya in India, the paṇḍitas held a council to examine this new source of Dharma.

"We have heard rumors about an unknown religious tradition recently introduced as the Chöd of Mahāmudrā. Its influence has spread throughout Tibet, Kham and Nepal. It claims to pacify and cut through the four hundred and four diseases and the eighty thousand demonic influences. Its founder is said to be a woman with three eyes who is considered to be an emanation of the Great Mother of Wisdom. Either she is indeed an emanation of the Mother Prajñāpāramitā, or she is Māra or some other evil spirit incarnate, in which case she will be difficult to subjugate. Moreover, it is equally difficult to know how to do so, for after having perverted the whole of Tibet, she is quite capable of contaminating India as well. We should therefore send someone out to Tibet to assess the situation."

While all agreed with the idea, the next question was whom to send. It had to be not only one very learned but also realized, someone endowed with magical powers, and he must be powerful enough to come back to India without falling under this woman's spell.

So three powerful yogins were chosen, and they took off like Mongol hunting falcons let loose. They rose up into the sky, and by sunrise the next day reached the hermitage at Zangri Khangmar. Machig's attendant Sönam Gyen noticed them first and told her, "Right above our hermitage there are three men of bluish complexion, with piercing eyes and black silken shoulder blankets. They're definitely not from around here. They're Nepalis or something."

"They're swift-footed travellers from India. Prepare them some fine seats," Machig told her. Sönam Gyen laid out triple-cushion seats, and Machig told her to let them in. Upon the attendant's inviting gesture, the three entered and sat down. In the language of India Machig inquired about their health. She further asked them various questions about recent events in their country, still in the language of India. They answered all her questions and, in turn, asked her, "How do you know our language?"

"I have often taken birth in India, and so I also learned the language!"

"You mean that you also remember your previous lives?"

"I know my present, past and future lives."

The ācāryas thereupon insisted that she tell them about her lives, but Machig realized that if she were to explain all of that to them in the language of India, her disciples wouldn't understand a word.

"Since these three Indians obviously want to debate and hear about my previous lives, I would rather have the Tibetans benefit from it as well. Therefore, our conversations should be translated into the languages of India, Nepal and Tibet."

While extending her hospitality to the three ācāryas, messengers were dispatched all the way to Amdo, Central Tibet and Kham, as well as to Nepal, informing one and all about the imminent debate between Machig and the ācāryas, in which she would also give a full account of her previous and future lives. Anyone who wished to attend was asked to bring along a month's provisions.

A crowd of 500,573 eventually assembled. Among them were four erudite translators who had come from India. When Machig started to teach Dharma, she also opened her own doors to help feed the crowd, which included some seventy thousand members of the sangha. With the lotsāwas translating, the three ācāryas fired off their questions to Machig, who answered them flawlessly and could not be defeated. They said, "All the Dharma teachings come from India, and it has never been said that any will originate in Tibet."

"That is true, India is the source of all the Buddhas and their teachings. Please tell us in detail the circumstances and time in which the Buddhas appeared, the various teachings they gave and their motivation to give them."

The three ācāryas were puzzled: "We don't know when exactly the Buddhas appeared, which cycle of teachings they gave, and how they guided their disciples. But if you know, please tell us."

Machig spoke for a full seven days, with the four translators barely managing to keep up with her. Then the ācāryas inquired, "This is very nice indeed, but do you have any means to prove your claim about recollecting your previous births? And can you prove the authenticity of your doctrine?"

Machig now addressed all present: "Listen carefully, all of you assembled here. The Indians have no confidence in either myself or my teachings. So they've sent these three ācāryas here to test me. 'Let's check this doctrine of yours,' they tell me, 'and if you do indeed recollect your previous lives, well, let's hear about them!' Obviously, if I can't provide sufficient proof and justify my Dharma teachings, not only the people of India, but also my own disciples, as well as all of you who have come here and everyone else in the Land of Snows will lose confidence in my instructions. If I don't give an account of my previous lives, no one will believe me anymore. So all of you listen carefully!

"First of all, I've studied the Buddha's precepts in their extensive, medium and abbreviated versions. Then, having demonstrated liberation by means of his words, I have composed *The Great Collection of [Chöd] Precepts*."[35]

Machig taught the full cycle of the *Great Collection of Chöd Precepts*, followed by descriptions of all the meditative experiences that had flowered in her mind. She further described the teachings received from her lamas and their spiritual lineage, the transmissions obtained from yidam deities such as Tārā, and the various prophecies they had made. Then, concerning her previous lives, she explained how through the kindness of Tārā, the Vajradhātu ḍākinī had appeared from the heart of the Great Mother Yum Chenmo, and had taken one hundred and seven human births, the last one being the present Shining Light of Lab.

"In the life preceding this one, I took birth in India, as paṇḍita Pranidhāna Siddhi and meditated in the Bhadra Cave at Potari. By the blessing of majestic Tārā, this previous body of mine remains there even now. It is still intact, without having lost its splendor or youthful appearance. If you cremate this body in white sandalwood, a sweet perfume will pervade the entire region, celestial music will resound, and precious victory banners, umbrellas, and all sorts of offerings will come down with a rain of multicolored flowers. Besides rainbows and lights filling the sky, you will see numerous extraordinary signs. On the skull there will appear, forming a diadem and as if embossed, the five Buddhas with Vairocana the Resplendent at the center, each of them embracing one of the five goddesses such as Buddha Locanā. On each vertebra there will appear a stupa of Total Victory. Each of the teeth will be marked by a clockwise spiralling conch shell. On the jaw you will see a white syllable *A*. At the waist you will see the protectors of the three classes of beings, at the shoulders the white and green Tārās, at the heart the Buddha Śākyamuni with Vajradhara in the center of his chest. All around the body you will find numerous multicolored relics the size of nuts.

"If everything I have just described does not happen like that, then my words are but a web of lies. You three paṇḍitas from India, go and verify my statements and return once you have made sure. As for myself, I have accomplished half of my work here on earth for the happiness of beings. I am fifty-two years old. At the age of ninety-nine[36] I'll leave for the Akaniṣṭha pure land, thereby demonstrating the transference of consciousness."[37]

All those who had witnessed the debate and listened to her teaching and retelling of her previous lives were moved by a deep faith in her words, and all their doubts were dispelled. However, in order to cut through the controversy once and for all, they asked Dampa Sangyé to come and asked him to accompany the three yogins to India. For the sake of beings in the Land of Snows, they asked him to bring back some of the relics mentioned by Machig. Dampa agreed and left for India right away with the three ācāryas. The assembly dispersed and everyone went home.

At Bodhgaya, Dampa and the ācāryas called together all the Indians and reported Machig's words, without leaving out anything. They decided to travel to Potari in order to verify her claims. Fifty-two paṇḍitas were sent to the cave, where they found the body intact, exactly as Machig had foretold. They cremated it in accordance with her instructions, and as the relics appeared, they exclaimed, "This Machig really is an emanation of the Wisdom Mother. No doubt about it! We should definitely invite her here, for these barbarians of Tibet are not worthy of her and her incarnation may just disappear!" They shared out the relics among them as objects of devotion, and the diadem of the five Buddhas was preserved at Bodhgaya. Dampa and the three yogins set out for Zangri, carrying with them the heart relic shaped as a Buddha image.

Upon their arrival, they offered Machig homage with full prostrations, circumambulated her three times, and presented her with vast offerings.

"Machig Labdrön, marvelous Wisdom Mother, each of your words proved true, without a single error. We also brought you the Buddha image found among the bodily relics."

All those present, assembled from Amdo, Central Tibet and Kham, were filled with joy and she gave her blessing to all. Dampa asked to keep the relic as a support for his personal meditation, and he carried it with him to Latö.

Indians and Tibetans alike were moved by an unshakeable faith, and even her detractors, now divested of any lingering doubts, offered her homage. In this way the Chöd doctrine which eradicates demonic forces became famous and was propagated throughout Tibet and India. When the Indians extended their invitation to come and settle in India, Machig replied, "For me to go to India would not in any way benefit beings. The moment has now come to guide my able disciples here in Tibet. In the course of this present life, I won't go to India. You are Indian, and India is the source of all the Buddhas and their teachings. At present, the Buddhism of India is being propagated in Tibet and this is the place to make it prosper. Previously, not a single teaching of Tibet became famous in India. Since I have often taken birth in your country, we have karmic connections. This time I have been born in Tibet where I teach a precious tradition unknown to you, called the Chöd of Mahāmudrā. This tradition which is now famous in even the remotest valleys of the Land of Snows should be transmitted to you also."

In this way, the extraordinary teachings born in Machig's mind were brought to India.

Machig studied and realized the concise, medium and extensive words of the Buddha. She perfectly studied the chapter on demons, in particular teachings such as:

> Attachment to any phenomenon whatsoever,
> From coarse form to omniscience,
> Should be understood as the play of a demon.

and:

> Form is neither white,
> Red, blue nor green....
> Form is devoid of presence,
> Devoid of appearance,
> Devoid of cessation.

and:

> All phenomena are equanimity;
> The Perfection of Wisdom herself is equanimity.

and so forth. Having obtained liberation through these teachings, she gained the extraordinary experience of naturally eliminating the four demons,[38] and then taught these extremely profound experiences through texts such as (1) *The Great Collection of [Chöd] Precepts*; (2) *The Great Collection of the Advanced [Precepts]*; (3) *The Great Collection of the Quintessence [of Chöd Precepts]*; (4) *The Appendices*; (5) *The Series of Pith Instructions*; (6) *Answers to Detractors*; (7) *The Secret Sign Teachings*; (8) *The Three Cycles of Recitation*; (9) *Using the Ground as the Path*; and (10) *Particular Oral Instructions*.[39] These ten texts were taken to India. The Indians, now moved by a sincere faith in this teaching, practiced it too, and in this way, a Tibetan tradition was propagated in India.

This tradition, born from Machig's meditative experiences, branched out from her in different lineages, some in the family line through her sons and daughters, some as the spiritual lineages of the hundred and sixteen holders of her teachings, and so on, but of all these lineages she is the one and only source.[40]

The numerous Perfection of Wisdom teachings which she passed on in a non-systematic way allowed 1,263 disciples to gain maturity and reach liberation. Among them were Tongdé Dagyi Wangchuk, Dröldé Gyalwé Jungné and her sixteen main disciples, holders of her tradition. They, in turn, became an inexhaustible source of benefit for others. Machig, furthermore, helped innumerable patients suffering from physical and mental disease, and completely cured 437 lepers, all of whom regained their earlier features. She guided them on the path to liberation, which became the source of inconceivable benefits.

Finally, at the age of ninety-nine, Machig entered the sphere of bliss.

When he was forty-two, her son Drupa had run into trouble and come to see her. Having noticed that he was ready for spiritual progress, she had instructed him. He had taken the vows of a lay practitioner under the name of Gyalwa Döndrup. At the age of forty-eight, he attained realization and showed great creativity, expressing his realization in spiritual songs.

Gyalwa Döndrup had two sons: the eldest, Tsangwang Gyel, married; and the younger, Khambu Yalé, became a monk. Tsangwang in turn had three sons, the eldest named Dampa Tönchung and the youngest, Kyémé Ösel Chenpo. As for the middle son, known as Thönyön Samdrup, during a debate which left him speechless, his daughter was born. She was named Lentogma [Lightning Reply] and was an emanation of Machig Labdrön. She propagated the Chöd of Mahāmudrā and the lineage flourished all the more.

Statue of the standing Machig Labdrön, located in her meditation cave at Zangri Khangmar. Photo: J. Edou.

Machig's Last Instructions

Then Machig spoke:[1]

For ninety-nine years, I have worked for the benefit of beings.
Now this work is almost complete.
I will not take birth again in this human realm in a physical form,
Nor will I leave behind any remains or relics.
But my emanations in the world will be innumerable;
And many will recognize them.
They will be perceived in different ways,
Depending on karma, pure or impure.
Understand this, my sons.

Fortunate sons, keep this in your heart.
My instructions on Chöd
Are the authentic teaching of Mahāmudrā [*phyag rgya chen po*].
This Mahāmudrā cannot be explained in words.
It cannot be explained, but it is like this:

Phyag is the nature of emptiness [of the mind].
Gya is liberation from the vastness of saṃsāric [appearances].
Chen po is the inseparable union [of appearances and emptiness].
Primordially co-emergent, [this inseparability] like empty space
Does nothing, is not dependent on anything.

In the same way, mind itself, [natural and co-emergent]
Has no support, has no object:
Let it rest in its natural expanse without any fabrication.
When the bonds [of negative thoughts] are released,
You will be free, there is no doubt.

As when gazing into space,
All other visual objects disappear,
So it is for mind itself.
When mind is looking at mind,

All discursive thoughts cease
And enlightenment is attained.

As in the sky all clouds
Disappear into sky itself:
Wherever they go, they go nowhere,
Wherever they are, they are nowhere.
This is the same for thoughts in the mind:
When mind looks at mind,
The waves of conceptual thought disappear.

As empty space
Is devoid of form, color or image,
So too, mind itself
Is free of form, color or image.

As the heart of the sun
Cannot be veiled by an eternity of darkness
So too, the realization of the ultimate nature of the mind
Cannot be veiled by an eternity of saṃsāra.

Even though empty space
May be named or conventionally defined,
It is impossible to point it out as "this."
It is the same for the clarity of mind itself:
Although its characteristics may be expressed,
It cannot be pointed out as "this."

The defining characteristic of mind
Is to be primordially empty like space;
The realization of the nature of the mind
Includes all phenomena without exception.

Once discursive thoughts are totally abandoned,
Dharmakāya is no other than that.
Once the five poisons are totally abandoned,
The five wisdoms are no other than that.

Once the three poisons are totally abandoned,
The three kāyas are no other than that.
Once conventional mind is totally abandoned,
Buddhahood is no other than that.

Once saṃsāra is totally abandoned
Nirvāṇa is no other than that.
Once mental agitation is totally abandoned,
Skillful means are no other than that.

Once emptiness is totally abandoned,
Discriminating wisdom [*prajñā*] is no other than that.
Once mind is totally abandoned,
Fearsome places are no other than that.

Once virtue and non-virtue are totally abandoned,
Gods and demons are no other than that.
Once the six consciousnesses are totally abandoned,
The six classes of beings are no other than that.
Once the eight consciousnesses are totally abandoned,
The eight armies of demons are no other than that.

Once wandering thoughts are totally abandoned,
Magical displays are no other than that,
Meditative absorption is no other than that,
The practice of the four daily sessions is no other than that.

Once discursive thoughts are totally abandoned,
The practice of Chöd is no other than that.
Once mindfulness is achieved,
The level of final accomplishment is no other than that.
Once the [ultimate nature] of the mind is realized,
The definitive sign of realization is no other than that.

Abandoning all bodily activities,
Remain like a bunch of straw cut loose.
Abandoning all verbal expressions of speech,
Remain like a lute with its strings cut through.
Abandoning all mental activity,
That is Mahāmudrā.

In the Dharma tradition of this old lady
There is nothing to do other than this.

Ah, fortunate sons and disciples gathered here,
This body of ours is impermanent like a feather on a high mountain pass,
This mind of ours is empty and clear like the depth of space.
Relax in that natural state, free of fabrication.
When mind is without any support, that is Mahāmudrā.
Becoming familiar with this, blend your mind with it—
That is Buddhahood.

You may recite mantras, be diligent in offering tormas,
Be versed in the entire Tripiṭaka teachings,
Including the Vinaya and the philosophical schools with their respective tenets,
But it will not make you realize Mahāmudrā, the nature of the mind.

Attached to your own point of view,
You merely obscure the clear light of your mind.
Protecting vows which are merely conceptual
Harms samaya in the ultimate sense.
Remain free of mental fabrications, free of consideration for yourself.

Like the waves in the water, naturally arising, naturally subsiding,
Without conceptualizations, without abiding in extreme [views].
In the primordial purity of mind,
There is no transgression of your samaya.
Free of desire and attachment and of extreme [views],
Like a single light dispelling the darkness,
You realize at once the teachings of Sūtra, Tantra and all other scriptures.

If you aspire to this path, you will be free from the infinity of saṃsāra.
If you enter this path, you will defeat all mental afflictions without exception.
If you achieve this path, you will attain the highest enlightenment.

Those who don't aim for this are deluded fools.
Those who don't enter this path are in darkness like the blind
And certain to be carried away by the river of saṃsāra's suffering.
This suffering is unbearable—have compassion for these fools.

If you wish to be freed from the suffering of saṃsāra,
At all times rely on a qualified lama, an erudite and realized spiritual friend.
Pray to the lama with respect and devotion,
Serve the lama well and request the oral instructions.
Having analyzed the master's words, practice accordingly.
Once the blessing has entered your heart,
You will come to recognize [the true nature of] your mind.

Alas, the phenomena of saṃsāra have no essence.
They are the cause of the suffering we experience
Which increases and remains.
Don't you realize that this life is being spent in agitation?
If you imagine you will practice Dharma when you have the leisure,
You will lose this opportunity.
Human life is wasted in the thought, "I will practice Dharma later."
What would happen if you were to die in an accident?
If you don't meditate with perseverance now,
And if you died tomorrow, who then would provide you with authentic Dharma?

If you don't do it yourself,
What good will the Dharma practice of others do you?
It is like a beggar's dream,
In which he is rich in splendor, food and wealth.
Upon awakening all is gone without a trace,

Like the passing of a bird in the sky.
All composite phenomena in the world are just like that.

Right now you have the opportunity.
Look for the essence of mind—this is meaningful.
When you look at mind, there's nothing to be seen.
In this very not seeing, you see the definitive meaning.

Supreme view is beyond all duality of subject and object.
Supreme meditation is without distraction.
Supreme activity is action without effort.
Supreme fruition is without hope and fear.

Supreme view is free from reference point.
Supreme meditation is beyond conceptual mind.
Supreme activity is practice without doing.
Supreme fruition is beyond all extremes.

If you realize this, enlightenment is attained.
If you enter this path [of Mahāmudrā], you will reach the essential nature.
You cut wrong conceptions about inner, outer and in between,
You understand all the teachings of the higher and lower paths,
You defeat the 84,000 kleśas,
You perfect simultaneously the symptoms,
The sign [of realization] and the level of final accomplishment
And you cross over the ocean of saṃsāra.

This old lady has no instructions more profound than this to give you.

Thus she spoke.

Then, on the morning of the fifteenth day in the sixth month of the Fire-Monkey year,[2] just as the sun rose glittering on the mountain top, Machig spoke: "All of my disciples, gather here. Prepare an excellent ganacakra to please all the ḍākas and ḍākinīs. For ninety-nine years, I have done vast amounts of work for the benefit of beings. Now I'm going to the realm of Khecari."

Her body shone with a blaze of pink light that emanated like sun rays, and then it rose about one cubit into space, from where she spoke:

My authentic teaching, the unique doctrine of the unborn,
Is the greatest of all systems of profound instructions.
This separation of body and mind and its blessing
Is the greatest of all transferences of consciousness.
This offering of the bodily aggregates
Is the greatest of all banquets.
This wandering in mountain solitudes and fearsome places
Is the greatest of all monasteries.

This entourage of illusory gods and demons
Is the greatest of all benefactors.
This practice free of the extremes of hope and fear
Is the greatest of all virtuous activities.
This action, the unobstructed experience of single taste
Is the greatest of all paths of action.
This essence of ultimate meaning, beyond thought and
expression,
Is the greatest of all Dharma practices.

I, Labdrön, the Shining Light of Lab,
Am the greatest of all women.
Now my death in the unborn expanse
Is the greatest of all ways to pass away.

Three times with a thundering voice she spoke the syllable *PHAT*. Then without moving away from the essence of reality, her mind left her body through the brahmanic aperture and in a rainbow disappeared into the vastness of space. Thus she departed into the expanse of suchness.

Abbreviations

Banquet
Pawo Tsuglag Trengwa
Dharma History: A Banquet for the Learned
Chos 'byung mkhas pa'i dga' ston

A Biography of Machig
Anonymous
Ma gcig ma'i rnam thar

The Blue Annals
Gö Lotsāwa
Deb ther sngon po

The Chöd Lineage of Ganden
Lobsang Zöpa
The Ruby Rosary: A Chronological Account of the Chöd Instructions, Means and Wisdom according to the Hearing Lineage of Ganden
dGa' ldan snyam brgyud kyi thabs shes gcod kyi gdams pa'i byung rabs pad rag gi 'phreng ba

Compendium
Jamgön Kongtrul Lodrö Thayé
Compendium of Knowledge
Shes bya kun khyab

The Concise Life Story
Kunpang Tsöndrü Sengé
The Concise Life Story of Machig Labdrön, Derived from An Exposition of Transforming the Aggregates into an Offering of Food
Phung po gzan skyur ba'i rnam par bshad pa las ma gcig lab sgron ma'i rnam par thar pa mdor msdus tsam zhig

Definitive Instructions
Karma Chagmé
Abiding in the Middle: Slightly Abridged Definitive Instructions on Chöd
gCod kyi gdengs bshad nyung ngur bsdud pa bzhugs pa'i dbu phyogs

The Fording Place

Jamyang Shényen

A Chöd Guide from Barpa College, Called 'A Fording Place for the Fortunate': The Heart Essence of Oral Instructions that are Uncommon and Kept Secret in other Tenet Systems

Bar pa grwa tshang gi gcod khrid skal ldan 'jug ngogs zhes bya ba thun mong min pa grub mtha' gzhan la gsang ba man ngag gi snying po

The Grand Poem

Āryadeva the Brahmin

The Grand Poem on the Perfection of Wisdom

Shes rab kyi pha rol tu phyin pa'i tshigs su bcad pa chen mo

Great Collection

Machig Labdrön

The Great Collection of [Chöd] Precepts

bKa' tshom chen mo

Guide

Jamyang Kyentsé Wangpo

A Seed of Faith: A Rough Outline of the Sacred Spots and Images of Ü-Tsang

dBus gtsang gi gnas rten rags rim gyi mtshan byang mdor bsdus dad pa'i sa bon

Heart Essence

Karmapa IX, Wangchuk Dorjé

Radiating the Light of the Activity: A Profound Commentary on the Heart Essence of the Ocean of Definitive Meanings

lHan cig skyes sbyor gyi zab khrid nges don rgya mtsho'i snying po phrin las 'od 'phro ba

The Marvelous Life

Namkha Gyaltsen

An Exposition of Transforming the Aggregates into an Offering of Food, Illuminating the Meaning of Chöd

Phung po gzan skyur rnam bshad gcod kyi don gsal byed, chapters 1 and 2

Path Profound

Tsongkhapa Losang Dragpa

The Path Profound, a Textual Commentary on Chöd

Zab lam gcod kyi khrid yig ma ti bha dra kirti sbyar ba

Quintessence

Machig Labdrön

Oral Instructions on the Perfection of Wisdom: The Great Collection of the Quintessence of Cutting through Demonic Objects

Shes rab pha rol tu phyin pa'i man ngag bdud kyi gcod yul las snying tshom [chen mo]

The Single Seat
Je Monlam Thayé Gyatso
The Treatise of the Single [Meditation] Seat: Profound Instructions on Cutting Through Demonic Objects
Man ngag zab mo bdud kyi gcod yul stan thog gcig ma'i gzhung

Synopsis
Karmapa III, Rangjung Dorjé
Synopsis of the Great Collection of Chöd Precepts
gCod bka' rtshom chen mo'i sa bcad

Transforming the Aggregates
Attributed to Machig Labdrön, edited by Jampa Sönam
An Exposition of Transforming the Aggregates into an Offering of Food, Illuminating the Meaning of Chöd
Phung po gzan skyur rnam bshad gcod kyi don gsal byed

Transmission History
Khamnyön Jigdral Chökyi Sengé
An Ornament to Liberation: The Precious Garland of the Transmission History of the Pacification and Chöd
Zhi byed dang gcod yul gyi chos 'byung rin po che'i 'phreng ba thar pa'i rgyan

Universal Geography
Lama Tsenpo Mindrol Nomun Khan
A Mirror Illuminating Container [World] and [Beings] Contained: An Extensive Universal Geography
'Dzam gling chen po'i rgyas bshad snod bcud kun gsal me long

Victorious Banner
Lobsang Donden
Commentary on the Practice of the Single [Meditation] Seat [according to] the Practice of the Profound Path of Wisdom and Means, Called the All-Victorious Banner over the Enemy
Lam zab mo thabs shes kyi spyod yul stan thog gcig tu nyams su len tshul 'khrid chog dgra las rnam par rgyal ba'i rgyal mtshan

Notes

Preface

1. *Phung po gzan skyur rnam bshad gcod kyi don gsal byed* (*An Exposition of Transforming the Aggregates into an Offering of Food, Illuminating the Meaning of Chöd*). Chapters 1 and 2 make up the sacred biography translated here as *The Marvelous Life*.

2. *Phung po gzan skyur ba'i rnam par bshad pa las ma gcig lab sgron ma'i rnam par thar pa mdor bsdus tsam zhig* (*A Concise Life Story of Machig Labdrön, Derived from An Exposition of Transforming the Aggregates into an Offering of Food*). This larger work, which seems to be the source for *Transforming the Aggregates,* is said in its colophon to be derived from Machig's *Grand Exposition of Transforming the Aggregates into a Food Offering,* a version which is no longer extant.

3. This undated and anonymous biography, published at the request of an unknown Rin bzang grags pa dbang phyug, is divided into seven chapters: (1) How Machig renounced the worldly life and left her family; (2) How Machig opened the gates of Dharma; (3) How Machig followed Thöpa Bharé and taught Dharma to her husband and her son Gyalwa Döndrup; (4) How Machig gained realization and subjugated demons in fearful places; (5) How Machig taught the ultimate meaning (of her doctrine) to Lhatag Khenpo and others; (6) How Machig settled at Zangri and worked to propagate her doctrine for the benefit of beings; (7) How Machig departed for the state beyond suffering.

Introduction

1. Bönpo priests: adepts of Bön, which is generally considered the earliest religion of Tibet. Prior to the introduction of Buddhism in the seventh century they exerted a powerful influence over the Tibetan rulers which lasted well into the eleventh century. Although there also exists a Bön tradition of Chöd, it will not be treated in detail in the present study.

2. Atiśa was a master at the monastic university of Nālandā. He spent twelve years in Tibet, where his teachings gave rise to the Kadampa school. His system

of the stages of the path (*lam rim*) pervades most Tibetan schools up to the present day. See Sherburne, 1983.

3. Mahāsiddha (*grub thob*): a tantric adept with supernatural powers (*siddhi*), usually living in the world without connection to any institution. The Tibetan tradition usually refers to the eighty-four mahāsiddhas of India as the main sources of the Vajrayāna transmitted to Tibet.

4. Trungpa, 1986 and Lhalungpa, 1985.

5. Roerich, 1976: 225. Error repeated in the index, p. 1216, and first detected by Janet Gyatso, 1985: 329, n. 34.

6. An account not accepted by all the sources, but prevalent in the popular view. See below, Chapter VI.

7. Apart from the well-known Yeshé Tsogyal, Machig Labdrön and Shukseb Lochen Jetsun Rigdzin Chönyi Zangmo (Shug gseb lo chen rje btsun chos nyid bzang mo, 1852-1953), an incarnation of Machig Labdrön, some of the oustanding women teachers of Tibet were Jomo Menmo (Jo mo sman mo, 1248-1283); Jetsun Mingyur Paldrön (Mi 'gyur dpal sgron, 1699-1769), the daughter of Minling Terchen Terdag Lingpa, Gyurmé Dorjé (1646-1714); Jetsun Trinley Chödrön, one of the teachers of Jamyang Kyentsé Wangpo (1820-1892); and Sera Khandro Kunzang Dekyong Wangmo, also known as Dewai Dorjé (bDe ba'i rdo rje, 1899-1952). List given by Matthieu Ricard, personal communication.

8. It might be worthwhile to study certain similarities between the society of twelfth-century Tibet and the historical conditions of medieval France that produced the witch. In present-day Nepali, the term *ḍākinī*, pronounced "ḍānkinī," still means "sorceress."

9. Templeman, 1981: 12.

10. Ibid.

11. A complete description (with the corresponding sādhana) of the feminine transmission of wisdom, as Yum kun tu bzang mo, is to be found in *The Concise Life Story*, fols. 8 ff.

12. Āryadeva the Brahmin, *The Grand Poem*; translated below in Chapter I.

13. Buddhism generally considers a system or tradition to be authentic and complete if it combines the right view (*lta ba*), right meditation (*sgom pa*) and right action or behavior (*spyod pa*).

14. *Dam chos phyag rgya chen po'i gcod yul.*

15. *bDud kyi gcod yul*. The translation provided here is only an approximate one. For a detailed discussion and definition, see Chapter III below.

16. The expression *bod gcod* occurs in Karma Chagmé's *Definitive Instructions*, where he draws a distinction between the *bka' ma* from the scriptural transmission to which these different lineages belong and the *gter ma* of Guru Rinpoché discovered by Rinchen Lingpa, Sangyé Lingpa and others. However, Machig herself was also the source of Recovered Treasure traditions. She herself hid texts so that

in the future, at the time of their discovery, they would correct the perverted tradition of Chöd. On the distinctions between *bka' ma* and *gter ma*, see Chapter V, n. 16, and Tulku Thondup Rinpoche, 1986: 101 and 224, n. 93 and 94.

17. Kapstein, 1980: 139.

18. Patrul Rinpoché, 1994: 297.

19. To the best of my knowledge, Janet Gyatso's "The Development of the Gcod Tradition," in *Soundings in Tibetan Civilization*, ed. Aziz and Kapstein (Delhi: Manohar, 1985), pp. 320-341, is the only serious study published so far; it has been used as a starting point for the present study. The unpublished dissertation by Savvas (1990) contains important translations of ritual texts. See also Orofino, 1987; the various references in Tucci, 1980 and Stein, 1972. For a fine translation of the commentary to the practice, see Anila Rinchen Palmo, 1987. *The Marvelous Life* is also presented in Allione, 1984.

20. Bleichsteiner, 1950: 194-195, as quoted by Eliade, 1964: 436.

21. David-Neel, 1993: 107.

22. Evans-Wentz, 1958: 277 ff. The text is the *gCod yul mkha' 'gro'i gad rgyangs* (*Cutting Through the Object—the Laughter of the Ḍākinīs*), an extract from the *Klong chen snying thig* (*Longchenpa's Essential Drop*).

23. Eliade, 1964: 108, 436.

24. *Jātaka*, or previous lives of the Buddha, about which see below, Chapter III.

25. Van Tuyl, 1979: 38.

26. *The Concise Life Story*, f. 118.

27. Patrul Rinpoché, 1994: 302.

28. Lacarrière, 1975: 159.

29. Tucci, 1980: 163

PART ONE: THE CHÖD TRADITION

I The Grand Poem on the Perfection of Wisdom

1. The general title, *'Phags pa shes rab kyi pha rol tu phyin pa'i man ngag* (*Instructions on the Perfection of Wisdom*), added on by the Tibetan editor, does indeed differ from the Tibetan translation after the Sanskrit title. This original Tibetan title, *Ārya de was mdzad pa'i shes rab kyi pha rol tu phyin pa'i tshigs su bcad pa chen mo*, is the one here translated as the heading, *The Grand Poem on the Perfection of Wisdom, by the Brahmin Āryadeva*. The translation of the verses owes much to the oral commentary offered by Khenpo Tsultrim Gyamtso Rinpoché (of Marpa Institute, Bauddha, Kathmandu) and by Geshé Lobsang Gyatso (School of Dialectics, Dharamsala).

2. The two aims (*don gnyis*): the bodhisattva's own aim of cutting through ignorance and realizing the nature of mind; and others' aims, the bodhisattva's compassionate activity for others.

3. Left out here, at the suggestion of Geshé Lobsang Gyatso, is the line

bca' bzhi gsum gyi bka' yi thog tu bzhag

which seems to refer to the fourfold *dam dca'* ("thesis," Skt. *pratījñā*) of the Madhyamaka system.

4. The altruistic mind set on enlightenment (Skt. *bodhicitta,* Tib. *byang chub kyi sems*), with the motivation of freeing all beings from the suffering of saṃsāra.

5. *mThun 'gyur legs pa brjod par bya;* literally, "Recite them perfectly such as they are."

6. Skillful means (Skt. *upāya,* Tib. *thabs*). The text suggests the union of transcendent wisdom (Skt. *prajñā,* Tib. *shes rab*), and skillful means, i.e., the other five perfections (Skt. *pāramitā,* Tib. *pha rol tu phyin pa*). This perspective is the very basis of the Mahāyāna in general and of the Prajñāpāramitā in particular.

7. The great clear light (*'od gsal chen po*): according to the most general definition, mind's essence is emptiness, its nature is clarity and its manifestation is without limits. This clarity is not a characteristic of mind, since, in the Madhyamaka context, mind is emptiness. The clear light is devoid of any reality and, being the fruit of the yogi's meditative experience, cannot become an object of analysis.

8. To unite space and awareness (*dbyings dang rig pa bsre bar bya*): The disciple is introduced to this practice through the initiation of the Opening of the Gates of Space which Dampa transmitted to Machig. Starting from this verse, the text corresponds exactly to the Chöd tradition of Machig.

9. The Golden Islands (*gser gling dag*) refers to the Sumatra archipelago.

10. The text here has the expression *snyems byed,* literally "arrogance" or "pride," but in the context of the Chöd tradition is better rendered as "the erroneous grasping at reality" or "ego-clinging," the fourth demon described in the Chöd tradition.

11. The "tangible demons" (*thogs pa'i bdud*) are perceived by the five senses, sometimes as agreeable, sometimes as disagreeable, sometimes as indifferent. These demons give rise to attachment, aversion or ignorance.

12. If the meditator's practice is excellent, he or she cuts through all reference points, all idea of direction, a state which resembles being lost in a vast forest. In the second case, the meditator annihilates the demons the very moment they appear in the mind, as if he or she were already endowed with supernatural powers. Finally, the sharpened axe represents transcendent wisdom that cuts attachment to the reality of these demons by means of reason.

13. The imaginary or intangible demons (*thogs med bdud*) are those that cannot be perceived by the senses. Some of them are purely imaginary, others possess a degree of relative reality.

14. Moxibustion (*me btsa'*) as applied in Tibetan medicine to certain points on the meridian lines of the body.

15. Regarding the technical terms related to Chöd—*chod tshad*, "definitive sign of realization" and *tshar tshad*, "level of final accomplishment"—see the explanations in Chapter III, section 4 and Chapter IV, section 4 below.

16. This sentence is often attributed either to Dampa or Machig. It refers to the tranference of consciousness practice (*'pho ba*) known as Opening the Gates of Space.

II The Prajñāpāramitā

1. Among the numerous commentaries to this sūtra, see Rabten, 1983; Trungpa, 1973; Conze, 1958; Geshe Kelsang Gyatso, 1986; Lopez, 1988; Khenpo Tsultrim Gyamtso, 1986.

2. However, "all silence is not to be exaggeratedly taken as the profoundest teaching, but only such a silence in the special context of profound thought on the ultimate....As the Goddess says to Śāriputra: '...do not point to liberation by abandoning speech!'" (Thurman, 1976: 132). See also Thurman, 1984: 91, n. 124; and especially pp. 129-130:

> The definite teaching turns out ultimately to be sheer silence, an absolute negation of the ultimate expressibility of reality. And yet we must never mistake this silence of non-imposition of authoritarian dogma about the absolute for a portentous or referential silence that joins in the non-rational mysticism of the reificational, naively realistic use of language to refer mysteriously to essences and substances. It is a silence rather that by its pure negation of anything beyond us affirms our absoluteness and perfection, affirms our own reason's ability to understand for ourselves without being dominated by any outside authority. It is a silence of restraint on the part of the Buddhas, a refusal to put a barrier between ourselves and them, as if only they knew and we did not, and they had to tell us what It is.

3. Skt. *śūnyatā*, Tib. *stong pa nyid*. The term *emptiness* actually refers to the ultimate nature of phenomena, that they are empty of inherent existence or devoid of self-nature. A Śūnyavādin does not assert nothingness, but points out that any phenomenon whatsoever is empty of inherent existence, of own-nature (*svabhava śūnya*).

4. Among the various Madhyamaka schools, the Svātantrikas view ultimate reality as similar to empty space; for the Prāsaṅgikas, it is beyond all conceptualization (*spros bral*). This latter definition is the highest analytical statement about ultimate nature, for it establishes the emptiness of inherent existence of all phenomenon (*rang stong*—intrinsic emptiness). However, the school of qualified emptiness (*gzhan stong*—extrinsic emptiness) adds to this definition the clear light of mind, viewed not as a phenomenon, but as the yogi's meditative experience. Hence, the ultimate nature of mind is defined as the inseparable union of clarity and emptiness.

5. Dalai Lama, 1977: 55.

6. The two veils that prevent the realization of the true nature of mind are the veil of mental afflictions (*nyon mongs pa'i sgrib pa*) and the veil of obstructions to omniscience (*shes bya'i sgrib pa*).

7. *The Marvelous Life*, pp. 61-62; translated below, pp. 151-152.

8. Ibid., p. 33; translated below, p. 132.

9. Gyatso, 1985: 323.

10. *The Single Taste* (*Ro snyoms*) is not quoted among the texts attributed to Nāropa in the Dergé edition of the bsTan 'gyur (Guenther, 1963: 268). Janet Gyatso (1985: 327) likewise admits she never saw "any statement explicitly asserting that Nāropa taught Gcod." Dzatrul Ngawang Tenzin Norbu (1867-1940) in the *sPyod yul khrid gzhung* mentions two Chöd texts by Nāropa, the *Ro snyoms* and the *gSang gcod.* Most sources quote one or the other and sometimes both. *A Biography of Machig* (fol. 87) mentions that Machig received from Dampa Sangyé "the five cycles of *ro snyoms*," without specifying its author.

11. Karma Chagmé, in his *Definitive Instructions* (p. 3) quotes *The Grand Poem* of Āryadeva, *The Single Taste* of Nāropa, *The Pacification* (*Zhi byed*) of Dampa and *The Elimination of Confusion* (*Khrul chos* or *'Khrul bcod*) of Padmasambhava/Orgyen. Jamgön Kongtrul in his *Compendium* (p. 423) omits the text by Āryadeva and replaces it with "the Chöd of the ultimate meaning of the lineage transmission," i.e., the instructions according to the tradition of the Prajñāpāramitā, transmitted since the Buddha by Nāgārjuna, Āryadeva the philosopher,...Āryadeva the Brahmin and Dampa. He is, however, familiar with the text of the Brahmin Āryadeva, which he refers to as *gZhung chung* (*The Short Treatise*) and which he integrates in his *gDams ngag mdzod* (*Treasury of Profound Instructions*), vol. 14, on Chöd.

12. According to the *Transmission History*, passim.

13. *sLob dpon.* The Tibetan tradition, which recognizes the eighty-four Indian mahāsiddhas, confuses two Nāgārjunas: the second-century philosopher and founder of the Madhyamaka system, and the ninth-century yogin, disciple of Saraha. Both of them are said to have had a disciple by the name of Āryadeva; the one here referred to as "the Brahmin" would then be the disciple of the second Nāgārjuna. A short biography of both Āryadevas is given in the *Transmission History*, p. 431. For the most recent assessment on the Nāgārjuna / Āryadeva chronology, see Ruegg, 1982. For an antithetical view, see Guenther, 1969: 12.

14. Referred to as the "Gaṅgā-like Mahāmudrā [Teaching]" (*Phyag chen gang ga ma*) in Je Monlam Thayé Gyatso's *The Single Seat* treatise (p. 361).

15. *Transmission History*, p. 432 ff.; according to the *Blue Annals* (Roerich: 868), he was born in Carasimha in the region of Bebala.

16. See note 13 above. The *Blue Annals* (Roerich: 868) only mentions Nāgārjuna and Āryadeva, seemingly conflating both Nāgārjunas and both Āryadevas.

17. According to *The Geography of Tibet according to the* 'Dzam-gling-rgyas-bshad (Wylie, 1962: 31) he meditated in the cave of Sankhu (Tsam khu), located close to the present-day Vajrayoginī temple.

18. Swift-footedness (*rkang mgyogs*) is one of the ordinary siddhis (powers), also attributed to Dampa in *The Marvelous Life*.

The path of vision (*mthong lam*) is the third of the five paths (*lam lnga*) and refers to a stage of direct perception of emptiness. Supreme Mahāmudrā corresponds to the fifth, the path of no more learning (*mi slob pa'i lam*) and is identical to Buddhahood.

19. On Dingri and Langkhor see Aziz in *Tibetan Studies in Honour of Hugh Richardson*, ed. by Aris and Aung (Delhi: Vikas, 1980): 21-29.

20. According to Karma Chagmé's *Oral Instructions for Mountain Retreats*, this version of Dampa's life is viewed as the esoteric oral tradition. However, for Gene Smith (quoted in Hopkins, 1987: 451, n. 26), this identification of Dampa Sangyé with Bodhidharma is "a strange flower produced by lCang-skya's fertile imagination."

21. *The Concise Life Story*, fols. 95-101.

22. Roerich, 1976: 982.

23. *Transmission History*, pp. 436 ff.

24. *The Concise Life Story,* fols. 135 ff.

25. *Transmission History,* pp. 436 ff. and *The Marvelous Life*, p. 32; translated below, p. 131.

26. Decleer, 1992.

27. Eliade, 1960: 23. Regarding the distinction between *chos 'byung* (transmission history) and *rnam thar* (sacred biography), see below, Chapter VI, and Decleer, 1992.

28. For a short biography of Kyotön Sönam Lama (sKyo ston bsod nams bla ma), see the *Transmission History*, p. 439, from which this passage was extracted.

29. In the colophon of his *The Path Profound: A Textual Commentary on Chöd* (p. 45), author Matibhadrakirti (Tsongkhapa Losang Dragpa) states that he composed his text while using for his sources, among others, Āryadeva's *Grand Poem*, Machig's *Collection of Precepts* (*bKa' tshom*) and a work by Dampa known as *The Set of Six Fragments on Chöd* (*gCod brul tsho drug pa*). In *The Single Seat* (p. 296), this latter treatise is first referred to as *Six Fragmentary Treatises on Chöd* (*gCod kyi gzhung brul tsho drug*) and later (p. 358) as *Six Fragments on Chöd* (*gCod brul tsho drug*), said to be composed of six parts (*tshen drug*). The *Transmission History* (p. 437) mentions a *gCod drug tsho drug* (*Six* [*Treatises?*] *on the Sixfold Chöd* [*Practice?*]) to which both the Opening of the Gates of Space and a *gZhung drug tsho drug* (*Six* [*Commentaries to* (?)] *the Six Treatises* [?]) are said to belong; but later quotes (p. 546) a *sKor brul tshogs drug* (*Six Collections on* [*the Main?*] *Cycle and Fragments* [?]) supposedly taught first by Dampa, and later by Mara Serpo. The *Blue Annals*, finally, mentions a *Khrul tsho drug pa* (*Set of Six Downfalls* [?]) (Roerich, 1976: 997) and a *gZhung brul tsho drug* (*Six Fragmentary Treatises* [?]) (ibid.: 998).

30. Roerich, 1976: 871.

31. *Chos dbang sems la bskur*, an "initiation of the ultimate meaning to the mind," as opposed to the *lha dbang lus la bskur*, an "initiation of a deity transmitted to the body." Jamgön Kongtrul (*Compendium*, p. 424) attributes this distinction to Machig; according to him, the former refers to the Opening of the Gates of Space and to the means for recognizing the nature of mind. This initiation, distinctly belonging to the Chöd tradition, would then correspond to the fourth (or word) initiation (*tshig dbang*) of Highest Yoga Tantra.

32. *'Khrul ['khor] gcod bka' rgya ma'i man ngag*, the oral instructions sealed by secrecy, concerning the yogic exercises of the Chöd tradition. These exercises are forceful techniques to make the winds enter the central channel, as opposed to the peaceful techniques of progressive visualization. Generally they belong to the completion stage (*rdzogs rim*). No text related to these exercises in connection with Chöd has been found.

33. According to Lama Chönze-la of Serkong Gompa, Swayambhū, these visualizations of the eight great cremation grounds are both outer and inner. The inner visualizations of the eight great cremation grounds are applied during the visualizations on the subtle body. If the yogi manages to obtain little stones or other ingredients from these eight great cremation grounds, they may be placed beneath the meditation mat and visualized as these spots, with no need to actually go there to practice Chöd, for example.

34. *Definitive Instructions*, p. 232.

35. *Compendium*, p. 421.

III The Chöd of Machig

1. *bDud kyi gcod yul sher phyin zab mo'i spyod* (*Compendium*, p. 420). In this case, the system is called *spyod yul*, "the sphere of action (or practice) of the bodhisattvas."

2. Respectively *gsang spyod, rig spyod, tshogs spyod* (*Compendium*, p. 421). *Rig spyod* here stands for *rig pa'i brtul zhugs kyi spyod pa*, literally "knowledge action of yogic behavior." Rangjung Dorjé, in his *Synopsis* (p. 71), considers *brtul zhugs* ("yogic behavior") and *spyod pa* ("action practice") as synonymous.

3. *Compendium*, p. 421.

4. Ibid., p. 422.

5. Explanation and description of the eight groups of guests after *Transforming the Aggregates*, pp. 149 ff.

6. Quoted by Patrul Rinpoché, 1994: 303.

7. *Quintessence*, pp. 140 ff.

8. Dalai Lama, 1977: 58.

9. *The Concise Life Story*, fol. 193.

10. *Transmission History*, pp. 418-419.

11. *Transforming the Aggregates*, p. 106.

12. Mahāmudrā, literally the "Great Hand-Seal" (*mudrā* being originally a ritual hand gesture), in Tibetan, accordingly, becomes *phyag* (hand) *rgya* (seal) *chen po* (great). The verse is part of a long poem (*The Concise Life Story*, fol. 446), translated below as "Machig's Last Instructions."

13. *Phyag chen smon lam*, the "Mahāmudrā Aspiration Prayer," exists in several translations, with Kunzang, 1992 among the most recent.

14. For a fine presentation of Mahāmudrā, see the First Paṇchen Lama, *The Great Seal of Voidness*, trans. by Geshe Ngawang Dhargyey et al. (Dharamsala: Library of Tibetan Works and Archives, 1975).

15. *Transforming the Aggregates*, p. 106.

16. *The Marvelous Life*, p. 64.

17. *Transforming the Aggregates*, pp. 106-107.

18. *Phyi'i rdzas kyi dam tshig*. Tsepak Rigzin (1986: 189) mentions the five meats of samaya, *dam tshig gi rdzas sha lnga*. The main outer sacred substances are the five meats (*sha lnga*) and the five nectars (*bdud rtsi nga*); one also finds the eight root substances (*rtsa ba brgyad*) and their thousand branches (*yan lag stong*).

19. This description of the four mudrās does not differ from the ones encountered in all standard Vajrayāna treatises. The four mudrās (*phyag rgya bzhi*)—karmamudrā, samayamudrā, dharmamudrā and śūnyatāmudrā—are well known in the Vajrayāna tradition, but here Machig describes four mahāmudrās (*phyag rgya chen po bzhi*). Whereas the first two are identical, the last two—the mahāmudrā of bliss emptiness and the mahāmudrā of clear light emptiness—differ from the standard explanation. Suggested here are gradual meditative experiences. For a parallel, see Guenther, 1963.

20. Quoted in *Heart Essence*, f. 61a.

21. Quoted ibid., f. 63b.

22. *gCod kyi lugs srol dang 'brel ba'i phyag rgya chen po* (personal communication, Kathmandu).

23. *Transforming the Aggregates*, pp. 107-108.

24. Ibid., pp. 108-109.

25. *gCig shes kun don rtogs pa'i gdengs thob shog.*

26. *Dam chos bdud kyi gcod yul.*

27. *Compendium*, p. 426.

28. *Kleśa* (Tib. *nyon mongs*) covers all negative emotions such as attachment, aversion, jealousy, etc., but also erroneous views and doubts. Hence one may translate *kleśa* by "mental afflictions."

29. *Skandha* (Tib. *phung po*) or the five psycho-physical aggregates: form (*gzugs*), feelings (*tshor ba*), perceptions (*'du shes*), compositional factors (*'du byed*) and con-

sciousness (*rnam shes*). They are the constituents of individuality, wrongly identified as a real and permanent self.

30. *bDag med rtogs pa'i shes rab. The Marvelous Life*, p. 33.

31. *dByings dang rig pa bsre bar bya*, a terminology frequently encountered with Dampa and Machig.

32. The essence of reality, "thatness" and "suchness," translate the Sanskrit terms *dharmatā* and *tathatā* (Tib: *chos nyid* and *de kho na nyid*, respectively). Phenomena abide in their true nature, emptiness, as opposed to their illusory manifestation as *dharmas*. For a position that contrasts "thatness" and "suchness," see Thurman, 1984: 149-150 ff.

33. *Ngo sprod 'pho ba*. Numerous *'pho ba* traditions of transference of consciousness exist, such as the one at the moment of dying, or the *'pho ba* to make one's consciousness enter into a corpse, the transmission of which died out with the death of Marpa's son Tarmadodé. There is also the transference of consciousness into empty space known in the Chöd tradition as Opening the Gates of Space (*nam mkha' sgo 'byed*).

34. *Cig car gyi 'pho ba*, simultaneous transference, or *rim gyi 'pho ba*, transference by stages; a description of these techniques is provided in *Transforming the Aggregates*, pp. 177 ff.

35. Jamgön Kongtrul, *The Garden of Joy*, translated by Anila Rinchen Palmo in *Cutting Through Ego-Clinging*, p. 26.

36. Quoted in the *Compendium*, p. 423, after the *Great Collection*.

37. Jamgön Kongtrul, *The Garden of Joy*, translated by Anila Rinchen Palmo in *Cutting Through Ego-Clinging*, p. 27.

38. *Compendium*, p. 424.

39. *Zab don thugs kyi snying po*, quoted in the *Transmission History*, p. 548, and in the *Compendium*, p. 424.

40. Quoted in the *Quintessence*, p. 155.

41. *Lha dbang lus la bskur ma yin, chos dbang sems la bskur ba yin* (*Compendium*, p. 424). See Chapter II, n. 30 above. Occasionally one encounters the variant *gcod dbang* (Chöd initiation) instead of *chos dbang* (Dharma, as ultimate meaning, initiation), for instance in Tāranātha's title *gCod yul dbang nam mkha' sgo 'byed du grags pa* (*The Chöd Empowerment Known as Opening the Gates of Space*).

42. The *Quintessence*, pp. 158-164.

43. Translated in *The Garden of Joy* by Lama Lodo Rinpoche, f. 20, p. 85.

44. *The Grand Poem*, above, p. 20.

45. Quoted in *The Single Seat*, pp. 371-372:

bem rig phral la dbyings rig bsre
dbyings dang rig pa dbyer med bsre

stong pa'i ngang du ci nus bzhag
nyams len phung po zan du bskyur

46. *The Concise Life Story*, fol. 314.

47. According to Khenpo Tsultrim Gyamtso, techniques for offering the other aggregates may have existed at one time, but if so, they have since been lost.

48. Patrul Rinpoché, 1994: 302.

49. Further details are given in the *Fording Place*, pp. 67 ff.

50. This red banquet too is divided into three kinds, peaceful (*zhi ba*), wrathful (*drag po*) and extremely wrathful (*shin tu drag po*). *The Fording Place* provides detailed descriptions of each (p. 74 ff.), as well as of the secret multicolored banquet (*gsang ba'i sna tshogs 'gyed*) (p. 85 ff.).

51. Extracts from Karma Chagmé's *Concise Exposition of the Daily Practice of Offering the Body.* The root text and commentary by Jamgön Kongtrul, under the title *Lus mchod sbyin gyi zin bris mdor bsdus kun dga'i skyed tshal* (*The Garden of Joy, Short Notes on Presenting the Body as an Offering*), have been translated by Anila Rinchen Palmo and also by Lama Lodo Rinpoche. This text gives a detailed explanation of the various white and red banquets as practiced in the *lus sbyin* tradition of Zurmang Monastery. Lama Lodo's translation, also entitled *The Garden of Joy*, contains very useful drawings. Other offering banquets are described in this commentary, as well as in *Transforming the Aggregates*, pp. 218 ff.

52. *Quintessence*, pp. 162-163.

53. Speyer, 1971: 4 ff. (free adaptation).

54. Frye, 1981.

55. *bSod nams thams cad bsdus pa'i mdo*, quoted in the *Transmission History*, p. 420.

56. Chang, 1977, vol. 1: 303. This episode is also cited by Van Tuyl (1979) in his attempt to classify the Chöd ritual as shamanistic dismemberment.

57. On this subject, see Lacarrière, 1975.

58. *Compendium*, p. 420: *gcad par bya ni nyon mongs yin la...rnal 'byor pas yul nyer bcug nas bag chags blangs te tshul bzhin ma yin pa'i yid la byed pa sngon du 'gro ba'i nyon mongs rnams yul gyi thog de nyid du gcod par byed pas gcod yul zhes bya'o.*

59. Karma Chagmé, *Oral Instructions for Mountain Retreats*, p. 182.

60. *The Garden of Joy*, trans. Anila Rinchen Palmo, p. 27.

61. The Tibetan text has: *phung po gzan du bskyur ba 'di bdag 'dzin 'dul ba'i lam mkhen yin.*

IV Gods and Demons

1. For an excellent introduction to the subject, see Smith, 1969; Stearns, 1980: chapter V; also Trungpa, 1986.

2. Stearns, 1980: 151, after *Thang stong snyan rgyud* (*Thangtong Gyalpo's Hearing Transmission*), vol. 1, p. 53.

3. *Synopsis*, p. 71.

4. See Chapter III, n. 2 above; also Snellgrove, 1959 and Avalon and Samdup, 1919.

5. Snellgrove, 1959, vol. 1: 63.

6. *The Concise Life Story*, fol. 455; this is part of the long poem translated below as "Machig's Last Instructions."

7. Stein, 1972: 170.

8. Smith, 1969: 1.

9. Chang, 1977, vol. 2, ch. 34.

10. Numerous monographs provide eloquent descriptions: Eliade, 1964 and the collection edited by Hitchcock and Jones, 1976.

11. Similar status was given to medieval European shepherds: not quite outdated here is Michelet's classical *La Sorcière*.

12. Dorjé and Ellingson, 1979. A description of the *rkang gling* is found in *Transforming the Aggregates*, p. 153.

13. *The Marvelous Life*, p. 36; translated below, p. 134.

14. Ibid., p. 49; translated below, p. 144.

15. Private audience, Dharamsala, 1989.

16. Patrul Rinpoché, 1994: 305-306.

17. This section occurs in chapter IV of *Transforming the Aggregates*; for a translation, see Anila Rinchen Palmo, 1987.

18. *Ngo bo gnas tshul gyi lha 'dre.*

19. Respectively, *gzugs med khams, gzugs khams, 'dod khams*—the Triple World.

20. *mThong snang sgro btags kyi lha 'dre.*

21. *Transforming the Aggregates*, p. 126.

22. *bSlu med las dbang gi lha 'dre.*

23. *mThar thug gyi lha 'dre.*

24. *Transforming the Aggregates*, pp. 136 and 140.

25. Ibid., pp. 109 ff.

26. *Great Collection*, p. 7. For a complete translation of this text, see Orofino, 1987: 17.

27. Sources for this section are *Transforming the Aggregates* (pp. 109 ff.), the *Great Collection* (pp. 7 ff.) and oral explanations provided by Khenpo Tsultrim Gyamtso.

28. *dNgos po'i yul la snyems zhugs pas thogs bcas bdud du bstan pa yin. Great Collection*, pp. 7 ff.

29. *The Grand Poem*, p. 19 above.

30. *Great Collection*, pp. 10-11.

31. Ibid., p. 12.

32. *'Jig rten chos brgyad.* Rigzin, *Tibetan-English Dictionary of Buddhist Terminology*, p. 117.

33. *bDag 'dzin*, "ego-clinging" and hence "ego," since egoism is defined as an excessive attachment to oneself, with the provision that, from a Buddhist point of view, this self or ego is devoid of inherent existence.

34. *Rig pa ye shes*, an abbreviation of *so so'i rang rig pa'i ye shes*, "self-knowing or self-experiencing wisdom," a term used by the Cittamātra (Mind Only) school, which considers it as really existing, and in the qualified emptiness (*gzhan stong*) philosophy, where this wisdom is viewed as emptiness.

35. *Transforming the Aggregates*, p. 115.

36. *The Marvelous Life*, pp. 33-35; translated below, pp. 132-133.

37. *A Biography of Machig*, fol. 109b. Except for the emptiness of suchness (*de bzhin nyid stong pa nyid*) these various emptinesses belong to the classification of the sixteen emptinesses (*stong pa nyid bcu drug*). See, for example, Rigzin, p. 160.

38. *Transforming the Aggregates*, p. 119.

39. The latter explanation after the *Great Collection*, pp. 10 ff.

40. *Transmission History*, p. 416.

41. Explanation according to *Transforming the Aggregates*, pp. 288 ff.

42. Definition after *Bod rgya tshigs mdzod chen mo*, p. 3112.

43. *The Grand Poem*, p. 20.

44. On these different kinds of gods and demons, see Nebesky-Wojkowitz.

45. *Heart Essence*, p. 163.

46. At this point, Machig describes the means within Mahāmudrā to bring these miraculous displays to a stop and uses expressions related to the direct Mahāmudrā experience which are impossible to translate literally; for example, *bal le* and *sig ge*, which refer to the mind's nature of clarity, are here freely rendered as "natural," "serene," "relaxed," "open" and so forth.

47. *Heart Essence*, p. 164.

48. Chang, 1977, vol. 1: 15 ff. The corresponding stage is the episode at the Tree of Serlag (*Marvelous Life*, pp. 36-38; translated below, pp. 133-136) described in the same terms and according to a similar procedure in *The Concise Life Story*, fols. 118-119.

V Transmission

1. See Stearns, 1980.

2. *Transmission History*, p. 550. The *Collected Works* (*gsung 'bum*) of Götsangpa (rGod tshang pa) do not contain any text specifically called Chöd, but the *Tshogs bsog mchod sbyin gyi zhal gdams* (*Oral Instructions on Completing the [Two] Accumulations [of Merit and Wisdom] through Presenting Homage and Offerings*) does mention an offering of the aggregates to the lamas, yidams, and to the demons, for the benefit of beings, after separating one's own body and mind, thereby completing the accumulation of meritorious activity. This technique seems quite close indeed to Machig's Chöd tradition. For Götsangpa's text, see his *Collected Works*, vol. 2: 375 ff.

3. See Chapter II, section 4 above.

4. See Chapter VI, section 2 below. For a complete sādhana centered on her, see *The Concise Life Story*, fols. 8 ff.

5. Ibid., fols. 350 ff.

6. According to Khenpo Tsultrim Gyamtso's oral comments, the seed syllable *PHAT* is pronounced in three different ways:

(1) In the context of presenting offerings, the sound should be similar to the smoke of an incense stick that softly rises and is drawn out effortlessly. Sound and mind are united without any conceptualization and without interruption.

(2) In the context of calling and assembling gods and demons, the sound is similar to a yak's tail that gradually widens, then again thins to nothing. The sound is also like the call for a crowd to assemble at a large feast.

(3) In the context of cutting through conceptualization, the sound is like a sesame seed, round and dry. After this *PHAT* the mind remains in a state free from the threefold cycle of subject, object and act.

7. These great systemized treatises (*gzhung krig chen*) are also called the great specific [teachings] (*bye brag chen po*). They consist of the *mDo kyi rnam bshad chen mo* (*The Grand Exposition according to Sūtra*), *sNgags kyi rnam bshad chen mo* (*The Grand Exposition according to Tantra*), and *mDo sngags kyi rnam bshad chen mo* (*The Grand Exposition according to Sūtra and Tantra [Combined]*). See ChapterVI, section 3 below.

8. *Le'u lag*. For all these texts and teachings of Machig, see Chapter VI, section 3.

9. *Kha thor krig med*, also called *Bye brag chung ngu* (*The Minor Specific [Teachings]*). See *The Concise Life Story*, fols. 351 ff., which classifies these teachings according to Sūtra, Tantra, or Sūtra and Tantra Combined.

10. For example, *Definitive Instructions*, p. 229 ff.; *Transmission History*, p. 477 ff.; *Path Profound*, p. 45. For details about the different (often contradictory) interpretations, see Janet Gyatso, 1985.

11. *The Concise Life Story*, fols. 400-401, where an eighth pair goes unmentioned. Missing here, judging by other lists, would be the male and female Chöd (*pho gcod, mo gcod*). See, for instance, *Definitive Instructions*, p. 229.

12. Possibly a reference to the Avalokiteśvara sādhana texts that miraculously appeared (came down from heaven) at Yambu Lakang in the Yarlung Valley, but no source was found to confirm this.

13. See p. 29 above.

14. Chimpug (mChims phug), the retreat center above Samyé with a Guru Rinpoché cave at its summit (not to be confused with the Chipug ['Chi phug] cave where Machig went to meditate at the age of forty-five). However, neither Khyentsé's *Guide* nor the *Universal Geography* mention either these Chöd termas or those hidden at Lhasa's Plain of Sorrows (*lha sa'i skyo thang*).

15. Explanations according to the *Definitive Instructions*. Kunpang Tsöndrü Sengé (Kun spang brtson 'grus seng ge), author of *The Concise Life Story*, is supposed to have been such a tertön (*gter ston*), and is linked with the discovery of a text named *Ma gcig shes rab gsal ldan (The Resplendent Transcendent Knowledge [by Machig])*. However, the text is not mentioned in *The Concise Life Story*, nor does its colophon refer to Kunpang as a tertön. See below Chapter VI, section 3; for further details on the Chöd of the Recovered Treasure tradition, see *Transmission History*, p. 557.

16. See Dargay, 1981: 24. As Matthieu Ricard explains in *The Life of Shabkar*, p. 555, the Oral Transmission tradition (*bka' ma*) is the long lineage of canonical scriptures (*ring brgyud bka' ma*) transmitted from master to disciple without interruption from the primordial Buddha Samantabhadra to Padmasambhava and other great Awareness Holders, as opposed to the terma (*gter ma*) tradition or short direct lineage of the Recovered Treasures, concealed for the sake of future generations, which represents the quintessence of the *bka' ma*. A third tradition is called the Profound Pure Vision (*zab mo dag snang*), which arises through direct vision of the deity.

17. See above, Chapter II, n. 29.

18. *The Concise Life Story*, fol. 196, lists four root texts of Machig related to the Sūtra tradition:

(1) *The Great Collection of Precepts*, which is outer
(2) *The Appendices*, which is inner (partly enumerated in *Transmission History*, p. 546)
(3) *The Sign Teachings* (*brDa chos*), which is secret and used by Tārā to evoke Machig's memory of her former lives
(4) A so-far unkown and untraceable *Don khang rgol gnad them su bstan pa* (?).

19. *Victorious Banner*, pp. 231 ff.

20. *Transmission History*, p. 475.

21. *The Concise Life Story*, fol. 353.

22. Ibid., fols. 6 ff.

23. *Transmission History*, pp. 421 ff. *A Biography of Machig*, fol. 39b, seems to follow the sūtra tradition of Chöd and names five transmission lineages: the lineage of means, the lineage of knowledge, the personal hearing lineage (*gang zag snyen gyi brgyud pa*), the combined lineage through signs (*brda*) and the blessing lineage of the (Buddhas') words. The biography also gives the names of Machig's spiritual and natural sons and daughters as well as those of the various holders of her tradition, fols. 145-147.

24. *The Concise Life Story*, fol. 193.

25. *rGyal thang lugs kyi gcod dbang nam mkha' sgo 'byed kyi cho ga*, passim.

26. *The Marvelous Life*, pp. 61-63; translated below, pp. 151-152. For the visualization of Yum chen mo and her maṇḍala, see *The Concise Life Story*, fols. 8 ff.

27. *Transforming the Aggregates*, p. 81, quotes this tantra as *bKa' brgyud gnas 'gyur yang thig me long* (*The Essential Mirror of the Transformation of the Oral Transmission*), a set of one hundred initiations also called *Bla ma gnas 'gyur gyi dbang brgya* (*The Hundred Initiations of the Transformation of the Lamas*) as in the *Compendium*, p. 424. For the titles of the treatises on generation and completion stages, and their commentaries, see *The Concise Life Story*, fols. 237 ff., and *Transforming the Aggregates*, pp. 81 ff.—the two sources used for the above section.

28. *The Concise Life Story*, fol. 238, names Vārāhī; *Transforming the Aggregates* names Mahāmāyā, apart from which the passage in both texts is absolutely identical — not suprisingly, since the latter derives from the former. According to Jamgön Kongtrul's *Compendium*, p. 424, these three cycles of the hundred initiations of the transformation of the lamas, the hundred initiations of the transformation of the Buddhas of the ten directions, and the hundred initiations of the transformation of the ḍākinīs, which correspond respectively to these three tantras, "are known as the three hundred Chöd initiations."

29. Enumeration in *The Concise Life Story*, fols. 351-352:

- *rGyu 'phrul chen mo rig pa'i rtsal 'don (For a Skillful Understanding of Mahāmāyā)*
- *Nang rig pa'i dmar khrid (Explicit Commentary on Inner Knowledge)*
- *Bla ma rnal 'byor zab lam ma (On the Profound Path of Guru Yoga)*
- *'Pho ba lhag pa'i lam zhugs ma (On Entering the Most Excellent Path of [Consciousness] Transference)*
- *'Jam dpal la sogs rigs gsum mgon la brten pa'i dmigs pa bskor gsum (Three Cycles on Visualization, Centered on the Lords of the Three Families, Mañjuśrī and Others)*
- *sPyan ras gzigs sgom pa'i snying rje bskor gsum (Triple Cycle on Compassion in Avalokiteśvara Meditation)*
- *rDo rje tshig rkang las bzhi'i sbyor ba (Vajra Stanzas to be Applied during the Four Activities)*

30. *Transforming the Aggregates*, p. 81.

31. *Compendium*, chapter 3, p. 424, where the author uses the expression "the hundred initiations of the hundred ganacakras" (*tshogs brgya dbang brgya*). *Transforming the Aggregates* (p. 83) has "the hundred initiations and the hundred ganacakras" (*dbang brgya dang tshogs brgya*).

32. The mudrās of action, commitment, bliss emptiness and clear light emptiness, a detailed explanation of which is provided in *Transforming the Aggregates*, pp. 106 ff. See also Chapter III, section 2 above.

33. *Transfoming the Aggregates*, p. 83.

34. *sNgags kyi rig brtul spyod pa dang rjes su 'brel ba*, the behavior or action by the yogi who has achieved stabilization in the completion stage yoga by mastery of the winds in the central channel.

35. Opening lines of *The Garden of Joy*. Compare *Cutting Through Ego-Clinging*, p. 11.

36. *Transforming the Aggregates*, p. 82.

37. These four kinds of fire offerings are called the "four activities": peaceful, increasing, powerful and wrathful. See the fire offering text in *The Precious Garland*, p. 561.

38. *'Phrul gcod bka' rgya ma* (*The Sealed Precepts on Cutting Through Magical Transformations*) and *Zhi byed dmar khrid HUNG bskor* (*The Practical Guide to Pacification's HUNG Cycle*) are two texts which Machig received from Dampa. See *The Marvelous Life*, p. 41; below, pp. 137-138.

39. *The Concise Life Story*, fols. 352-353.

40. Mentioned in *Transmission History*, p. 559.

41. For a short biography of Gyalwa Döndrup, see *Transmission History*, p. 494 ff.; for some lines on Nyenchung (sNyan chung) Lotsāwa, see ibid., pp. 507-508.

42. *Sras rgyud, nyams kyi rgyud pa*, in *Definitive Instructions*, p. 231.

43. On this Vajrayāna lineage, see *Transmission History*, pp. 532 ff. Khyentse's *Guide* (p. 142) mentions a *sham bu rtse dgu* or *rtse chen* as a rocky hill north of the valley of Gyantse, but nothing proves this is the same spot.

44. *Transforming the Aggregates*, p. 82.

45. His meditation cave is still honored in the Nyemo (sNye mo) Valley, in Tsang.

46. *Transmission History* (pp. 559-560). Since the author, Khamnyön (also known as Jigdral Chökyi Sengé, nineteenth century), quotes Jamyang Khyentsé Wangpo (1820-1892) (see Rossi-Filibeck, 1983), he seems to have known this Vajrayāna tradition as a living force. Today, it seems to be practiced mainly in the Gelugpa school.

47. *Transmission History*, p. 545. This latter lineage will be discussed below in Chapter VI, section 3.

48. Among others, Zurmang Monastery preserved the *gCod tshogs yon tan kun 'byung* (*Source of All Qualities, a Collection of Chöd [Treatises]*) of the Third Karmapa, which also provides details about its lineage, as does *The Precious Garland*. The *Transmission History* (p. 542) also describes this second lineage, but at first calls it "Chöd's Hundred Initiations lineage that unites the Oral Transmision [*bka' ma*] and Recovered Treasures [*gter ma*]," and later, "the long lineage of the Sūtra tradition," which seems contradictory.

49. Quoted from memory by Khenpo Tsultrim Gyamtso, as *sKyabs che dgon pa, rGyu gnas dgon pa* and *Phyag gcod* (spellings only approximate), all three situated in Kham. The former two are cited by Tucci, 1980: 92.

50. The *dGa' ldan gcod rabs* (*Chöd Lineage of Ganden*) presents a complete treatment of the Gelug Chöd, while drawing a distinction between the short lineage of Vajradhara, Mañjuśrī, and Tsongkhapa, and the distant lineages from Machig and Khugom Chöseng till Khedrub Chöjé of Samding and then on till Paṇchen Lungrig Gyatso and so forth. According to the *Path Profound* (p. 3 ff.), the distant lineages came down from Khugom Chöseng; with a few minor differences, they correspond to the Second Dalai Lama's listings (Rossi-Filibeck, 1983). Compare also with Janet Gyatso, 1985.

51. Information received from Tashi Tsering (Library of Tibetan Works and Archives) and Geshé Georges Dreyfus. Elements of this debate are to be found in the *Collected Works* of sTong dpon rin po che, published by Dharamsala's Buddhist School of Dialectics. The standard Gelugpa point of view, by contrast, is expressed in various texts of the *gCod tshogs* (*Chöd Collection*) edited by Tsering Dorje (Dharamsala: Library of Tibetan Works and Archives, 1986).

52. Volume XIV of the *Treasury of Profound Instructions* contains two Chöd texts by Tāranātha, *gCod yul zab mo'i khrid yig gnad don snying po* (*The Essence of Definitive Meaning: A Written Commentary on Profound Cutting Through the Object*) and *rGyal thang lugs kyi gcod dbang nam mkha' sgo 'byed kyi cho ga* (*The Chöd Initiation in the Tradition of Gyalthangpa: A Ritual for Opening the Gates of Space*).

53. The biographies of Sangs rgyas ston pa, mKhas grub chos rje and Zhangs ston pa are to be found in the *Transmission History*, p. 522 ff. On the Shangpa tradition, see Kapstein, 1980: 138-144.

54. Janet Gyatso, p. 337.

55. See Patrul Rinpoche's chapter entitled "The Kusali's Accumulations" in *The Words of My Perfect Teacher*, pp. 297-307.

56. Tarthang Tulku, 1983: 102.

57. *gCod pa'i brtul zhugs sam smyo lta bu bzhes*, quoted in Stearns, 1980: 153.

58. *The Laughter of the Ḍākinīs* starts off with a Yeshé Tsogyal invocation, but applies the visualization of the Secret Wisdom Ḍākinī. *The Words of My Perfect Teacher* (*Kun bzang bla ma'i zhal lung*) of Patrul Rinpoché is a commentary to the preliminary practices of the *Innermost Drop* and applies the visualization of Machig's wrathful aspect as the Wrathful Black Lady (Khros ma nag mo).

59. *gDan thog gcig m'ai khrid yig 'khor 'das rang grol* (*Self-liberation from Saṃsāra and Nirvāṇa: A Guide to the Single Seat Treatise*) and *dBang bskur chos kyi sgo 'byed kyi chog sgrigs dbang chog 'khor 'das gzhi grol* (*Release from the Base [Duality] Saṃsāra-Nirvāṇa: An Empowerment Rite Composed after the Initiation [known as] Opening the Gates of Dharma [in the Definitive Meaning]*), in *Transmission History*, p. 549. Both texts have remained elusive so far. It is worth noting, however, that Dampa transmitted to Machig a *gDan thog gcig tu gcod pa'i gdams pa* (*Chödpa Instructions on the Single Seat*): see *The Marvelous Life*, p. 41; translated below, p. 138. For further details on the Chöd in the Nyingma context, see Janet Gyatso, 1985.

60. *Zhi ba'i gcod, rgyas pa'i gcod, dbang gi gcod* and *drag po'i gcod*. Tenzin Namdak, personal communication. For a list of the available Bön Chöd texts, see bibliography.

61. Janet Gyatso, p. 340.

VI Biographies of Machig Labdrön

1. *Transforming the Aggregates*, p. 406.

2. *Phung po gzan skyur ba'i rnam par bshad pa las ma gcig lab sgron ma'i rnam par thar pa mdor bsdus tsam zhig*. In a new edition of *Transforming the Aggregates* published by the mTsho sngon mi rigs dpe skrun khang (1992), the title reads *Dus gsum rgyal ba kun gyi yum gcig 'phags ma lab kyi sgron ma'i rnam par thar pa phung po gzan bsgyur gyi rnam par bshad pa mkha' 'gro bye ba'i gsang lam*. This version, which includes the term *rnam thar* in its title, is actually the same as *Transforming the Aggregates* except for a few minor differences.

3. Katz, 1977: 13.

4. Letter from Templeman, November 1989.

5. Decleer, 1992, vol. 1: 13.

6. Tibetan tradition knows of three kinds of hagiographies (*rnam thar*): the outer, dealing with the main "outer" events in the life, including birth and death; the inner, describing teachings, initiations, and spiritual progress of the subject; and the secret, revealing primarily meditative experiences (*nyams*). *The Marvelous Life* does not refer to any of these levels, but would seem to belong to the first category. No mention has been encountered to date of an inner or secret biography of Machig.

7. See Boureau, 1984 for an excellent study on the legendary saints' lives and the marvelous in the Christian context.

8. See Ruegg, 1966.

9. On the Profound Pure Vision (*zab mo dag snang*), see Chapter V, n. 16 above.

10. *The Concise Life Story*, fols. 307 ff.

11. Ven. Lobsang Tenzin, 1990: 106.

12. *sKor lo bde mchog gi grub thab chen po sprul pa'i dkyil 'khor mngon sum du bzhengs pa. Transforming the Aggregates*, p. 14.

13. Ibid., p. 147.

14. Beyer, 1978: 45, citing Guenther, 1971: 103, n. 1.

15. Ven. Tenga Rinpoché, oral explanation of the Chod practice, Swayambhunath, Nepal, 1988.

16. Private audience with students' group, Dharamsala, March 1990.

17. Snellgrove, 1975: 175.

18. "To despise women, whose nature is wisdom" is considered a tantric root downfall.

19. Hopkins, 1987: 240, n. 72; Guenther, 1986: 219 ff.

20. *A Biography of Machig*, fols. 89ff. See also Preface, note 3 and note 28 below.

21. *Transforming the Aggregates*, p. 281, where Machig defines a sacred spot (*gnas*) as a place blessed by the Buddhas, or the residence of protectors or ḍākinīs, such as the twelve *bstan ma*.

22. Ibid., p. 146.

23. Ibid., p. 145, where Thönyön asks his mother Machig how to see her as Vajravārāhī. In her identification with Vārāhī, she occupies the central place, is surrounded by four ḍākinīs who represent the four Buddha families (Buddha, Ratna, Padma, and Karma). As a group of five, they are associated with the five elements, five wisdoms and five Buddha bodies (Skt. *kāya*, Tib. *sku*), with Machig herself being the bliss body.

24. Dalai Lama, 1977: 27-28.

25. Khenpo Tsultrim Gyamtso, Boulder, Colorado, October 1994.

26. *Transmission History*, p. 472. City of the rākṣasas, Tib. *srin po'i grong khyer*.

27. See Bibliography for complete titles, editions and translations where available. The *Chos 'byung ngo mtshar rgya mtsho* (*Dharma History [Called] an Ocean of Wonders*) written by sTag lung pa Ngag dbang rnam rgyal (Taglung Ngawang Namgyal) is not mentioned here since it follows word for word the other five main sources.

28. We recently found a third version of Machig's biography in Dolpo, a manuscript written in cursive script, unfortunately without date or author. This text, *Ma gcig ma'i rnam thar* (*A Biography of Machig*), also called *rNam thar mgur ma*, appears to be quite old. The text includes many of Machig's spontaneous songs (*mgur*). It follows the general historical trends of Machig's life, but devotes for example an entire chapter to the young Machig's fight with her parents to avoid marriage and dedicate herself to the practice of Dharma. Another chapter covers Machig's wanderings in fearful places subjugating demons. Due to its late discovery, we only managed to include here a few quotes from the manuscript where

it differs on main points from other available sources. For the outline of this biography, see note 3 of the Preface.

29. A xerox copy of this rare *dbu med* manuscript was graciously provided by Cyrus Stearns. The original was found by the late Prof. T. Wylie and is deposited in the rare manuscripts section of the University of Washington, Seattle.

30. Edited by Jampa Sönam (Byams pa bsod nams), said to be the thirtieth holder of the hearing lineage (*lung brgyud*). If one estimates twenty years per generation, he would have lived in the nineteenth century, and hence be a contemporary of Jamgön Kongtrul Lodrö Thayé. All references to the Tibetan text given in the translation below follow Jampa Sönam's edition. A third edition has been recently published by mTsho sngon mi rigs dpe skrun khang (Shinhua: 1992), under the title *Dus gsum rgyal gyi yum gcig 'phags ma lab kyi sgron ma'i rnam pa thar pa phung po gzan bsgyur gyi rnam bshad pa mkha' 'gro bye ba'i gsang lam* (*A Hagiography of the Venerable Labdrön, the Unique Mother of All the Victorious Ones of the Three Times, called The Exposition of Transforming the Aggregates into a Food Offering, the Secret Path of the Ḍākinīs' Activity*).

31. The Tibetan text, for most of the chapters, provides no other titles than the name of the person who addresses his or her questions to Machig. The titles follow the chapter contents established by Lama Denis Töndrup, Karma Ling, France; personal communication.

32. *The Concise Life Story*, fols. 305 ff.

33. *Phung po zan skyur gcod kyi gsal byed ma cig rnam bshad chen mo* (*Machig's Grand Exposition of Transforming the Aggregate into a Food Offering, Illuminating the Meaning of Chöd*) in: *Bod kyi bstan bcos khag cig gi mtshen byang dri med shel dkar phreng ba*, referred to as the *Labrang Karchag*, edited by mTsho sngon mi rigs dpe skrun khang, in the *rnam mthar* chapter, p. 70. Access to this text would tell us whether it is Namkha Gyaltsen's version of *The Grand Exposition* mentioned below (see n. 36), an earlier version of Machig's *Grand Exposition of Transforming the Aggregates into an Offering of Food* which could be the source of all the later versions and currently unknown, or a different text altogether.

The *Labrang Karchag* also mentions another biography of Machig by rGyal thang ri khrod pa, called *Ma cig lab sgron rnam mthar pad ma dkar po'i phreng ba*, unknown to us.

34. *rNam bshad chen mo'i brgyud pa*, in *Transforming the Aggregates*, p. 406. According to the colophon of the 1992 edition of *Transforming the Aggregates* (*mKha' 'gro bye ba'i gsang lam, The Secret Path of the Ḍākinīs' Activity*), p. 648, the compiler Sangs rgyas dpal received this *rNam bshad chen mo'i brgyud pa* from Mönchöd Tsöndrü Sengé (Mon gcod brtson 'grus seng ge).

35. The *Transmission History*, pp. 546-548, provides a detailed table of contents for Namkha Gyaltsen's *Grand Exposition*. Next to *Yid ches lo rgyus* (*A Devotional Account [of Machig's Life]*), it includes some of her own original compositions, such as the *bKa' tshom chen mo* (*The Great Collection of [Chöd] Precepts*), *Yang tshom chen mo* (*The Great Advanced Collection [of Chöd Precepts]*) and *sNying tshom chen mo*

(*The Great Quintessence [of Chöd Precepts]*); as well as commentaries such as Rangjung Dorjé's *gCod bka' tshom chen mo'i sa bcad* (*Synopsis of the Great Collection of Chöd Precepts*) and other general commentaries on Chöd; the ordinary, extraordinary and specific *Le'u lag* (*Appendices*) of Machig; the Recovered Treasures; and so forth. A number of these texts are included within vol. XIV of the *gDams ngag mdzod* (*Treasury of Profound Instructions*).

According to the *Transmission History*, Namkha Gyaltsen also received the Chöd of Mahāmudrā from Kunga Gyaltsen, and the colophon of the two first chapters of *Transforming the Aggregates* states that he received Machig's Vajrayāna Chöd, being the eighth in the line for this lineage coming from Machig's son Thönyön Samdrup.

36. Khetsun Sangpo, 1977, vol. VII: 407 mentions one Namkha Gyaltsen born in 1370, but the biography given there does not provide any clue that would allow a definitive identification with the compiler of *The Grand Exposition*. For a short biography of Namkha Gyaltsen, see also *Transmission History*, pp. 540 ff.

37. *Transforming the Aggregates*, p. 406.

38. *Kun sbangs* (or *spangs*) *kyi ming can sprang po brtson 'grus seng ge*. Even with the spelling error, identification with the author seems definite. Out of humility he refrains from calling himself a renunciate, merely stating that others call him so, while [in reality] he is only a beggar. See Roerich, 1976: 744; *Transmission History*, p. 522, and p. 541 ff.

The lineage given in *Transforming the Aggregates*, mentioned above on p. 107, and this one seem to indicate that Kunpang Tsöndrü Sengé and Namkha Gyaltsen were contemporary, since both appear before Nyima Gyaltsen and Mönchöd Tsöndrü Sengé. If this is so, *The Concise Life Story* could be the source of Namkha Gyaltsen's *Grand Exposition* and of *Transforming the Aggregates*. However, in this lineage the Second Karmapa, Karma Pakshi (1204-1284), is listed after them. This is contradicted both by the fact that Namkha Gyaltsen included in his *Grand Exposition* a text by the Third Karmapa, Rangjung Dorjé (1284-1339), and by the date of his birth given by Khetsun Sangpo, 1370 (see n. 36 above).

39. *Transmission History*, p. 557.

40. Ibid., p. 513 ff. These four sources are: a *gSal sgron*, a *mTha' rnam gsal ba'i yig bkras*, a *Dam tshig nyi zhu rtsa gcig* and a *gCod kyi lo rgyus* (the latter including?) a *Don rnam thar bsdus don*. It seems that none of these texts is available. *The Twenty-one Vows* is mentioned as related to an Avalokiteśvara practice.

41. *Transmission History*, p. 514.

42. Dorjé Drönma was Machig's son Gyalwa Döndrup's great-granddaughter. She was also called Lentogma [Lightning Reply] and was considered an emanation of Machig. See the last lines of *The Marvelous Life*, p. 163 below.

43. *Transforming the Aggregates*, p. 85, has the following note:

> Starting from "and in this way, a Tibetan tradition was propagated in India," [the section immediately following] does not belong to the [original] treatise. Also, starting from "this tradition, born from Machig's meditative experience" all the way till "so that her lineage flourished all the more" has been added by me, Namkha Gyaltsen.

44. This statement seemed true until we found the manuscript entitled *A Biography of Machig* in Dolpo. Tashi Tsering from the Library of Tibetan Works and Archives agreed that this manuscript seems to be one of the oldest sources available, apparently coming from an oral transmission.

45. In the colophon of *A Biography of Machig*, the compiler adds: "In the ocean-like life of Machig, this *rnam thar* is but a drop of water. Among the various versions [of her life] which I have gathered, I have composed this short version." Unfortunately he does not quote his sources.

46. Norbu, 1987: 47.

47. See p. 3 above; Roerich, 1976: 225 and 919; Snellgrove, 1987: plate 80a. The date 1150 and the age of 88 for the death correspond to the dates of Machig Zhama, not to those of Labdrön. See also Orofino, passim.

48. According to Stearns, she received it from Se mkon chung ba. This *Lam 'bras zha ma lugs* of hers is also known as the middling (*'bring po*) transmission since she didn't receive all the instructions. It seems that Zhama Lotsāwa, the translator of Āryadeva's *Grand Poem on the Perfection of Wisdom*, was the brother of Machig Zhama.

49. Roerich, 1976: 223, 229.

50. *Marvelous Life*, p. 89; translated below, pp. 138-139.

51. Roerich, 1976: 984.

52. *Banquet*, p. 1565.

53. Roerich, 1976: 983.

54. *Transmission History*, p. 451.

55. Ibid., p. 453.

56. *Guide*, p. 51.

57. *A Biography of Machig*, fols. 39b-67b.

58. For example, Roerich, 1976: 984 and *The Marvelous Life*, p. 36, translated below on p. 134.

59. In Tibetan the same term (*nang*) signifies inner and Buddhist, with the non-inner being considered outsiders (*phyi*).

60. *Transforming the Aggregates*, p. 107.

61. Ibid., p. 50.

62. *Transmission History*, p. 455.

63. Ibid., p. 483.

64. In *A Biography of Machig*, fols. 87-103, Bhadra (who is called Bharé ['Ba' re]) is not described as an Indian yogi but as a local master (*slob dpon*) from the Echung region. Machig actually becomes his Dharma teacher, as suggested in the title of

chapter 3, "How Machig followed Thöpa Bharé and taught Dharma to her husband and son Gyalwa Döndrup." Even though Machig is called "Ani" (nun) by her co-disciples, the text does not mention anywhere that she took monastic vows. For the titles of the chapters of *A Biography of Machig*, see note 3 of the Preface.

65. *Transmission History*, p. 463 ff.

66. *Banquet*, p. 1371.

67. Roerich, 1976: 985.

68. For more detailed descriptions of the life of Gyalwa Döndrup, see *The Concise Life Story*, fols. 361 ff.

69. *The Concise Life Story*, fols. 495 ff. *A Biography of Machig*, fols. 145-147, gives the names of Machig's natural and spiritual sons and daughters: four sons and four daughters, the eight equal to herself (*rang dang snyams pa*), the eight scholars, the three early liberated and the three late liberated, her two heart sons (*thugs sras*) Khugom Chökyi Sengé and Gyalwa Döndrup, who are also mentioned later as the holders of her transmission, and her four other spiritual children.

70. *A Biography of Machig* does not mention Machig's encounter with the Indian ācāryas, but contains an entire chapter (5) about Machig's debate with one Lhatag Khenpo (lHa stag mkhan po) and others to eliminate all doubts concerning her teaching.

71. *Transmission History*, p. 475.

72. Roerich, 1976: 984.

73. *The Concise Life Story*, fol. 456.

74. *Bod rgya tshigs mdzod chen mo*, vol. III: 3216 provides the dates for Machig Zhama (1062-1149), but strangely omits those of Machig Labdrön. 1153 is a Water-Bird year, 1152 is a Water-Monkey year. One may suppose that *The Concise Life Story* mistakenly put in a Fire element, with Machig's death being dated 1152.

75. *The Concise Life Story*, fols. 454 ff.

76. *Guide*, pp. 47-48.

PART TWO: THE MARVELOUS LIFE

VII Machig's Previous Life, Her Birth and Her Childhood

1. Cakrasaṃvara ('Khor lo bde mchog) is one of the main Highest Yoga Tantra deities. His entourage consists of sixty-four deities. The master is able, by the power of his practice and accomplishments, to make the maṇḍala mansion of the deity visibly appear to others.

2. The highest of the four classes of tantra (Action, Performance, Yoga, and Highest Yoga), each with two stages of generation and completion, respectively with and without support.

3. Supreme siddhi (*mchog gi dngos grub*). There are ordinary supernatural powers and the supreme or extraordinary siddhi, which is Buddhahood — the only siddhi that should be pursued. The ordinary siddhis or feats should only be applied for others' benefit.

4. *Dur khrod*, cemetery, or, according to the local custom, either cremation ground, charnel field or sky-burial site. The *Concise Life Story* adds a name for the spot—*Dur khrod ro gling*, "the charnel field Isle of Corpses," which does not figure, however, among the eight great cremation grounds (*dur khrod chen po brgyad*) of the tradition.

5. Khaṭvāṅga (*kha tvam*): metal trident that represents the renunciation of the wandering yogin. For ḍākinīs, the trident is replaced by a half-vajra. In the tantric tradition the khaṭvāṅga symbolizes the yogic partner or consort. It is usually adorned with a skull, a half rotten head and a bleeding head, as well as a horizontal double vajra. As mentioned by Templeman (1989: 103), it is a weapon that clearly proclaims the yogi's intrepid stance in the face of absolute truth.

6. Kālikā (Khros ma nag mo), in other Chöd texts described as the secret and wrathful form of Vajravārāhī.

7. *Tshul mdzad*, literally "enacting" or "showing" the action of killing.

8. *A* is the primordial syllable of emptiness and of the Perfection of Wisdom. *HA RI NI SA* is part of the root-mantra of Vajravārāhī (rDo rje phag mo).

9. *HRI* is the primordial syllable of compassion as represented by Avalokiteśvara (sPyan ras gzigs).

10. *The Concise Life Story* (fol. 68) describes the child's extraordinary characteristics in further detail, and, for instance, specifies that she possessed the thirty-two signs [of a Buddha].

11. These are all signs of a ḍākinī. Usually texts distinguish a set of five major signs, such as the frontal ("third") eye, slightly webbed fingers, pink fingernails like mother-of-pearl (*nya phyis*), a multicolored halo of light similar to a rainbow in which appear the syllables *OM AH HUNG*, and so forth. Here, in *Transforming the Aggregates* (p. 24), these characteristics seem to have been added on, most likely by the editor.

12. The capital or printed letters (*dbu can*) as contrasting with cursive writing (*dbu med*). The text here has the expression *yig chen*, "large letter," the most usual type for printed works. Children learning how to write first trace the letters on smooth short boards. Only once they have perfectly mastered writing are they allowed to write on paper, in Tibet a rare and hence precious commodity.

13. Ten bodhisattva bhūmis: the ten levels or grounds (Skt. *dasabhūmi*, Tib. *sa bcu*) a bodhisattva must cross after having realized emptiness, on the first ground, till ultimate enlightenment. Thus one speaks of a "third-bhūmi bodhisattva," a "seventh-bhūmi bodhisattva," etc. The five paths (*lam lnga*) are the paths of accumulation, of application, of vision (first bhūmi), of meditation (second to ninth bhūmi) and of no more learning (tenth bhūmi).

14. Chöné (*mchod gnas*) is a rather vague term, sometimes referring to the one in charge of the offerings; but it does not correspond to any particular monastic function today; hence "the one officiating," in whatever function.

15. Modes (*skad 'gyur*), literally "different languages." Lamas questioned on this topic could not come up with any definitive answer. It would seem to refer to different kinds of modulation, tone or melody pattern in the recitation.

16. Khecari (*mkha' spyod*, literally "Active in Space"): one of the pure lands or paradises; also translated sometimes as "Ḍākinī Realm." According to Khenpo Tsultrim Gyamtso, the ultimate paradises are the realization of mind's clear light. From this realization, the clear light's limitless play and the power of previous aspirations may cause pure lands to appear. Rigzin (1986: 35) further describes it as a Buddha Field "which a yogi can reach, without abandoning his ordinary form or body, in one lifetime through proper practice."

17. *Atsāra* is a deformation of the Sanskrit term *ācārya*, "master" (Tib. *slob dpon*), often used for pseudo-masters and eventually for the clowns during the comic interludes of the ritual *'cham* dances. Here either ironic (referring to any Indian with the airs of a master) or just an erroneous Tibetan pronunciation of an Indian word.

18. A Tibetan custom. When two people consider each other of equal spiritual rank, they don't prostrate but touch heads. By this gesture Dampa shows he considers Machig his equal.

19. *Mi phod pa rdzis.*

20. *'Khrib chod.*

21. *The Concise Life Story* (fol. 104) quotes this entire teaching, but here has: "Understand that mind itself (*sems nyid*) is similar to empty space," rather than "understand that [all] sentient beings (*sems can*) are similar to empty space." Although both interpretations are possible in the Chöd context, the *Concise Life Story*'s reading seems preferable here.

22. The Tibetan uses the expression *gad bdar*, to sweep or cleanse. According to the oral commentary, the meaning is to analyze or observe the nature of mind.

23. *sGra dbyangs mi grags* means that not the slightest trace of ego's existence remained with her.

24. The three whites are milk, yoghurt, and butter; the three sweets are sugar, molasses, and honey.

25. Experience of the single flavor of the expanse of dharmatā (*chos nyid kyi dbyings ro snyoms*). In the essence of reality, the very nature of phenomena, or emptiness, there is no difference between friends and enemies, pleasant or unpleasant, happiness or suffering, but the equanimity of a single flavor regarding all phenomena.

26. "Brother" here is the Tibetan *ming po*, which might also refer to close or distant cousins.

27. There is a mistake in our version, which gives *e'i gongs ba* but is clearly referring to Machig's birthplace of *e'i gangs ba*. This is confirmed by *The Secret Path of the Ḍākinīs' Activity*, pp. 250 and 268, which gives both places as *dbye ba'i gangs ba*.

28. This distinction between the four yogins (*sngags pa*) and Machig (*jo chung ma*) *might* indicate that she was not considered a lay yoginī, and hence was considered a nun, to which the name *jo chung ma* might also refer. Still, in itself this would not prove that she had taken the monastic vows. In Tibet many women lived (and dressed) like nuns without having received the ordination. Moreover, this remark seems to be added as a gloss, most likely by the editor, for it does not appear as an integral part of the text. *The Concise Life Story* (fol. 114) seems rather to distinguish between four men and one woman (*pha jo bzhi, lab sgron dang lnga*) without mention as to whether they were monks or lay yogins.

29. *Chos dbang sems la bskur*: see above, Chapter II, n. 30 and Chapter III, section 3.

30. *Nam mkha' sgo 'byed*, about which see Chapter III, section 3.

31. Vajrayāna tradition distinguishes a visualized ("provisional") deity (Skt. *samayasattva*, Tib. *dam tshig sems dpa'*) from the actual or wisdom deity (Skt. *jñānasattva*, Tib. *ye shes sems dpa'*).

32. The twenty-four dance postures of the dance by the peaceful deities (*zhi ba'i gar thabs*) have come down from Indian tradition. The sixty melodious qualities of Brahmā's voice (*dbyangs yan lag drug bcu*) include qualities such as purity, clarity, ability to be heard throughout the universe, and so forth.

33. Tib. *rDo rje lta bu'i ting nge 'dzin*: the profound meditation generally described as being like the Buddha's beneath the pipal tree at Bodhgaya, just before his enlightenment. See also Rigzin, 1986: 145.

34. Skt. *nāga*, Tib. *klu*: subterranean deities of the waters who are sometimes helpers, sometimes obstructers. One often hears the expression "the gods above and the nāgas below."

35. *Phung po 'dre rnams kyi gzan du bskyur*, similar to the title of *The Marvelous Life*, and the core practice of Chöd. *The Concise Life Story* (fol. 117) offers a more elaborate version of Machig's battle with the demons.

36. Tib. *rjes gnang*: formal authorization to read the means of achievement (Skt. *sādhana*) of a deity, to visualize the deity and to recite the mantra. Apart from the hearing transmission (Tib. *lung*, usually a ritual recitation), the disciple requires this formal authorization in order to practice; but only in the course of an empowerment (Tib. *dbang*) will he or she receive the profound and detailed meditational instructions, and also engage him- or herself to preserve the initiatory bond (Skt. *samaya*, Tib. *dam tshig*) that accompanies the empowerment.

37. *Thugs bcud ma rig mun sel rgyud*, one of the three major tantras which Tārā transmits to Machig through direct inspiration. These three constitute the Vajrayāna Chöd tradition.

38. Wisdom (*shes rab*) here refers to the ultimate truth of emptiness, and the skillful means (*thabs*) to realize that truth refers to compassion (on the Mahāyāna

level) and to particular yogic techniques (on the Vajrayāna level). Realization, then, can only be the fruit of the union of these two principles, the first feminine and the second masculine. Hence, in the present context, sexual union is the symbol of the union of these two principles.

39. *Phyir mi ldog pa'i sa non pa*: to reach the level or ground of a non-returner. This characteristic applies to the practitioner who has reached the path of vision (*mthong lam*).

40. *Yi dam* (Skt. *iṣṭadevatā*), literally "the mind-bound." It is the meditation or personal deity which in Vajrayāna is the bond by means of which mind is yoked on the path to awakening. This deity is usually assigned by a personal teacher. As Nāropa told Marpa, "The fact is that they [the *yi dams*] are his [the guru's] manifestations" (Guenther, 1963: 107).

41. The eight consciousnesses are the five sense consciousnesses, the mental consciousness (*yid kyi rnam shes*), the afflicted mind (*nyon yid*) and the foundation, or mind basis of all, consciousness (Skt. *ālayavijñāna*, Tib. *kun gzhi rnam shes*).

42. *Rang rig 'od gsal*.

43. Clarity (or clear light) emptiness (*gsal stong*) is a term generally used in Mahāmudrā to describe the ultimate nature of mind. It corresponds to the union of emptiness and the means (*thabs*) for its realization.

44. According to *The Concise Life Story*, Machig presents this offering for the third initiation (*shes rab ye shes kyi dbang*), curiously absent here; she then presents another maṇḍala for the fourth or word initiation (*tshig dbang*). This is no doubt an error of our *Transforming the Aggregates* version.

45. *Byams chos sde lnga* are the five treatises which Maitreya transmitted to Asaṅga.

46. The text here uses the technical term *nyams len drod tshad*, "the measure of heat in the practice." Just as when approaching a fire one experiences its heat first as a sign of being close, likewise, when the yogin approaches the realization of a practice, some precursory signs of this realization occur, which are known as heat.

47. *Nā ro chos drug* are spiritual exercises such as dream yoga, clear light yoga, and yoga of the intermediate state, which constitute the path of means (*thabs lam*) in Nāropa's Mahāmudrā tradition. For a description of these six yogas, see Guenther, 1963: 131ff.

48. *Dohā* (Skt.) belong to the Indian tradition of spontaneous symbolic songs by means of which Vajrayāna masters express their meditative experiences and realization, and transmit their definitive instructions.

49. *Bya ba rgyud*, Action Tantra, is the first of the four classes of tantra, which emphasizes the outer practices related to deity yoga.

50. The image of the Buddha in the Jo khang of Lhasa representing his glorious form. It is considered the most sacred and most ancient statue of Tibet, the original having been brought by Songtsen Gampo's Chinese bride in the seventh century.

51. *Chos dbang sems la bskur*: the same initiation which Sönam Lama bestowed on Machig.

52. See Chapter II, n. 29. According to *The Concise Life Story* (fol. 437), Machig requested one empowerment from Dampa Sangyé who gave her, "from among the *Six [Treatises?] on the Sixfold Chöd [Practice?]*, the Opening of the Gates of Space and four kinds of instructions. Without any other instructions, Machig attained liberation."

53. Explicit commentary, *dmar khrid* or experiential guide, i.e., teachings on the very essence of a practice, often on the nature of mind, orally provided by the guru following his or her own experience. *The Concise Life Story* does not differ here from *The Marvelous Life* regarding initiations and transmissions listed, only adding that the explicit commentary concerns the *HUNG* cycle (*dmar khrid HUM bskor*).

54. *bKa' brgyud bla ma rnal 'byor zab lam ma*, part of the Chöd tradition according to the Tantras.

55. *'Pho ba lhag pa'i lam zhugs pa*, a Vajrayāna treatise belonging to the Chöd tradition according to the Tantras, which gives instructions on a completion stage technique to make the coarse winds/minds enter the central channel (Skt. *avadhūti*, Tib. *rtsa dbu ma*), here called "the supreme path." See Trungpa, 1986: 234. As noted above, Dampa was familiar with the form of consciousness transference known as entering a corpse.

56. *The Concise Life Story* (fol. 136) adds to these three yogas (of Nāropa) a fourth, the clear light yoga.

57. For this section, *The Concise Life Story* has been followed, as it is more explicit for this episode. In the *Precious Garland* (pp. 241-253) are contained the prayers associated with the means of achievement (Skt. *sādhana*), under the title *gCod khrid gdan thog gcig ma'i sgrub thabs ldeb* (*A Guide to Chöd, Augmented with the Means of Achievement of 'The Single Seat'* [i.e., without leaving one's seat]).

58. Skt. *nirmāṇakāya*, Tib. *sprul pa'i sku*: the emanation body. Machig pays homage to this form of Dampa, which has become manifest in the world and operates here. It is different from the other two Buddha bodies, the subtle bliss body (Skt. *sambhogakāya*, Tib. *longs spyod sku*) and the truth body (Skt. *dharmakāya*, Tib. *chos sku*).

59. *The Concise Life Story* (fol. 137) adds this further clarification: *ma rgyud mkha' 'gro ma thams cad kyi gros phug*, source (literally, *phug* means "cave," thus "source" or "origin") of all ḍākinīs of the Mother Tantras.

60. Skt. Kālikā, Tib. Khros ma nag mo, the wrathful form of Vajravārāhī.

61. *mDo dangs snyigs 'byed* (*Transforming the Aggregates*, p. 42), whereas *The Concise Life Story* (fol. 138) has *mDo sde dang snyigs 'gyed* (with *'gyed* seemingly a copy error for *'byed*). The Kongtrul edition of *Transforming the Aggregates*, however, has *sngags 'byed.*

62. Tib. *'Jam dpal rtsa ba'i rgyud kyi rgyal po.*

63. "The four teachings of Mahāmudrā through symbols" (*phyag rgya chen po'i brda chos bzhi*) as previously explained, are karma (mahā-)mudrā, samaya (mahā-) mudrā, bliss-emptiness (mahā-)mudrā, and clarity-emptiness (mahā-)mudrā. See, for instance, *Fording Place*, p. 106; on karmamudrā, see Guenther, 1963: 207 ff.

64. These four ḍākinīs represent the main streams of the four main Tibetan schools during the eleventh century—Sakya, Nyingma, Kagyü and Chöd, the latter thus elevated to the rank of a major school. Missing is Atiśa's *Lamp for the Path* tradition. He passed away the year prior to Machig's birth. Possibly the passage is an interpolation by the compiler of the *Transforming the Aggregates* volume, if not of a later editor.

VIII Her Achievements

1. Skt. *Pratītyasamutpāda*, Tib. *rten 'brel [yan lag bcu gnyis]*. The twelve links of dependent arising is the doctrine that shows how all physical and psychic phenomena are conditioned and interdependent. These twelve links, from ignorance to old age and death, illustrate the world as conditioned by suffering, with each link being the cause of the next: for example, rebirth in a body produces old age and death, and so forth. By purifying these twelve links in reverse order one reaches enlightenment, which then replaces the first link of fundamental ignorance. See Napper, 1989.

2. *bDe mchog gi dbang blangs*, "taking the Saṃvara initiation," is to be understood, according to Khenpo Tsultrim Gyamtso, as the self-entering (*bdag 'jug*) of the maṇḍala, i.e., self-initiation.

3. According to *The Concise Life Story*, fol. 160, the lama tells her: "If you had taken [monastic] vows, that would be negative; but since you are not [bound by nuns' vows], there is no harm." According to the *Transmission History*, he tells her: "Lady Little Hat, in my presence you took the vows; I hereby restore you to your earlier [lay] status."

4. *Tshul bstan*, "showing the action of." Being a ḍākinī from the beginning, Machig does not actually act, but shows the action (for instance, for didactic purposes); in the same way, a Buddha does not reach liberation, but enacts the procedure for the sake of disciples. Compare Chapter VII, n. 7 for a similar expression.

5. Skt. *Pañcakāmaguna*, Tib. *'dod yan lnga*: the five objects of enjoyment of the five senses: the most beautiful visual objects, the most sublime sounds, the finest flavors and smells, the most delicate contacts.

6. The eight-branch prayer: more common is the seven-branch version (*yan lag bdun pa*). It includes prostrations, offerings, confession, rejoicing in others' merits, requesting the teaching of Dharma, requesting the teachers to remain in the world, and dedication.

7. Generation stage (Skt. *utpattikrāma*, Tib. *bskyed rim*) and completion stage (Skt. *sampannakrāma*, Tib. *rdzogs rim*), the former involving a support, the latter usually without support.

8. Skt. *Vajradhātu*, Tib. *chos kyi dbyings*: the expanse of all manifestation.

9. Avalokiteśvara (Tib. sPyan ras gzigs) is the bodhisattva who personifies compassion, Mañjuśrī (Tib. 'Jam dpal dbyangs) symbolizes wisdom, and Vajrapāṇi (Tib. Phyag na rdo rje) stands for enlightened energy—the three fundamental qualities of a Buddha.

10. Mudrā (Tib. *phyag rgya*, literally "ritual hand gesture,") represents here the spiritual transformation of illusory appearances into pure vision, by the power of aspiration. This offering is treated *in extenso* in Karma Chagmé's *Concise Body Offering*.

11. *bKa' brgyud* here is the transmission lineage of the meaning of the Prajñāpāramitā (*bka 'brgyud don kyi brgyud pa*), corresponding to the Sūtra tradition.

12. *dBu ma'i lam*, central channel. The winds, drops and channels are the subtle elements that make up the illusory body. According to the Vajrayāna, mental purification is linked with the purification of these three subtle elements.

13. *The Concise Life Story* confirms this, but the *Transmission History* (p. 464) mentions that she stayed only three or four days with Dampa.

14. *Ma rgyud mkha' 'gro gnas 'gyur gyi dbang dang tshogs brgya*. For a description of these initiations, see Chapter V, section 1, above. The Mother Tantras are generally associated with the transmutation of passion into spiritual energy, as with the Cakrasaṃvara Tantra (Trungpa, 1986: 251). The cycle of empowerments here referred to belong to a tantra named *Thugs bcud ma rig mun sel* (*The Quintessence that Dispels the Darkness of Ignorance*), the third tantra which Machig received from Tārā.

15. *bsTan ma bcu gnyis*. These harmful mountain goddesses, associated with different mountains in Tibet, were subjugated by Padmasambhava who turned them into Dharma protectors. They often appear in the sacred biographies of yogins, such as that of Milarepa. See Nebesky-Wojkowitz, 1975: 181 ff.

16. The *Concise Life Story* (fols. 193 ff.) provides extra detail about Machig's reply. She first defines her tradition under five headings: generic name, transmission, essence, body offering and places of practice. Next she explains the Sūtra tradition on the basis of four root texts that further divide into twenty-five branches. These four root texts (fol. 196) are:

(1)*The Great Collection of Chöd Precepts* (*bKa' tshom chen mo*)
(2) *The Appendices* (*Le'u lag*) by name of *Instructions from the Meeting of Mother and Son* (*Ma bu ngo sprod du gdams pa*)
(3) *Recalling through the Sign Teaching* (*brDa chos la bzla ba*)
(4) *Don khang rgol grad thim su bstan pa* (?)

17. *bGegs* is a generic term covering different kinds of negative forces causing physical illnesses, mental suffering and obstacles.

18. This *Uḍumvara Tantra* is described in great detail in *The Concise Life Story* (fols. 237-241). *Transforming the Aggregates*, p. 81, cites this tantra as *bKa' brgyud gnas*

'gyur yang thig me long (*The Essential Mirror of the Transformation of the Oral Transmission*), a set of one hundred initiations also called the hundred initiations of the transformation of the lamas (*bla ma gnas 'gyur gyi dbang brgya*). Machig received it from Tārā during a vision and composed in line with it a sādhana on Yum Chenmo's lineage, coming down to herself.

19. The text here seems to mix up the *Uḍumvara Tantra* and the *Tantra on Taming the Nāgas [and] the Five Poisons* (*Dug lnga klu 'dul ba*), whereas *The Concise Life Story* draws a clear distinction between the two.

20. *Thugs bcud ma rig mun sel*, the third of the tantras Tārā transmits to Machig. See n. 14 above.

21. *The Concise Life Story* (fol. 205) adds: "even though, eventually, this tradition of the two stages will come to naught, still you'll remain [forever] the Ruling Lady of Secret Mantra." This deterioration of the Vajrayāna Chöd lineage is confirmed by a note in *The Marvelous Life* (p. 82), stating "Up to [Namkha Gyaltsen's] time this tradition...remained intact; but starting from [his successor] Tashi Gyaltsen it deteriorated."

22. Tib. *gSang sngags, gzungs sngags* and *rig sngags.*

23. According to *The Concise Life Story* (fol. 238), this name "Lady Ruling over the Vajradhātū" refers to a sādhana contained in the third tantra, *The Quintessence that Dispels the Darkness of Ignorance.*

24. *brDa.* This might be the teaching through signs of Machig's Sūtra tradition, the one referred to in *The Concise Life Story* (fol. 196) as *brDa chos la bzla ba* (*Recalling through the Sign Teaching*).

25. *Shes bya'i chos thams cad kyi grol phug.* As an emanation of the Great Wisdom Mother, primordial emptiness, she is at the origin or the source (*phug*, cave) for understanding the ultimate nature of phenomena, i.e., emptiness.

26. According to Ricard in *The Life of Shabkar*, note 4 of Author's Introduction, *'og min stug po bkod pa'i zhing khams*, means literally "which is not below," the unexcelled Buddhafield. Although it is generally considered to be Buddha Akṣobhya's Eastern Paradise, there are in fact several kinds of *'og min*. See Khenpo Yonten Gyatso's commentary on Jigme Lingpa's *Treasury of Spiritual Qualities* entitled *Yon tan rin po che mdzod kyi 'grel ba zla ba'i sgron me*, in *rNying ma bka' ma* (Kalimpong: Drubjung Lama, 1982-87), vol. 40, pp. 742-743.

27. This entire description faithfully follows the process of Vajrayāna sādhanas that aim to familiarize the meditator with the universe of marvels, so that he or she may be able to transform ordinary appearances into pure manifestations.

28. In this dream Machig sees her entire spiritual lineage, which will become the Chöd lineage. Sönam Lama is her root guru, seated on the crown of her head. Dampa is Sönam Lama's teacher and holds his teaching directly from Vajradhara, source of the tantras. Mañjuśrī, Āryadeva and the ḍākinī Sukhasiddhī too are mentioned in the Chöd lineages where Machig occupies a central position.

29. *The Concise Life Story* (fol. 220) indicates Thöpa Bhadra as the one who exhorted Machig to develop her Vajrayāna tradition and to commit it to writing for the benefit of future generations.

30. *Chos dbang sems la bskur*, see Chapter II, n. 30 above. The *Compendium* (p. 424) informs us that "at present, [in the Chöd tradition] one practices mainly the empowerment of ultimate meaning [directly] bestowed to the mind that opens the gates of space by means of oral instruction."

31. (1) *Phyogs bcu'i sangs rgyas gnas 'gyur ba'i dbang rgya* (*A Hundred Empowerments of the Transformation of the Buddhas of the Ten Directions*) belongs to the *Dug lnga klu 'dul ba'i rgyud* (*Taming the Nāgas [&] the Five Poisons Tantra*).

(2) *Ma rgyud mkha' 'gro gnas 'gyur ba'i dbang brgya* (*A Hundred Empowerments of the Transformation of the Dākinis according to the Mother Tantras*) derived from the Highest Yoga Mother tantra *The Quintessence that Dispels the Darkness of Ignorance*.

(3) *gTor ma la brten pa'i dbang brgya* (*A Hundred Empowerments with Ritual Cakes as a Support*) belongs to the Sūtra tradition.

Jamgön Kongtrul in the *Compendium* (p. 424) states that these three hundred initiations in groups of one hundred are no longer transmitted. *Transforming the Aggregates* (pp. 81-82, i.e., part of the short section left untranslated; see n. 40 below) has similar comments.

32. The twelve sources or doors of consciousness (Skt. *āyatana*, Tib. *skye mched*) cover the six sense faculties and their perceptual objects. The eighteen elements (Skt. *dhātu*,Tib. *khams*) cover the twelve doors plus the six corresponding sense consciousnesses.

33. Through pure vision (*dag snang*) or universal purity (*dag pa rab 'byams*), Vajrayāna practitioners transform ordinary appearances, the five aggregates, the twelve doors of consciousness and the eighteen elements into a divine palace to which is welcomed the deity being meditated upon. All phenomena transform into pure appearances and divine manifestations; all beings appear as deities. For this reason, the Vajrayāna tradition is often called the path of transformation.

34. *rNam snang gi chos bdun*. The meditation posture is explained by Vairocana in seven points: sitting cross-legged, hands in the gesture of meditative equipoise, back straight, neck bent slightly forward, shoulders straight, eyes looking at the tip of the nose, and the tongue touching the upper palate.

35. *bKa' tshom chen mo*.

36. Machig passed away at the age of ninety-nine according to the *Concise Life Story* and the *Transmission History*; at ninety-five according to the *Blue Annals* and the *Banquet*.

37. *'Pho ba tshul bstan*.

38. *bDud bzhi rang sar gcod*.

39. (1) *bka' tshom chen mo*
(2) *yang tshom* [*chen mo*]
(3) *nyid* (*snying* ?) *tshom* [*chen mo*]
(4) *le'u lag*
(5) *gnad them*
(6) *khong rgol*
(7) *gsang ba brda chos*
(8) [*gsang ba brda chos*] *la bzlas skor gsum*
(9) *gzhi lam du slong ba*
(10) *khyad par gyi man ngag*
The first four appear in Kongtrul's *Treasury*, volume XIV.

The Concise Life Story (fol. 287) gives the same titles with a few differences in the spelling but adds on a text (or group of texts?) called *Chos tshen brgyad dang gcod brgyad.*

40. This is where compiler Namkha Gyaltsen adds the note that the paragraph "and in this way a Tibetan tradition...." to "...the one and only source," (*Transforming the Aggregates*, p. 81, line 1) does not belong to the text proper but had been added by him. Following Khenpo Tsultrim Gyamtso's advice, the translation jumps here directly to p. 83, line 6, since this untranslated section consists of a very technical exposition of the differing lineages and lineage holders, as well as the empowerments passed on in each. These materials have been treated in Chapter 5 above.

Machig's Last Instructions

1. Machig's last instructions are translated from *The Concise Life Story*, fols. 445-457.

2. Clearly an error: the two Fire-Monkey years closest to the year of Machig's death being 1116 and 1176.

Tibetan-English Lexicon of Chöd Terminology

Ka

ku sa li	Skt. *kusali*; beggar, mendicant
kun brtags	labelled, imaginary
kun brtags lha 'dre	gods-demons that are merely labels
kun gzhi rnam shes	Skt. *ālayavijñāna*; fundamental consciousness
bka' gcod	Chöd lineage transmission
bka' gter zung 'jugs	union of the oral transmission and recovered treasures
bka' ma	lineage (scriptural) transmission
bka' tshom chen mo	(Machig's) *Great Collection of (Chöd) Precepts*
mkar 'gyed	white banquet
rkang gling	kangling; horn fashioned from human thigh bone
rkang mgyogs	the power (siddhi) of swift-footedness
klu	Skt. *nāga*
skad 'gyur	lit. translation, mode or modulation
skad 'don cho 'phrul	oral magical apparition or interference
bskyed rim	Skt. *utpattikrama*; generation stage (of the deity)

Kha

kha thor krig med	(Machig's) non-systematic teachings
kha tvam	Skt. *khaṭvāṅga*; trident
khra 'gyed	multicoloured banquet
khros ma nag mo	Skt. Kālikā; Wrathful Black Lady

mkha' 'gro ma	Skt. *ḍākinī*; celestial woman, sky-goer
mkha' spyod	Skt. *khecarī*, lit. active in space; ḍākinī realm
'khri chod	cutting through limitations
'khrul 'khor	yogic exercises

Ga

gang zag snyen gyi brgyud pa	personal hearing lineage
gad bdar	lit. to sweep; to observe (the nature of the mind)
grub thobs (chen po)	Skt. (*mahā*)*siddha*
glo bur	(91) negative contingencies
dga' brod bdud	demon of exaltation
bgegs	negative force
bgegs rigs	(80, 000) kinds of negative forces
mgron (pa)	guest
'gyed	banquet
rgya gcod	Indian Chöd
rgyas pa'i gcod	extended Chöd (old Bön)
sgo 'byed ('pho ba)	opening of the gate (transference of consciousness)
sgom lam	path of meditation
sgyu 'phrul	illusory play
sgyu lus	illusory body
sgrub brgyud	practice lineage

Nga

ngo sprod pa	to recognize or to point out (the nature of the mind)
ngo sprod 'pho ba	transference of consciousness through recognizing (the nature of the mind)
ngo bo gnas tshul gyi lha 'dre	gods-demons in their essential nature
sngags kyi rnam bshad chen mo	(Machig's) *Grand Exposition according to Tantra*
sngags skyes mkha' 'gro ma	mantra-born ḍākinī

Ca

gcod	Chöd, cutting through
gcod pa	Chödpa, Chöd practitioner

gcod dbang or chos dbang	Chöd initiation, initiation of the ultimate meaning
gcod yul	cutting through (in the presence of) the object
gcod log	erroneous Chöd (doctrine)

Cha

cho 'phrul	magical apparition or interference
chos	Skt. *dharma*; phenomena
chos kyi dbyings	Skt. *dharmadhātu*; sphere of manifestation
chos nyid	Skt. *dharmatā*; suchness, the essence of reality
chos nyid gyi dbyings ro snyoms	single flavor of the expanse of suchness
chos dbang sems la bskur	initiation of the ultimate nature transmitted to the mind
chos 'byung	lit. origin of the doctrine, historical account, transmission history
chod tshad	definitive sign of realization
mchog gi dngos grub	supreme or ultimate siddhi
'chi bdag gi bdud	demon lord of death

Ja

rjigs rten kyi mkha' 'gro ma	mundane ḍākinī
rjes gnang	formal authorization

Nya

nyam bzhags	meditative equipoise, absorption
nyams brgyud	lineage of experience
nyams len drod tshad	measure of heat in the practice
nye rgyud	short lineage
nyon mongs	Skt. *klesa*; mental afflictions
nyon mongs pa'i yid	afflicted mind (seventh consciousness)
gnyan pa	malignant spirits
gnyan sa	frightful places, wilderness
gnyis med brgyud	nondual lineage
gnyug ma	natural (mahāmudrā)
snying tshom chen mo	(Machig's) *Quintessence*
snyems *or* snyems byed	arrogance, ego-clinging
snyems byed kyi bdud	demon of arrogance or of ego-clinging

Ta

gtad pa	support (mahāmudrā)
gtu mo	inner heat (yoga)
gter ston	treasure discoverer
gter ma	recovered treasure
gtor dbang	torma initiation
gtor ma	offering cake
lta ba	view, philosophical tenet
stong pa nyid	Skt. *śūnyatā;* emptiness
brtul shugs spyod pa	action of yogic conduct, chosen behavior

Tha

thabs	skillful means, method
thig le	Skt. *bindu;* drop
thogs bcas bdud	tangible demon
thogs med bdud	intangible demon
mthar thugs don gyi lha 'dre	ultimate gods-demons
mthong snang sgro btags gyi lha 'dre	extraordinary or supernatural gods-demons
mthong lam	path of vision

Da

dag snang	pure vision
dag pa rab 'byams	(path of) universal purity
dam tshig pa	Skt. *samayasattva;* provisional or vow deity
dam tshig gi phyag rgya	Skt. *samayamudrā*
dur khrod	cremation or charnel ground, cemetery
don brgyud	lineage of ultimate meaning
drag po'i gcod	wrathful Chöd (new Bön)
gdon	demon
bdag med rtogs pa'i shes rab	knowledge or awareness that realizes the non-existence of a self
bdag 'dzin	lit. self-holding; ego-clinging
bdud gzhi rang sar gcod	lit. natural elimination of the four demons
bdud kyi gcod yul	cutting through demonic object
bde stong	bliss-emptiness

bde stong gi phyag rgya	mudrā of bliss-emptiness
mdo kyi rnam bshad chen mo	(Machig's) *Grand Exposition according to Sūtra*
mdo sngags kyi rnam bshad chen mo	(Machig's) *Grand Exposition according to Sūtra and Tantra Combined*
sde brgyad	eight kinds (of powerful demons)
sdang ba'i dgra	enemies that evoke anger
brda	sign or symbol
brda brgyud	sign or symbol lineage

Na

nag 'gyed	black banquet
nad rigs	(424) kinds of disease
gnas gdon	local demon
gnod par byed pa'i bgegs	negative forces that cause hindrances
rnam 'kha sgo 'byed	opening of the gates of space
rnam chos	celestial teaching
rnam thar	lit. complete liberation; hagiography, sacred biography
rnam bshad chen mo	(Machig's) *Grand Exposition*
rnal 'byor ma	yoginī
snang stong dbyer med	indissociability of manifestations and emptiness

Pa

spyod pa	action, practice
spyod yul	(Chöd) practice (of the bodhisattvas)
spros bral	(state) beyond conceptualization

Pha

pha brgyud	male lineage
phung po	Skt. *skandha;* psycho-physical aggregate
phung po gzan skyur	transforming the aggregates into food offering
pho gcod	male Chöd
pho brang	celestial palace
phyag rgya chen po	Skt. *mahāmudrā;* the great seal gesture
phyag rgya chen po'i gcod yul	Chöd of Mahāmudrā

phyag rgya bzhi	four mudrās, four seals
phyir mi ldog pa'i sa	stage of no return
'pho ba	transference of consciousness

Ba

bar du gcod pa'i rkyen	lit. conditions that cut apart; adversity, interference
bu lon	debt
bogs 'don	advantages, benefits
bod gcod	Tibetan Chöd
bye brag chen po	(Machig's) great specific teachings
dbang gi gcod	powerful Chöd (old Bön)
dbu chen	capital or printed letters
dbu med	cursive script
dbyangs yan lag drug bcu	60 melodious qualities (of Brahmā's voice)
dbyings rig bsre ba	to unite space and awareness
sbyin sreg	Skt. *homa;* burnt offering

Ma

ma brgyud	female lineage
ma bcos	non-artificial (state)
mi phod pa rdzis	to eradicate all resistance
me btsa'	moxibustion
mo gcod	female Chöd
dmar 'gyed	red banquet
dmigs pa	mental object, support, visualization
smyon pa	madman, mad saint

Tsa

btsan	spirit
rtsa	Skt. *nāḍī;* channel
rtsa dbu ma	Skt. *avadhūti;* central nāḍi or channel

Tsha

tshar tshad	level of final accomplishment
tshul bstan *or* tshul mdzad	to demonstrate a mode of acting
tshogs 'khor	Skt. *ganacakra;* offering ritual, feast offering

tshogs spyod — group practice or conduct

Dza

rdzogs chen — Skt. *mahāsandhi;* great perfection
rdzogs rim — Skt. *sampannakrāma;* completion stage

Zha

zhi gnas — Skt. *śamatha;* calm abiding
zhi ba'i gar stabs — (24) dance postures of peaceful deities
zhi ba'i gcod — peaceful Chöd (old Bön)
zhi byed — (Dampa's system of) the Pacification of Suffering
zhig po — hermit
zhing skyes mkha' 'gro ma — field-born ḍākinī
gzhan stong — lit. extrinsic emptiness; qualified emptiness
gzhung krig chen — (Machig's) great systematic treatises

Za

zang thal — unobstructed, limitless
zang ri — Copper Mountain (Machig's residence)
zang ri khang dmar — Red Fortress of the Copper Mountain
zan or gzan — food offering

'a

'og min — Skt. *akaniṣṭha;* lit. which is not below
'od gsal — clear light

Ya

yang tshom chen mo — (Machig's) *Great Collection of the Advanced Precepts*
yi dam — Skt. *iṣṭadevatā;* mind-bound or personal deity
yum chen mo — Great or Primordial Mother (Prajñāpāramitā)
yul — object, perceived object
yul can — subject, perceiving consciousness
ye 'grogs *or* 'brog — (360 kinds of) accident, danger
ye shes — Skt. *jñāna;* primordial wisdom
ye shes mkha' 'gro ma — wisdom ḍākinī
ye shes pa — Skt. *jñānasattva;* wisdom deity

Ra

rang stong	lit. intrinsic emptiness; empty of itself
rang babs	naturally (mahāmudrā)
rig pa'i ye shes	self-knowing wisdom
rig spyod	knowledge action or practice
rig ma	consort, knowledge woman
rigs gsum mgon po	protectors of the three families
ring brgyud	long lineage
ro snyoms	experience of single taste
rlung	Skt. *prāṇa*; wind

La

lan chags	karmic debt
lan chags bgegs	karmic creditors
lam du 'kyer	to carry onto the path, to utilize
las kyi phyag rgya	Skt. *karmamudrā*; action seal
las gdon	demon of karma
lus gdon	bodily demon
lus (mchod) sbyin	offering of the body (Chöd ritual)
le'u lag	(Machig's) *Appendices*
lo rgyus	chronicle
log gcod	perverted Chöd doctrine

Sha

shes rab	Skt. *prajñā*; knowledge, wisdom
shes rab kyi pha rol tu phyin pa	Skt. *prajñāpāramitā*; perfection of wisdom
shes rab ma	knowledge woman
bshad brgyud	explanatory lineage (Chöd)

Sa

sa chos	terrestrial teaching
sa bdag	owner of the land, lord of the soil (deity)
sems kyi gnas lugs	ultimate nature of the mind
sems nyid	mind itself
sras rgyud	son/daughter's lineage

srin po'i grong khyer	city of the rakṣāsas
slob dpon	Skt. *ācārya;* master
gsang spyod	secret practice or conduct
gsang ba'i sna tshogs 'gyed	secret multicolored banquet
gsar ma	new (tantras)
gsal stong	clear light emptiness
gsal stong gi phyag rgya	mudrā or seal of clear light emptiness
bslu med las dbang gi lha 'dre	unpredictable karmic gods-demons

Ha

lha 'dre	god-demon
lhags mthong	Skt. *vipaśyanā;* penetrating insight
lhan skyes	co-existing, co-emergent, innate
lhan skyes mkha' 'gro ma	innate or co-emergent ḍākinī
lhong or lhong tshad	symptom (of realization)

Bibliography

Sūtras and Tantras

Diamond-Cutter Sūtra
Ārya-vajracchedikā-nāma-prajñā-pāramitā
'Phags pa shes rab kyi pha rol tu phyin pa rdo rje gcod pa
Translation: E. Conze, *Buddhist Wisdom Books, The Diamond Sūtra and the Heart Sūtra*. London: Allen and Unwin, 1958.

Heart Sūtra
Bhagavatī-prajñā-pāramitā-hṛdaya
bCom ldan 'das ma shes rab kyi pha rol tu phyin pa'i snying po
Translation: E. Conze, *Buddhist Wisdom Books, The Diamond Sūtra and the Heart Sūtra*. London: Allen and Unwin, (1958) 1975.

Prajñāpāramitā Sūtra in Eight Thousand Lines
Aṣṭa-sāhasrikā-prajñā-pāramitā
Shes rab kyi pha rol tu phyin pa brgyad stong pa
Translation: E. Conze, *Aṣṭasāhasrikā Prajñāpāramita*. Calcutta: Asiatic Society, 1958 (Bibliotheca Indica 284); reprinted Bolinas, California: Four Seasons Foundation, 1962.

Prajñāpāramitā Sūtra in One Hundred Thousand Lines
Śata-sāhasrikā-prajñā-pāramitā
Shes rab kyi pha rol tu phyin pa stong phrag brgya pa
Translation: E. Conze, *The Large Sūtra on Perfect Wisdom*. Berkeley: University of California Press, 1975.

Prajñāpāramitā Sūtra in Twenty-Five Thousand Lines
Pañca-viṁśati-sāhasrikā-prajñā-pāramitā
Shes rab kyi pha rol tu phyin pa stong phrag nyi shu lnga pa
Translation: E. Conze, *The Large Sūtra on Perfect Wisdom*. Berkeley: University of California Press, 1975.

Sūtra of All Merits
bSod nams thams cad bsdus pa'i mdo
[does not appear in the bKa' 'gyur catalogues; quoted in the Jātaka literature]

Sūtra of the Wise and the Foolish
Dama-mūka-nāma-sūtra
mDzangs blun zhes bya ba'i mdo [*mDo mdzangs blun*]
Edition: Shinhua: mTsho sngon mi rigs dpe skrun khang, 1984.
Translation: Stanley Freye, *Sūtra of the Wise and the Foolish.* Dharamsala: Library of Tibetan Works and Archives, 1981.

Teachings of Vimalakīrti
Ārya-vimalakīrti-nirdeśa-nāma-mahāyāna-sūtra
'Phags pa dri ma med par grags pas bstan pa zhes bya ba theg pa chen po'i mdo
Edition: J. Oshika, in *Acta Indologica*, pp. 137-240. Narita: Naritasan Shinshoji, 1970.
Translation: R. Thurman, *The Holy Teaching of Vimalakīrti, A Mahāyāna Scripture.* University Park: Pennsylvania State University Press, 1976. E. Lamotte, *L'Enseignement de Vimalakīrti.* Louvain: Peeters, 1962. C. Luk, *The Vimalakīrti Nirdeśa Sūtra.* Berkeley and London: Shambhala, 1972.

Sanskrit and Tibetan Sources on Chöd

Anonymous
Ma gcig ma'i rnam thar
A Biography of Machig
Edited at the request of Rin bzang grags pa dbang phyug
Blockprint, n.p., n.d.
[Copy in author's possession from Lang(?) Gonpa, near Phyger, Dolpo.]

Āryadeva the Brahmin (Ā rya de wa, ca. ninth century)
Shes rab kyi pha rol tu phyin pa'i tshigs su bcad pa chen mo
The Grand Poem on the Perfection of Wisdom
In: *gCod kyi chos skor* (A Cycle of Teachings on Chöd), pp. 1-9. Delhi: Tibet House, 1974.

Dzatrul Ngawang Tenzin Norbu (rDza sprul ngag dbang bstan 'dzin nor bu, 1867-1940)

sPyod yul nyon mongs zhi byed log 'dren zil gnon ltas ngan gyang 'gug gyi khrid gzhung ma rig mun sel
Dissipating the Darkness of Ignorance: A Scriptural Commentary on the Action Spheres of Pacifying the Delusions, Subduing Through Splendor Erroneous Guides and Countering Wrong Views
In: *Rare Tibetan Texts from Nepal*, pp. 375-576. Dolanji: Tibetan Bonpo Monastic Centre, 1976.

gCod yul nyon mongs zhi byed kyi bka' gter bla ma brgyud pa'i rnam thar byin rlabs gter mtsho
Treasure Lake of Blessings: Sacred Biographies of the Guru Lineage on the Scriptural and Treasure [Traditions of] Chöd which Pacifies Kleśas
In: *A Collection of Biographies of Gurus in the Transmission Lineage of the gCod*

Teachings, ed. by Ngag dbang bstan 'dzin nor bu of Rong phu. Ngagyur Nyingmay Sungrab Series, XXI. Gangtok: Sonam T. Kazi, 1972.

Götsampa Gompo Dorjé (rGod tshams pa mgon po rdo rje)
Tshogs bsog mchod sbyin gyi zhal gdams
Oral Instructions on Completing the Accumulations [of Merit and Wisdom] Through Giving Homage and Offerings
In: *gSung 'bum*, vol. II, pp. 375-382. Thimphu: Kunzang Tobgay, 1976.

Jamgön Kongtrul Lodrö Thayé ('Jam mgon kong sprul blo gros mtha' yas, 1813-1899)
Shes bya kun khyab
Compendium of Knowledge
3 vols. Lhasa: Mi rigs dpe skrun khang, 1982, 1985.

Lus mchod sbyin gyi zin bris mdor bsdus kun dga'i skyed tshal
The Garden of Joy: Short Notes on Presenting the Body as an Offering
Reproduced and translated in: Anila Rinchen Palmo, *Cutting Through Ego-Clinging*. Landrevie, St. Leon sur Vézère, Montignac: Edition Dzambala, 1987. Also: Lama Lodo Rinpoche, trans. *Garden of All Joy.* San Francisco: KDK Publications, 1993.

Jamgön Kongtrul Lodrö Thayé, editor
Shes rab kyi pha rol tu phyin pa'i zab don bdud kyi gcod yul gyi bzhung
Śāstra on Cutting through Demons: The Profound Meaning of the Prajñāpāramitā
Collection of Chöd texts in: *gDams ngag mdzod* (Treasury of Profound Instructions), vol. XIV. Delhi: N. Lungtok and N. Gyaltsan, 1971.

Jamyang Shényen ('Jam dbyangs bshes gnyen)
Bar pa grwa tshang gi gcod khrid skal ldan 'jug ngogs zhes bya ba thun mong min pa grub mtha' gzhan la gsang ba man ngag gi snying po
A Chöd Guide from Barpa College, Called 'A Fording Place for the Fortunate': The Heart Essence of Oral Instructions that are Uncommon and Kept Secret in other Tenet Systems
In: *gCod tshogs: The Collected Gcod Teachings of the Dge-lugs-pa Tradition*, pp. 49-104. Dharamsala: Library of Tibetan Works and Archives, 1986.

Je Monlam Thayé Gyatso (rJe smon lam mtha' yas rgya mtsho)
Man ngag zab mo bdud kyi gcod yul stan thog gcig ma'i gzhung
The Treatise of the Single [Meditation] Seat: Profound Instructions on Cutting through Demonic Objects
In: *gCod tshogs, The Collected Gcod Teachings of the Dge-lugs-pa Tradition*, pp. 291-436. Dharamsala: Library of Tibetan Works and Archives, 1986.

Jigmé Lingpa ('Jigs med gling pa, 1730-1798)
gCod yul mkha' 'gro'i gad rgyangs
Cutting through the Object, the Laughter of the Ḍākinīs
In: *Klong chen snying gi thig le* (Longchenpa's Essential Drop)
Translation by Kazi Dawa Samdup in W. Y. Evans-Wentz, *Tibetan Yoga and Secret Doctrines*, pp. 301-334. London: Oxford University Press, 1958.

Khamnyön Jigdral Chökyi Sengé (Khams smyon 'jigs 'bral chos kyi seng ge, ca. end of nineteenth century)

Zhi byed dang gcod yul gyi chos 'byung rin po che'i 'phreng ba thar pa'i rgyan

An Ornament to Liberation, the Precious Garland of the Transmission History of the Pacification and of Chöd

In: *gCod kyi chos khor, A Cycle of Teachings on Chöd*, pp. 411-597. Delhi: Tibet House, 1974.

Karma Chagmé (sKar ma chags med, 1609-1672)

gCod kyi gdengs bshad nyung ngur bsdud pa bzhugs pa'i dbu phyogs

Abiding in the Middle: Slightly Abridged Definitive Instructions on Chöd

In: *gCod tshogs rin chen 'phreng ba* (The Precious Garland, a Collection on Chöd), pp. 229-239. Paro: Lama Ngödrup and Sherab Drimay, 1981.

rGyun khyer gyi lus sbyin bsdus pa

Concise Exposition of the Daily Practice of Offering the Body.

Blockprint, n.p., n.d.

[gCod rituals according to the Zurmang tradition]

gCod tshogs gcod khrid sogs

Collection of Texts on Chöd: Guides on Cutting Through, and So Forth.

Sonada, Darjeeling: Könchog Lhadripa edition, 1985; printed Delhi, Jayyed Press, Ballimaran.

[Collection of texts on Chöd practice as followed in Kham, after Karma Chagmé's teachings]

Karmapa III, Rangjung Dorjé (Rang byung rdo rje, 1284-1339)

gCod bka' rtshom chen mo'i sa bcad

Synopsis of the Great Collection of Chöd Precepts

In: *gDams ngag mdzod*, vol. XIV, pp. 53-79.

gCod tshogs yon tan kun 'byung

Source of All Qualities, a Collection of Chöd [Treatises]

Ed. by Pema Lodroe. Bir: Tibetan Medical Store, Nangchen Division, 1979.

[Collected Chöd teachings from the Zur mang bka' brgyud tradition]

gCod kyi lus sbyin ngag 'don mu tig 'phreng ba

The Pearl Garland: An Oral Transmission on Chöd's Body Offering

Ed. by Pema Lodroe. Bir: Tibetan Medical Store, Nangchen Division, 1979.

gCod tshogs las rin po che'i 'phreng ba

A Precious Garland [Compiled] from the Collected Chöd [Teachings]

Edition: *The Complete Liturgy for the Practice of the gCod Tradition*. Paro, n.p., n.d. Reprint Delhi: 1981.

gCod lugs phun sum tshogs pa'i me mchod bltas mchog bkod pa

A Most Excellent Fire Offering in the Chöd Tradition, Arranged as a Grand Spectacle

In: *gCod tshogs las rin po che'i phreng ba*, pp. 386-419. Delhi: 1981.

Kunpang Tsöndrü Sengé (Kun spangs btson 'grus seng ge, thirteenth century)

Phung po gzan skyur ba'i rnam par bshad pa las ma gcig lab sgron ma'i rnam par thar pa mdor msdus tsam zhig

The Concise Life Story of Machig Labdrön, Derived from An Exposition of Transforming the Aggregates into an Offering of Food
Unpublished *dbu med* ms., 519 fols. Seattle, University of Washington, East Asia Collection.

Lobsang Donden (Blo bzang don ldan)
Lam zab mo thabs shes kyi spyod yul stan thog gcig tu nyams su len tshul 'khrid chog dgra las rnam par rgyal ba'i rgyal mtshan
Commentary on the Practice of the Single [Meditation] Seat [according to] the Practice of the Profound Path of Wisdom and Means, Called the All-Victorious Banner over the Enemy
In: *gCod tshogs, The Collected Gcod Teachings of the Dge-lugs-pa Tradition*, pp. 191-251. Dharamsala: Library of Tibetan Works and Archives, 1986.

Lobsang Zöpa (Blo bzang bzod pa)
dGa' ldan snyam brgyud kyi thabs shes gcod kyi gdams pa'i byung rabs pad rag gi 'phreng ba
The Ruby Rosary: A Chronological Account of the Chöd Instructions, Means and Wisdom according to the Hearing Lineage of Ganden
In: *gSung 'bum*, vol. IV, pp. 1-90. New Delhi: Dorje Tsering, 1985.

Machig Labdrön (Ma gcig lab sgron, 1055-1153)
Phung po gzan skyur rnam bshad gcod kyi don gsal byed
An Exposition of Transforming the Aggregates into an Offering of Food, Illuminating the Meaning of Chöd
Ed. by Jampa Sönam (Byams pa bsod nams)
In: *gCod kyi chos skor* (A Cycle of Chöd Teachings), pp. 10-410. Delhi: Tibet House, 1974. Also see edition published by mTsho sngon mi rigs dpe skrun khang (Shinhua: 1992) under the title *Dus gsum rgyal ba kun gyi yum gcig 'phags ma lab kyi sgron ma'i rnam par thar pa phung po gzan bsgyur gyi rnam par bshad pa mkha' 'gro bye ba'i gsang lam* (Hagiography of the Venerable Labdrön, the Unique Mother of All the Victorious Ones of the Three Times, Called the Exposition of Transforming the Aggregates into an Offering of Food, the Secret Path of the Ḍākinīs' Activity)
Translation: Chapters 1 and 2 (*The Marvelous Life*) in this volume.

bKa' tshom chen mo
The Great Collection of [Chöd] Precepts
In: *gDams ngag mdzod*, vol. XIV, pp. 7-16.
Translation: G. Orofino, *Contributo allo studio dell' insegnamento di Ma gCig Lab sGron*. Naples: Istituto Universitario Orientale, 1987.

Shes rab pha rol tu phyin pa'i man ngag bdud kyi gcod yul las snying tshom [chen mo]
Oral Instructions on the Perfection of Wisdom: The Great Collection of the Quintessence of Cutting through Demonic Objects
In: *gDams ngag mdzod*, vol. XIV, pp. 116-164.

Shes rab kyi pha rol to phyin pa'i man ngag yang tshom zhu len ma
Oral Instructions on the Perfection of Wisdom, the Great Collection of Advanced [Chöd Precepts], Questions and Answers
In: *gDams ngag mdzod*, vol. XIV, pp. 101-115.

Mati bhadra kirti: see Tsongkhapa

Namkha Gyaltsen (Nam mkha' rgyal mtshan)
Phung po gzan skyur rnam bshad gcod kyi don gsal byed
An Exposition of Tansforming the Aggregates into an Offering of Food, Illuminating the Meaning of Chöd, chapters 1 and 2.
See Machig Labdron, *Phung po gzan skyur rnam bshad gcod kyi don gsal byed*

Shongchenpa (gShongs chen pa)
Ma gcig gi rnam thar mdzad pa bco lnga pa
The Fifteen Deeds, a Sacred Biography of Machig
In: *Thang stong snyan brgyud* (Thangtong [Gyalpo]'s Hearing Lineage). 2 vols. Delhi: Trayang, 1973.

Tāranātha (Kun dga' snying po, 1575-1635)
gCod yul zab mo'i khrid yig gnad don snying po
The Essence of Definitive Meaning: A Written Commentary on Profound Cutting Through the Object
In: *gDams ngag mdzod*, vol. XIV, pp. 185-200.

rGyal thang lugs kyi gcod dbang nam mkha' sgo 'byed kyi cho ga
The Chöd Initiation in the Tradition of Gyalthangpa: A Ritual for Opening the Gates of Space
In: *gDams ngag mdzod*, vol. XIV, pp. 361-370.

Thugsé Künga (Thugs sras kun dga')
Zhi byed snga bar phyi gsum gyi skor
The Cycle on the Early, Middle and Later [Practice] of the Pacification
Ed. by B. Nimri Aziz, 4 vols. Thimphu: Kunzang Tobgay, 1979.
[Collection of Dampa's teachings as transmitted by Thugsé Künga]

Tsering Dorje, editor
gCod tshogs: The Collected Gcod Teachings of the Dge-lugs-pa Tradition, by Mati Bhadra-kirti, Blo-bzang-don-ldan and others.
Dharamsala: Library of Tibetan Works and Archives, 1986.
[Reproduced from rare blockprints preserved in the LTWA]

Tsongkhapa Losang Dragpa (Tsong kha pa Blo bzang grags pa)
Zab lam gcod kyi khrid yig ma ti bha dra kirti sbyar ba
The Path Profound, a Textual Commentary on Chöd
In: *gCod tshogs, The Collected gCod Teachings of the Dge-lugs-pa Tradition,* pp. 1-48. Dharamsala: Library of Tibetan Works and Archives, 1986.
Translation: Carol Savvas, "A Study of the Profound Path of gCod: The Mahāyāna Buddhist Meditation Tradition of Tibet's Great Woman Saint Machig Labdron." Ph. D. dissertation. Madison: University of Wisconsin-Madison.

Sources on Bön Chöd

Khandro Dechen Wangmo (mKha' 'gro bde chen dbang mo, b. 1868)
Yum chen kye ma 'od mtsho'i zab gsang gcod kyi gdams pa las phran dang bcas pa'i gsung pod

Ed. by Tshering Wangyal. Dolanji: Tibetan Bönpo Monastic Centre, 1974.
[Collection of "new" Bön Chöd precepts from the revelations of mKha' 'gro bde chen dbang mo]

Kyangtrul Namkha Gyaltsen (sKyang sprul nam mkha' rgyal mtshan, b. 1868)
mKha' ' gro gsang gcod kyi lag len skor
Cycle of Chöd Practices of the Secret Ḍākinīs
Ed. by Tashi Dorje. Dolanji: Tibetan Bonpo Monastic Centre, 1974.
[Texts outlining various practices of the Bönpo Chöd precepts from the mKha' 'gro gSang gCod cycle]

Nagter Sang-ngag Lingpa (Nag gter gsang sngags gling pa, b. 1864)
Zab mo gcod kyi gdams nag yum chen thugs rje sgrol ma
Profound Instructions on Chöd, called Liberation through Yum Chenmo's Compassion
Ed. by Patshang Lama Sonam Gyaltsen. Dolanji: Tibetan Bönpo Monastic Centre, 1973.
[Bonpo Chöd precepts rediscovered by gSang sngags gling pa]

Tülku Tronyen Gyaltsen (sPrul sku Khro gnyan rgyal mtshan, fourteenth century)
Zab lam mkha' 'gro gsang ba'i gcod kyi gdams pa
The Profound Path of Chöd Instructions of the Secret Ḍākinīs
Ed. by Tashi Dorje. Dolanji: Tibetan Bönpo Monastic Centre, 1973.
[A collection of Bönpo gCod tantras and related texts]

Other Sanskrit and Tibetan Sources

Atiśa (Dīpaṁkara-śrī-jñāna, 982-1054)
Bodhi-patha-pradīpa and *Bodhi-mārga-pradīpa-pañjikā*
Byang chub lam gyi sgron ma and *Byang chub lam gyi sgron ma'i dka' 'grel*
Translation: R. Sherburne, *A Lamp for the Path and Commentary*. London: Allen and Unwin, 1983.

Bod rgya tshigs mdzod chen mo
Tibetan-Chinese Dictionary
Compiled by Tshe tan zhabs drung et al. 3 vols. Beijing: Mi rigs dpe skrun khang, 1985, 1986.

Candrakīrti (Zla ba grags pa)
Madhyamaka-avatāra
dBu ma la 'jug pa
Entering the Middle Way
Translation: J. Hopkins, *Compassion in Tibetan Buddhism*. London: Rider, 1980.
[Contains first five chapters of Tsongkhapa's commentary, with quotation of Candrakīrti's verses]

Gö Lo [tsāwa] Zhonnu Pel ('Gos lo gzhon nu dpal)
Deb ther sngon po
The Blue Annals
Edition: 2 vols. Shinhua: Si khrom mi rigs dpe skrun khang, 1982.

Translation: N. Roerich and G. Chöphel, *The Blue Annals.* Delhi: Motilal Banarsidass, 1949, 1976.

Gyurmé Dechen ('Gyur med bde chen)
dPal grub pa'i dbang phyug brtson 'grus bzang po'i rnam par thar pa kun gsal nor bu'i me long
A Jewel Mirror Illuminating Everything: A Sacred Biography of the Glorious Lord among Siddhas, Tsöndrü Sangpo [Thangtong Gyalpo]
Shinhua: Si khrom mi rigs dpe skrun khang, 1982.
Translation (partial): C. Stearns, "The Life and Teachings of the Tibetan Saint Thang-stong rgyal po, 'King of the Empty Plain'." Unpublished M.A. thesis. Seattle: University of Washington, 1980.

Jamyang Kyentsé Wangpo ('Jam dbyangs mkhyen brtse'i dbang po, 1820-1892)
dBus gtsang gi gnas rten rags rim gyi mtshan byang mdor bsdus dad pa'i sa bon
A Seed of Faith: A Rough Outline of the Sacred Spots and Images of Ü-Tsang
Ed. and trans. by A. Ferrari and L. Petech, *mK'yen brtse's Guide to the Holy Places of Central Tibet.* Rome: Istituto Italiano per il Medio ed Estremo Oriente, 1958.

Karma Chagmé (sKar ma chags med)
Ri chos mtshams kyi zal gdams
Oral Instructions for Mountain Retreats
Tashi Jongs, Palampur, Himachal Pradesh, India

Karmapa IX, Wangchuk Dorjé (dBang phyug rdo rje, 1556-1603)
lHan cig skyes sbyor gyi zab khrid nges don rgya mtsho'i snying po phrin las 'od 'phro ba
Radiating the Light of the Activity: A Profound Commentary on the Heart Essence of the Ocean of Definitive Meanings
Edition: Rumtek Dharmachakra, n.d.

Khetsun Sangpo (mKhas btsun bzang po)
bKa' gdams gsar rnying rjes 'brangs dang bcas pa'i bla ma brgyud pa'i rnam thar kun btus nor bu'i do shal
The Jewel Necklace: Selected Biographies of Guru Lineages of Precepts and Instructions, New and Ancient, Including Their Historical Succession
A Biographical Dictionary of Tibet and Tibetan Buddhism, 12 vols. Dharamsala: Library of Tibetan Works and Archives, 1973-1979.

Lama Tsenpo Mindrol Nomun Khan (Bla ma btsan po smin grol no mon khan)
'Dzam gling chen po'i rgyas bshad snod bcud kun gsal me long
A Mirror Illuminating Container [World] and [Beings] Contained: An Extensive Universal Geography
Ed. and trans. by T. Wylie, *A Tibetan Religious Geography of Nepal.* Rome: Istituto Italiano per il Medio ed Estremo Oriente, 1970 (Nepal section). T. Wylie, *The Geography of Tibet according to the 'Dzam-gling-rgyas-bshad.* Rome: Istituto Italiano per il Medio ed Estremo Oriente, 1962.

Nāgārjuna (Klu sgrub)
Prajñā-nāma-mūla-madhyamaka-kārikā [*Madhyamaka-śāstra*]
dBu ma rtsa ba'i tshig le'ur byas pa shes rab ces bya ba [*dBu ma'i bstan bcos*]
Fundamental Treatise on the Middle Way Called Wisdom [also known as Treatise on the Middle Way]
Translation: F. J. Streng, *Emptiness.* Nashville and New York: Abingdon, 1967.

Panchen Lama I, Losang Chökyi Gyaltsen (Blo bzang chos kyi rgyal mtshan)
dGe dang bka' brgyud rin po che'i phyag chen rtsa ba rgyal ba'i gzhung lam
The Main Path of the Conqueror Buddhas, Root [Text] of the Mahāmudrā [Tradition] of the Precious Gelug and Kagyü Masters
Translation: Geshe Ngawang Dhargyey, Sharpa Tulku, Khamlung Tulku, A. Berzin and J. Landaw, *The Great Seal of Voidness.* Dharamsala: Library of Tibetan Works and Archives, 1975.

Patrul Orgyen Chökyi Wangpo (dPal sprul o rgyan chos kyi dbang po, 1808-1887)
Kun bzang bla ma'i zhal lung
Translation: Patrul Rinpoche, *The Words of My Perfect Teacher,* trans. by the Padmakara Translation Group. San Francisco: HarperCollins, 1994. Also: S. T. Kazi, *Kun Zang La May Zhal Lung.* Englewood Cliffs, New Jersey: Diamond Lotus, 1989.

Pawo Tsuglag Trengwa, Second Nehnang Pawo (dPa' bo gtsug lag 'phreng ba)
Chos 'byung mkhas pa'i dga' ston
Dharma History: A Banquet for the Learned
2 vols. Beijing: Mi rigs dpe skrun khang, 1985.

Taglung Ngawang Namgyal (sTag lung pa ngag dbang rnam rgyal)
Chos 'byung ngo mtshar rgya mtsho
A Dharma History [Called] an Ocean of Wonders
Edition: 2 vols. Tashi Jongs, Palampur, Himachal Pradesh, India: 1972.
[Account of the development of Buddhism in Tibet with special emphasis on the sTag lung bka' brgyud pa]

Tāranātha
sGrol ma'i rgyud kyi byung khung gsal bar byed pa'i lo rgyus gser gyi phreng ba
Golden Rosary, an Account that Illuminates the Origins of the Tārā Tantra
Translation: D. Templeman, *The Origin of the Tārā Tantra.* Dharamsala: Library of Tibetan Works and Archives, 1981.

Tsangnyön Heruka (gTsang smyon he ru ka, 1452-1507)
rNal 'byor gyi dbang phyug chen po mi la ras pa'i rnam mgur
Sacred Biography and Collected Songs of the Great Lord among Yogins, Milarepa
Shinhua: mTsho sngon mi rigs dpe skrun khang, 1981, 1989.
Biography: L. Lhalungpa, *The Life of Milarepa.* Boston and London: Shambhala, 1977. W. Y. Evans-Wentz, *Tibet's Great Yogi Milarepa.* London: Oxford University Press, 1928, 1969.

Songs: Garma C.C. Chang, *The Hundred Thousand Songs of Milarepa*. 2 vols. Boulder and London: Shambhala, 1977.

Mar pa lo tsā'i rnam thar
Sacred Biography of Marpa Lotsāwa
Shinhua: Si khrom mi rigs dpe skrun khang, 1980.
Translation: Chögyam Trungpa and Nalanda Translation Committee, *The Life of Marpa the Translator*. Boulder and London: Shambhala, 1982.

Tsongkhapa (Tsong kha pa)
gSung rab kyi drang ba dang nges pa'i don rnam par phye ba gsal byed pa legs par bshad pa'i snying po
The Essence of True Eloquence: A Clear Explanation Distinguishing the Provisional and the Definitive Meanings of the Scriptures
Translation: R. Thurman, *Tsong Khapa's Speech of Gold in the "Essence of True Eloquence"*. Princeton, New Jersey: Princeton University Press, 1984. Reprinted as *The Central Philosophy of Tibet*. Princeton, New Jersey: Princeton University Press, 1991.

sNgags rim chen mo
Grand Exposition of Secret Mantra
Translation: J. Hopkins, *Tantra in Tibet* (London: Allen and Unwin, 1977) and *Yoga in Tibet* (London: Allen and Unwin, 1981; reprinted as *Deity Yoga*, Ithaca: Snow Lion, 1987).

Works in Western Languages

Allione, Tsultrim. *Women of Wisdom*. London: Routledge and Kegan Paul, 1984.

Anila Rinchen Palmo. *Cutting Through Ego-Clinging*. Montignac: Dzambala, 1987.

Aris, Michael and Aung San Suu Kyi, eds. *Tibetan Studies in Honour of Hugh Richardson*. Delhi: Vikas Publishing, 1980.

Avalon, A. and Samdup. *The Chakra-samvara Tantra, a Buddhist Tantra*. London: 1919.

Aziz, Barbara and Matthew Kapstein, eds. *Soundings in Tibetan Civilization*. Delhi: Manohar, 1985.

Benard, Elizabeth. "Ma gCig Labs sGron, a Tibetan Saint." *Chö Yang* [Dharamsala] 3 (1990): 43-51.

Beyer, Stephan. *The Cult of Tārā: Magic and Ritual in Tibet.* Berkeley: University of California Press, 1978.

Bleichsteiner, E. *L'église jaune*. Paris: Payot, 1950. First published as *Die gelbe Kirche*. Vienna, 1937.

Boureau, A. *La légende dorée*. Paris: Edition du Cerf, 1984.

Chang, Garma C. C. *The Hundred Thousand Songs of Milarepa*. 2 vols. Boulder and London: Shambhala, 1977.

Conze, Edward. *Buddhist Wisdom Books: The Diamond Sūtra and the Heart Sūtra.* London: Allen and Unwin, 1958.

_______. *The Large Sūtra on Perfect Wisdom.* Berkeley: University of California Press, 1975.

_______. *The Perfection of Wisdom in Eight Thousand Lines and Its Summary.* Bolinas: Four Seasons Foundation, 1973.

Dalai Lama [XIV], Tsong-ka-pa and Jeffrey Hopkins. *Tantra in Tibet.* London: Allen and Unwin, 1977. Reprint. Ithaca: Snow Lion, 1987.

Dargay, Eva. "A gTer-ston Belonging to the dGe-lugs-pa School." *The Tibet Journal* VI/1 (1981): 24-30.

David-Neel, Alexandra. *Magic and Mystery in Tibet.* New York: HarperCollins, 1993. First published as *Parmi les mystiques et les magiciens du Tibet.* Paris: Librarie Plon, 1929.

Decleer, Hubert. "The Melodious Drumsound All-Pervading: Sacred Biography of Rwa Lotsāwa." *In* Ihara and Yamaguchi, eds. *Tibetan Studies, Proceedings of the International Association of Tibetan Studies, Narita, 1989*, vol. I, p. 13. Naritu Shinshoji, 1992.

Dhargyey, Geshe Ngawang, Sharpa Tulku, Khamlung Tulku, A. Berzin and J. Landaw. *The Great Seal of Voidness.* Dharamsala: Library of Tibetan Works and Archives, 1975.

Dorjé, R. and Ter Ellingson. "Exploration on the Secret gCod Da ma ru." *Asian Music* 10/2 (1979).

Driessens, Georges. *L'entrée au milieu.* Poneyrade: Éditions Dharma, 1988.

Eliade, Mircea. *Myths, Dreams and Mysteries.* Trans. by Philip Mairet. New York: Harper and Row, 1960.

_______. *Shamanism: Archaic Techniques of Ecstasy.* Trans by Willard R. Trask. Princeton: Princeton University Press, 1964.

Evans-Wentz, W. Y. *Tibetan Yoga and Secret Doctrines.* Oxford: Oxford University Press, 1958.

Facchini, M. "The Spiritual Heritage of Ma gCig Lab sGron." *Journal of the Tibet Society* [Bloomington] 3 (1983).

Ferrari, Alfonsa and Luciano Petech. *mK'yen brtse's Guide to the Holy Places of Central Tibet.* Rome: Istituto Italiano per il Medio ed Estremo Oriente, 1958.

Frye, Stanley. *Sūtra of the Wise and the Foolish.* Dharamsala: Library of Tibetan Works and Archives, 1981.

Gross, Rita. *Buddhism after Patriarchy.* Albany: State University of New York Press, 1993.

Guenther, Herbert V. *The Life and Teachings of Nāropa.* Oxford: Claredon Press, 1963. Reprint. Boston and London: Shambhala, 1986.

_______. *The Royal Song of Saraha*. Seattle and London: University of Washington Press, 1969.

_______. *Treasures on the Tibetan Middle Way*. Berkeley: Shambhala, 1971.

Gyatso, Geshe Kelsang. *Heart of Wisdom*. London: Tharpa, 1986.

Gyatso, Janet. "The Development of the Gcod Tradition." In Aziz and Kapstein, eds., *Soundings in Tibetan Civilization*, pp. 320-341. Delhi: Manohar, 1985.

_______. *Apparitions of the Self: The Secret Autobiographies of a Tibetan Visionary*. Princeton: Princeton University Press, forthcoming.

Hercus, L. A. et al. *Indological and Buddhist Studies*. Delhi: Sri-Satgur, 1982.

Hitchcock, J. and R. L. Jones, eds. *Spirit Possession in the Nepal Himalayas*. Delhi: Vikas Publishing, 1976.

Hookham, Shenpen. *The Buddha Within*. Albany: State University of New York Press, 1991.

Hopkins, Jeffrey. *Emptiness Yoga*. Ithaca: Snow Lion, 1987.

Ihara, S. and Z. Yamaguchi, eds. *Tibetan Studies, Proceedings of the International Association of Tibetan Studies, Narita, 1989*. 2 vols. Naritu Shinshoji, 1992.

Kapstein, Matthew. "The Shangs-pa bKa'-bgyud: An Unknown Tradition in Tibetan Buddhism." In *Tibetan Studies in Honour of Hugh Richardson*, Aris and Sung, eds. Delhi: Vikas, 1980.

Katz, Nathan. "Anima and mKha' 'Gro ma: A Critical Comparative Study of Jung and Tibetan Buddhism." *The Tibet Journal* 2/3 (1977), pp. 13ff.

Khenpo Tsultrim Gyamtso. *Progressive Stages on the Meditation on Emptiness*. Oxford: Longchen Foundation, 1986.

Klein, Anne Carolyn. *Meeting the Great Bliss Queen*. Boston: Beacon Press, 1995.

Kunzang, Erik P. *Song of Karmapa*. Kathmandu: Rangjung Yeshe, 1992.

Lacarrière, J. *Les hommes ivres de Dieu*. Paris: Éditions du Seuil, 1975.

Lhalungpa, Lobsang. *The Life of Milarepa*. Boston and London: Shambhala, 1985.

[Lobsang Tenzin.] "Biography of a Contemporary Yogi, Ven. Lobsang Tenzin." *Chö Yang* [Dharamsala] 3 (1990): 102-111.

Lodo Rinpoche, Lama, trans. *The Garden of All Joy*. San Francisco: KDK Publications, 1993.

Lopez, Donald, S. Jr. *The Heart Sūtra Explained, Indian and Tibetan Commentaries*. Albany: State University of New York Press, 1988.

Mercier, E. *Chamanisme et Chamans*. Paris: Éditions Dangles, 1987.

Napper, Elizabeth. *Dependent Arising and Emptiness*. Boston: Wisdom, 1989.

Nebesky-Wojkowitz, René de. *Oracles and Demons of Tibet*. Graz: Akademische Druck Universität Verlaganstalt, 1975.

Norbu, Namkhai. *The Crystal and the Way of Light*. New York and London: Routledge and Kegan Paul, 1987.

Orofino, Giacomella. *Contributo allo studio dell'insegnamento di Ma gcig Lab sgron*. Naples: Istituto Universitario Orientale, 1987.

Patrul Rinpoche. *The Words of My Perfect Teacher*. Trans. by Padmakara Translation Group. San Francisco: HarperCollins, 1994.

Rabten, Geshe. *Echoes of Voidness*. Boston and London: Wisdom, 1983.

Ricard, Matthieu. *The Life of Shabkar, The Autobiography of a Tibetan Yogin*. Albany: State University of New York Press, 1994.

Rigzin, Tsepak. *Tibetan-English Dictionary of Buddhist Terminology*. Dharamsala: Library of Tibetan Works and Archives, 1986.

Roerich, George, trans. *The Blue Annals*. Delhi: Motilal Banarsidass, 1976.

Rossi-Filibeck, E. de. "The Transmission Lineage of the gCod Teaching According to the Second Dalai Lama." In *Contributions on the Tibetan and Buddhist Religion and Philosophy, Proceedings of the Csoma de Körös Symposium, 1981*, vol.2, pp. 47-57. Vienna: 1983.

Ruegg, David Seyfort. *The Life of Bu sTon Rin po che*. Rome: Istituto Italiano per il Medio ed Estremo Oriente, 1966.

________. "Towards a Chronology of the Madhyamaka School." In L. A. Hercus et al., *Indological and Buddhist Studies*, 1982.

Savvas, Carol D. "A Study of the Profound Path of Gcod: The Mahāyāna Buddhist Meditation Tradition of Tibet's Great Woman Saint Machig Labdron." Ph. D. dissertation. Madison: University of Wisconsin-Madison, 1990.

Sherburne, Richard, S. J. *A Lamp for the Path and Commentary, by Atisha*. London: Allen and Unwin, 1983.

Smith, E. Gene. "Introduction" in *The Life of the Saint of gTsang*. Ed. by Lokesh Chandra. Delhi: Sāraswati Vihāra, 1969.

Snellgrove, David. *Buddhist Himalaya*. New York: Philosophical Library, 1975.

________. *The Hevajra Tantra*. 2 vols. London: Oxford University Press, 1959.

________. *Indo-Tibetan Buddhism*. 2 vols. Boston: Shambhala, 1970.

Speyer, J. *The Jātaka Māla, Garland of Birth-Stories of Ārya-śūra*. Delhi: Motilal Banarsidass, 1971.

Stearns, Cyrus. "The Life and Teachings of the Tibetan Saint Thang-stong rgyal po, 'King of the Empty Plain'." Unpublished M.A. thesis. University of Washington, 1980.

Stein, R. A. *Tibetan Civilization.* London: Faber and Faber, 1972.

_______. *Vie et chants de 'Brug-pa Kun-legs le Yogin.* Paris: Maisonneuve, 1972.

Tarthang Tulku. *The Enlightenment of Yeshe Tsogyel.* Berkeley: Dharma Publishing, 1983.

Templeman, David, trans. and ed. *The Origins of the Tārā Tantra, by Jonang Tāranātha.* Dharamsala: Library of Tibetan Works and Archives, 1981.

_______. *Life of Kṛṣṇācārya/Kānha.* Dharamsala: Library of Tibetan Works and Archives, 1989.

Thurman, Robert. *Tsong Khapa's Speech of Gold in the "Essence of True Eloquence".* Princeton, New Jersey: Princeton University Press, 1984. Reprinted as *The Central Philosophy of Tibet.* Princeton, New Jersey: Princeton University Press, 1991.

_______. *The Holy Teachings of Vimalakīrti, A Mahāyāna Scripture.* University Park: Pennsylvania State University Press, 1976.

Trungpa, Chogyam. "Dharmas Without Blame." In *Garuda,* vol. III, pp. 2-8. Berkeley and London: Shambhala, 1973.

Trungpa, Chogyam and Nalanda Translation Committee. *The Life of Marpa the Translator.* Boston and London: Shambhala, 1986.

Tucci, Giuseppe. *The Religions of Tibet.* Delhi: Allied Publishers, 1980.

Tulku Thondup Rinpoché. *Hidden Teachings of Tibet.* London: Wisdom, 1986.

Van Tuyl, C. "Mila-ras-pa and the gCod Ritual." *The Tibet Journal* 4/1 (1979).

Willis, Janice D. "Ḍākinī: Some Comments on its Nature and Meaning." *The Tibet Journal* 12/4 (1987).

Wylie, Turrell. *A Tibetan Religious Geography of Nepal.* Rome: Istituto Italiano per il Medio ed Estremo Oriente, 1970.

_______. *The Geography of Tibet according to the 'Dzam-gling-rgyas-bshad.* Rome: Istituto Italiano per il Medio ed Estremo Oriente, 1962.

General Index

Index of Tibetan and Sanksrit Names